Russia and its Neighbours

Russia and its Neighbours

Could History Have Predicted Russia's War on Ukraine?

Jonathan S. Swift

Pen & Sword
MILITARY

First published in Great Britain in 2026 by
Pen & Sword Military
An imprint of Pen & Sword Books Limited
Yorkshire – Philadelphia

ISBN 978 1 03613 928 5

A CIP catalogue record for this book is available from the British Library.

Typeset by Mac Style
Printed in the UK by CPI Group (UK) Ltd, Croydon, CR0 4YY.

FSC
www.fsc.org
MIX
Paper | Supporting responsible forestry
FSC® C013604

The Publisher's authorised representative in the EU for product safety is Authorised Rep Compliance Ltd., Ground Floor, 71 Lower Baggot Street, Dublin D02 P593, Ireland.
www.arccompliance.com

For a complete list of Pen & Sword titles please contact:

PEN & SWORD BOOKS LIMITED
47 Church Street, Barnsley, South Yorkshire, S70 2AS, England
E-mail: enquiries@pen-and-sword.co.uk
Website: www.pen-and-sword.co.uk
or
PEN AND SWORD BOOKS
1950 Lawrence Road, Havertown, PA 19083, USA
E-mail: uspen-and-sword@casematepublishers.com
Website: www.penandswordbooks.com

'Those who do not remember the past are condemned to repeat it.'

Jorge Santayana

Contents

Major Mike Shearer is a geopolitical defence analyst and commentator. He saw service during the Cold War patrolling the inner German border in a Main Battle Tank. He was the British Military Spokesman during the Iraq War (2007–2008) and has also seen active service in the Gulf War 1990–1991, Iraq 2003, 2007 and 2008, Cyprus, Bosnia and Northern Ireland. He is often seen commenting on UK national TV.

Foreword

An outstanding read as Dr Jonathan Swift takes a deep dive into the relationship between Russia and its neighbours. A must-read for the Prime Minister's Office, Foreign Office, Cabinet Office, MOD, all military officers, academics and students of international relations. As this book goes to print, it would also be beneficial for President Trump's administration to read and understand.

This book untangles the complex history of Russia and asks the question: 'Could history have predicted the war on Ukraine?' Swift gently guides the reader through a scholarly analysis, starting in the twelfth century with the Grand Duchy of Moscow, through to the illegal invasion of Ukraine or 'Special Military Operation' as Putin labelled it in February 2022. Please, do not recoil at the term 'scholarly analysis' – this is not a dusty read, the author has taken great care to employ normal vernacular while maintaining clear context.

Over the centuries, while the people of Russia suffered under the despotic Imperial Czars, they then opted to downgrade to the much more oppressive Bolshevik reign of misery. While the author charts the emergence and progress during the hardwiring of Communist ideology into the minds of the Russian/Soviet leadership, it is extraordinary how the people so readily acquiesced. Perhaps the answers rest in the common drivers throughout Russia's history: paranoia, insecurity, power, control, greed, spite and of course, envy.

As you read through this book, you may conclude, as I did, that without a heavy dose of high voltage therapy for the national leadership, there is little hope for Russia. Of course, the Russian leadership take a different view. They manage their psychotic cocktail of insecurity traits by deploying terror, not only to their close neighbours and beyond, but to their own people.

Further, as you read on, you quickly recognise that the notion of terror requires much more than just threats; it requires brutal action. Time and time again, this book highlights the Russian solution to all its perceived needs, territory by conquest. It's rather like Hitler's rationale for World War II, his requirement for *lebensraum* or 'living space' for the German people to flourish. The truth is, it's all about empire building under the umbrella of one ideology, and if anyone disagrees with it, exterminate! The term for such behaviour is fascism, the very ideology of Nazism that Putin ironically accused President Zelensky of when he invaded Ukraine. There are many examples of Soviet/Russian invasions into other countries here. If I have counted correctly in the past 103 years, from 1919 to 2022, twenty-two countries have suffered at the hands and might of Soviet/Russian aggression, some more than once and some more than twice. During that time, the longest period of peaceful stability was a mere sixteen years.

It is not unsurprising that a despot like Putin was drawn to Ukraine, after all, it is the breadbasket of Europe, has warm water ports, fossil fuels, and its rare-earth minerals are plentiful. Despite the opposing ideologies of Communism versus capitalism, and whichever way you choose to dress it up, I conclude from this book that Putin is nothing more than a common thief, murderer and genocidal megalomaniac.

Dr Swift exposes the tried, tested, ways and means by which Putin and his predecessors have skilfully played their hand. How they executed mendacious statecraft to justify naked aggression, while testing the resolve of the West. Too often, Soviet/Russian leaders have correctly judged, relied upon and got away with taking advantage of the failure of Western leaders, who are frequently distracted and engaged with their own political siloism. In addition, he lays bare the strategies that Putin adroitly bakes into everyday life, for the purpose of maintaining order and expanding the cause for 'Mother Russia'. In this case, Mother Russia may be interpreted to mean Putin's aspiration for imperial expansionism. It is in this cause that he employs a plethora of tactics, techniques and procedures, namely: propaganda, censorship, dis/mis and malinformation (fake news), subversion, *kompromat* and other nefarious sleight-of-hand activities.

With every page I turned, I developed a greater in-depth understanding that covers the wider events that led to the 2022 invasion of Ukraine. The skilful yet dastardly manner in which Putin covers all bases to serve his aims – is a masterclass in the art of self-application and attention to detail. Corruption, electoral fraud, censorship, dealing with opponents, third-country political interference, and even the manipulation of the UN Charter to justify his actions are all part of Putin's playbook.

Brilliantly written, this book joins the dots through the history of the leadership of Imperial, Communist, and Nationalist Russia. It exposes the single-minded determination of Putin and his predecessors in the quest for Russian expansionism. In Putin's case, he presents himself as a strong man leading a strong country. His ruthless and confident ability to politically outmanoeuvre presidents, chancellors, prime ministers and secretaries general over recent decades reinforces the question in the title of this book, 'Could history have predicted the war on Ukraine?' I encourage all with even the slightest interest in geopolitics, democracy and its associated freedoms to read this book and answer the question for yourself.

Major Mike Shearer

Preface

'These military exercises, drills are purely defensive and are not a threat to any other country.'

(Vladimir Putin: 18 February 2022)
Referring to the Russian build-up of military forces along the Russian and Belorussian frontiers with Ukraine.
The attack on Ukraine took place six days later.

The world was shocked by the Russian reinvasion of Ukraine on 24 February 2022 and horrified by the atrocities committed by Russian troops as they devastated their way through Ukrainian towns and villages.[1] However, given the history of Russo-Soviet aggression against Ukraine and other neighbouring states, and the record of excesses committed by Russian forces since the formation of the Soviet Union, this savagery was predictable. The Red Army has always been heavily implicated in atrocities, as to impose their Communist ideology on the world, Soviet leaders have relied on the military and actively encouraged its personnel to display unprecedented levels of aggression and violence as a means of striking fear into the populations they have attacked and occupied. The military historian James Lucas sums up the Russian military thus: 'the passive Slav mentality and the Communist ethos produced an army whose men had a callous indifference to brutality, to suffering and even to death.'[2] During the most recent attacks on eastern Ukraine, evidence was found that the Russian military were told to 'kill everyone'[3] and it was widely reported that rape was being used as a weapon against the civilian population.[4]

In October 1920 during the Civil War, the Red Army's elite *Konarmiia* (Cavalry Army) went on the rampage through the Ukrainian village of Prelacy, some 100 miles east of Kyiv. In a report on the incident, the Bolshevik Revolutionary Tribunal noted that the mutiny began when the soldiers murdered their commissar, and began an orgy of drunken violence against civilians:

> In Priluki, twenty-one Jews killed and twelve wounded. In Oveche, drunken Red Army men raped almost every woman. Soldiers broke into the offices of the Special Department and the Deserters Commission, demanding to know who was a Communist or a commissar. In Vakhov, eighteen homes were burnt, twenty men killed, women raped in the streets in full view of the townsfolk and the younger women taken away like slaves in transports.[5]

Unfortunately, it appears that much of the world has forgotten (or never really understood) the long history of politically inspired outrages committed by Russia against its neighbouring states, which means that the current invasion of Ukraine – with its associated atrocities – are in danger of being dismissed as a singular aberration of the Putin regime, when in fact they are a continuation of what has been happening for over a hundred years. Chronicled incidents of barbarity against the Ukrainian Jews and other citizens are many: Jeffrey Veidlinger claims that between 1918 and 1921 there were more than 1,000 'anti-Jewish riots and military actions…in about 500 different locales throughout what is now Ukraine'.[6] He points out that, whilst these 'actions' (generally known as 'pogroms') were not the first, they were probably the most barbaric in terms 'of the range of participants, the number of victims, and the depths of barbarity'.[7] Perhaps the most chilling aspect of these attacks on Ukrainian civilians, however, was the premeditated nature of the assaults as a form of genocide; Martin Latsis, the head of the Ukrainian Cheka (Lenin's secret police) set the tone when he wrote in November 1918 that they were not waging a war against individuals, but 'exterminating the bourgeoise as a class'. He advised Cheka interrogators that they need not look for evidence that the accused had committed a crime against the new state, but instead they should ask themselves to what class the accused belonged, his origin, and his 'education or profession' and concluded that his fate should be determined by the answers to these questions.[8]

Veidlinger also notes that the pogroms were also characterised by larceny on a grand scale: 'soldiers filled their trucks and carts with pilfered goods and took them away.'[9] But for the dates, both the genocide and the theft could have been a description of Putin's troops in Ukraine just over one hundred years later: some three months after Putin's troops invaded Ukraine, the Mgrublian Centre for Human Rights (Claremont McKenna College, California) published a translation of the 'genocide handbook', issued to Russian forces by RIA Novosti (the Russian official press agency) in which it outlined 'an explicit program for the complete elimination of the Ukrainian nation as such'.[10] Amongst other things, this encouraged invading Russians to use great levels of violence against the civilian population, and called for 'the liquidation of the Ukrainian state, and for abolition of any organization that has any association with Ukraine'. In terms of theft and wanton destruction, Putin's forces appear to be worse than those of Lenin; Shaun Walker and Andrew Roth reported that when a resident of Novyi Bykiv, whose house had been occupied by Russians for a month, eventually managed to return, she found that the occupiers had stolen 'perfumes, jewellery, some wine, a scooter, a novelty cushion and a collection of old coins'. In addition to this, they had looted 'computers, projectors and electronic equipment'[11] from the local school, with other villagers losing 'washing machines, food, laptops and even a sofa'; one woman complained that the Russians took 'literally everything, male and female coats, boots, shirts, jackets, even my dresses and lingerie'. There is photographic evidence of Russian soldiers looting toilet seats and even complete toilets! What they could not steal was deliberately vandalised, or made unusable, and returning residents found 'discarded alcohol bottles, food wrappers and cigarette butts strewn around the apartment, large piles of faeces blocking the toilets and family photographs torn and thrown around the house'.[12]

It is perhaps a cliché but nevertheless true, to say that history repeats itself and that humanity can only progress by learning from the past: as Jorge Santayana famously observed: 'Those who do not remember the past are condemned to repeat it.'[13] Rather than the invasion of Ukraine being a recent phenomenon, it has been going on in various forms for over 100 years. Taking just the twentieth century, how many people (outside Ukraine) know that Soviet forces invaded the country three times between 1918 and 1921? Whilst the deaths of millions of Ukrainians as a consequence of the deliberately caused famines of the early 1930s are relatively widely known, how many people have also heard of the other great Soviet-made famine in Ukraine in 1946–1947, in which thousands starved to death as the Soviets forcibly exported grain and foodstuffs from Ukraine to other Soviet republics? Do people understand that the Soviet Union, rather than liberating East European countries from the Nazis as they would have us believe, simply replaced Nazi occupation with Communist occupation? Stalin's forces instituted large-scale regime change throughout eastern Europe from 1944, initially controlling these countries through a military presence and later through puppet governments until 1991. Ironically, Soviet intentions towards Eastern Europe were known well in advance of 1945, yet the Western Allies persisted in their self-delusion that Stalin could be trusted to keep his word; Roosevelt was naïve in the extreme, and went out of his way to accommodate Stalin's demands for military supplies – even at the expense of US forces.[14] Official figures from the US Embassy & Consulates in Russia, show that between 1941 and 1945, the USA had supplied the USSR with 400,000 jeeps and trucks, 14,000 aircraft, 13,000 tanks, 8,000 tractors, 15 million pairs of army boots, 1.5 million blankets, 107,000 tons of cotton, 4.5 million tons of food and 2.7 million tons of petroleum products.[15] The extent and importance of Allied support was never fully acknowledged by the Russians, who even to this day, continue to give the impression that they alone beat Nazi Germany, and that Western military aid was of little consequence. As Denis Havlat concludes in his study of Western aid: 'Soviet claims about the irrelevance of Western aid can thus be dismissed as propaganda and inaccurate'.[16]

President Vladimir Putin covets the massive deep-water port of Sevastopol in Crimea. This is the real reason for the current Russian invasion of eastern Ukraine. Although Russian forces took Crimea in 2014 with a swift strike by Special Forces units, the problem that Putin had was in holding the region. The issue was how to physically link Crimea to Russian territory thus giving unrestricted access to Sevastopol, as it is at the end of a long supply chain that passes through the Ukrainian provinces of Donetsk, Zaporizhzhia and Kherson; other than by air, the only direct land connection that Russia had with Crimea was across the Kerch Bridge;[17] whilst this provided an immediate solution, it could not accommodate sufficient road and rail traffic indefinitely. Added to which, it was vulnerable to attack – as indeed proved to be the case on 23 July 2023, when it was heavily damaged by Ukrainian sea drones. Logically, Russia needed a land bridge or 'corridor' to provide a direct physical connection with Crimea, and the obvious place for this (geographically speaking) was through the Eastern Ukrainian provinces mentioned above. To this end, Russia actively encouraged and supplied so-called 'separatist' movements in Donetsk in the hope that it would fall sufficiently under pro-Russian control as to present a case for 'self-determination' leading to absorption into Russia. Following this, the next step would be the annexation of Zaporizhzhia and finally Kherson by similar means, giving them direct access to Crimea. This is a classic Russo-Soviet technique for territorial acquisition in which it presents the world with a series of 'reasonable' demands, masked as 'self-determination' – a core principle on which democratic governance is based – and consequently such demands appear reasonable and are likely to be met, whilst obviating the need for outright force to complete the annexation.

However, the Ukrainians understood what was happening, and resisted Russian destabilisation: but this has meant that the citizens of areas such as Donetsk have been subjected to a constant barrage of Russian threats, shelling and terrorist attacks. Whilst people outside Ukraine may remember the 2014 Russian invasion and annexation of Crimea, most will have dismissed it as a *fait accompli*, forgotten about it – 'nothing to do with me' – and got on with their lives. The Crimea, and parts of eastern Ukraine have, by contrast, been living through Russian occupation since 2014; they cannot get on with their lives as if nothing has happened. When Putin recommenced his invasion of Ukraine on 24 February 2022, there was a further outcry, and more comparisons made of his actions with those of Hitler;[18] by his words and deeds Putin has become a second Hitler, which is ironic as his excuse for the latest invasion of Ukrainian sovereign territory was his desire to 'de-Nazify' Ukraine!

This book suggests that the current danger posed by Vladimir Putin's Russia is a continuation of the threats from the Communist administrations that preceded the break-up of the Soviet Union in December 1991, and that anyone with a knowledge of Russo-Soviet history could have predicted the invasion of Ukraine. In a wider context, Western democracies in general are now faced with Putin's resurgent nationalism; the only real difference is that rather than being threatened by Russian Communism, which lacked an economic base on which to leverage the West, we are now threatened by Russian nationalism – which, until recently was underpinned by considerable economic power stemming from Russia's vast reserves of oil, gas, timber, gold, coal and other minerals.[19] These reserves of energy and precious metals (in particular gold, silver, and diamonds)[20] had been used by Putin in two ways: to bring in foreign earnings through export sales,[21] and as a means of blackmail by withholding sales from certain countries that displeased him.[22] This latter tactic was particularly effective in terms of Europe (and especially Germany) which relies heavily on Russian gas.

Ukraine is bearing the brunt of this current aggression and to date is miraculously keeping Putin's forces in check, but for how long can this last before sheer weight of numbers begins to tell? It is to be welcomed that the USA, the UK, and the EU are supplying Ukraine with weapons and money, but the danger exists that the public (voters) will begin to suffer from 'donor-fatigue', and especially in times of economic crisis, will begin to question the wisdom of such expenditure. Added to this is the unpredictability of the new US administration under President Trump,[23] which appears not to understand the importance of resisting Russia. If Western support for Ukraine were ever to be reduced or even withdrawn then it is likely that the war would be won by Putin. Such a military victory would (in his eyes), give him the legitimacy he needs to annex all of Ukraine, and to 'incorporate' Transdniestria into Russia, along with other nations such as Moldova. After that, he may well turn his expansionist gaze towards other countries – reports from May 2025 suggest that he was already amassing troops along the Russo-Finnish border.[24]

Despite his much-publicised lamentations on the collapse of the Soviet Union, Putin's long-term objective is not the restoration of the old Soviet borders, but in the view of this author it is the restoration of the boundaries of Imperial (Czarist) Russia. In tandem with this, Putin naturally sees himself as the Czar of this resurgent Russia, with absolute powers, rather than the leader of a government that is accountable to an electorate. Assuming this to be the case, then to fully restore these old Imperial borders, Putin would have to take not only Ukraine and Crimea, but Belarus, Finland, Moldova, Latvia, Lithuania, Estonia, and much of Poland and Finland. Ukraine, it is argued, is but a first step in this process of 'restitution'. However, Putin is faced with a big problem: leaving aside Belarus, which is his subservient 'lapdog',[25] all these states are independent republics, most are members of the European Union, and – with the exception of Ukraine and Moldova – all are members of NATO; thus, were Putin to continue his quest for the restoration of the Czarist Empire, it would bring him into direct conflict with NATO. It can only be speculated what his reaction to this would be – perhaps he thinks that if he were to attack a NATO member on the fringes of the Alliance (such as Finland), there would be no serious repercussions, and he could continue to destroy NATO through 'salami tactics'.[26] Or if he is sufficiently deluded, he may be willing to risk nuclear war in his quest for the restoration of the Russian Empire, believing that a nuclear first strike against NATO would be successful in eliminating resistance. However, despite threats[27] the use of nuclear weapons is unlikely, as if Putin were to subject Europe to nuclear strikes, there would be precious little left for him to occupy and incorporate into his new Russian Empire, other than a radioactive wasteland; the most likely scenario is that he will launch an all-out conventional and cyber war, during the course of which – while the West is otherwise occupied – Iran could move against Israel, ISIS could complete its take-over of Syria, the Chinese would take Taiwan, North Korea would invade South Korea, the Argentines would take the Falkland Islands, and citing reasons of 'security' or 'national emergency', Donald Trump might even send US forces to annex Greenland!

The key question that underpins this book is whether the current invasion of Ukraine could have been predicted? This question can never be answered definitively, as it lies within the territory of historical 'might-have-been', and consequently is highly subjective and at the mercy of circumstances. It is interesting to note, however, that in his foreword to Brian Moynahan's 1994 book on Russia, the Russian professor and poet Yevgeny Yevtushenko suggested that there could be a war between Russia and Ukraine in the future.[28] History shows that the Russian menace has the absorption of Europe as its goal, and consequently the attack on Ukraine was inevitable. Thus, the answer to the question must be a resounding 'YES'; paraphrasing Santayana, we can predict future events only if we understand and learn from the past, if not, then a repetition of history is almost inevitable due to the nature of mankind. Just as German territorial expansion was at the root of the last two world wars, the history of Russia provides a clear indicator of the nature of successive regimes, and shows that the country's appetite for expansion has not been diminished by its experiment in so-called 'democracy'; in fact, the supposed move to democracy since the break-up of the USSR in 1991 has arguably presented even greater dangers, as it has encouraged the West to assume that the Russian bear has lost its appetite for expansion, and has gone into the equivalent of territorial hibernation. This is dangerous, as the history of the twentieth century is full of catastrophes built on naïve assumptions: the Royal Families of Great Britain and Russia were convinced that their German cousin, Kaiser Wilhem, would observe the niceties of civilised co-operation over Serbia in 1914; British Prime Minister Neville Chamberlain tried to assure his countrymen that they were safe hiding behind his paper containing Hitler's signature promising 'peace for our time'; US President Roosevelt felt he could trust Stalin and gave in to his every demand, which Stalin simply interpreted as a sign of weakness, and more latterly, US President Obama felt that it was safe to trust Putin as the Cold War had ended – his response to the 2014 invasion of Crimea was weak and tardy, leading Putin to assume that he would have no problems in completing the total annexation of Ukraine at a time of his choosing. It is interesting to speculate as to the reason for his delay of eight years before re-commencing his invasion of Ukraine: it was most likely a consequence of the time taken to regroup and reorganise the Russian Armed Forces following the 2014 occupation of Crimea and the incursions into Donbas, to complete the building of the Kerch bridge, and to fully assess the implications of the Western response. After this his timetable was probably delayed by the Covid-19 pandemic.

In the final analysis, Putin cannot be allowed to violate sovereign borders with impunity, otherwise who knows where he will eventually stop? Whilst Russia and NATO continue to fight what is in effect a proxy war, escalation into World War III can be avoided, although Ukraine will (unfairly) continue to bear the brunt of Russian aggression. If Putin were to defeat Ukraine, however, a full-scale war in Europe would be bound to break out sooner rather than later. Everything must, therefore, be done to support Ukraine, and stop Putin's aggressive expansion. History has shown that, unless stopped, Russia will continue the way it has done for over one hundred years: the writing is on the wall – but does the West care to see?

Chapter 1

Imperial Russia – The Schizophrenic State

'We are two hundred years behind Europe in the development of our national political institutions. Russia is still more Asiatic than European and must therefore be governed by an autocratic government.'

Czar Nicholas II, St Petersburg, January 1902
Quoted in: Antony Beevor, *Russia: Revolution and Civil War 1917-1821* (London: Weidenfeld & Nicolson, 2023), p.1

This chapter is divided into three parts: the first deals with Imperial Russia which until the twentieth century had been an empire ruled by a succession of authoritarian royalty, the last of which was the Romanovs. It briefly traces the geopolitical development of the Russian Empire from 1147 and shows how it expanded its political influence and economic power through the annexation of vast swathes of neighbouring territory, culminating with the Romanov Imperial Empire by the end of the nineteenth century.

The second part shows how three events – World War I, the October Revolution of 1917, and the Treaty of Brest-Litovsk – led to a major upheaval within the Russian Empire. The twenty years from 1905–1925 was a period of great change for Russia, and following the October Revolution, the country was in the throes of a politico-socio transformation the like of which had not been seen since the French Revolution, some 150 years earlier. The vast Russian Empire was inherently unstable, and since the end of the nineteenth century, had been a hotbed of revolt, with the failed revolution of 1905 effectively the 'dress rehearsal' for that which followed in 1917. A key difference between 1905 and 1917 was that in 1905 the Russian military were able to play a major role in the maintenance of law and order, and to ensure the continuation of the Romanov dynasty. By 1917, however, the army was effectively a broken force, having suffered a series of humiliating military defeats, and it lacked a sense of purpose in addition to a new-found sympathy for the Bolshevik revolutionaries. The 1917 revolutionaries were more organised and coherent, and most anti-establishment groups had coalesced under the philosophical umbrella that was Bolshevism – later to be termed Communism. The instability throughout the country emerged along the lines of old ethnic/nationalistic groupings, added to which was the economic collapse, military defeat, social confusion and national humiliation of World War I. Following the collapse of the Russian Empire in 1917 and the confusion of the Russian Civil War, there were many groups that saw this as the perfect moment to seek their national independence. However, the Bolsheviks opposed this and ensured that the various 'Soviet Socialist Republics' remained firmly within the newly formed Union of Soviet Socialist Republics (USSR).

The third part looks briefly at the Russian Civil War, the theoretical basis of Communism, and how it was intended to 'internationalise' this radical philosophy through the Comintern. It is important to recognise that the November 1918 Armistice did not bring an end to the fighting. With the withdrawal of Russia from the war against the Central Powers (Germany, Austro-Hungary, and Turkey) the Allies feared that this would lead to German occupation of Eastern Europe, and that the Germans could seize the vast quantities of war materials that had been shipped to Russia. These concerns, coupled with the Communist repudiation of Imperial debts and the global threat posed by Bolshevism, sparked 'intervention' designed – in the words of Winston Churchill – to 'strangle Bolshevism at birth'. It could be argued that the presence of foreign troops on Russian soil (initially to counter advances by German forces, and later to oppose the growing threat of Bolshevism) was a provocative move by the Allied powers – certainly it has been portrayed as such by a succession of Soviet governments and used as a justification for their professed fear of invasion. Alternatively, it could be argued that the presence of Allied forces was the direct consequence of the international threat posed by Bolshevism itself.

The Russian Empire

Territorial Expansion

To understand the relationship between Russia and its neighbours, it is necessary to begin by explaining the historical interaction of nations within the geographical area that comprises Russia and its neighbours today. In 1972 Ivan Rudnytsky pointed out that the nations that comprised the then Soviet Union had long histories of independence, with different cultural and ethnic identities, up until their forced incorporation into the Russian Empire.[29] This longevity of ethnic and cultural identity is key to understanding why Ukraine is *not* part of Russia, despite the protestations of various Russian leaders from Lenin to Putin. The growth of the Russian Empire is a long and complex story and is of relevance in this book, in that it illustrates the schizophrenia underlying Russian psychology in their attitude to neighbouring states. Firstly, there is the Russian paranoia over invasion by foreign powers, and secondly their hypocrisy in annexing neighbouring territories as a perceived means of countering this.

Russian history has been the story of continued territorial expansion at the expense of its neighbours: territorial expansion allowed the Russian Empire to access new lands containing agricultural resources such as cereal crops, timber, sunflowers, sugar beet, and mineral deposits such as coal, gold, diamonds, aluminium, and copper, and more latterly, oil and gas. The second reason for this expansion was political – it provided territory (a 'buffer zone') between Russia and its enemies. As explained by Atzil and Kim: 'Generally speaking, geography, including distance, favours defenders. If the attacker must travel far to reach the defender's territory, its power projection capability is significantly reduced by the costs of transporting and supplying the projected military force.'[30] There is a logic in this, as in the case of Russia, a sufficiently large buffer zone would mean that an invader would have to cross a considerable distance, and their forces would be continually vulnerable to attack, in addition to extending their supply lines.

However, it would appear that the Russians have never quite understood that by annexing adjoining territories, they have actually *weakened*, not *strengthened* their position in this respect. Ironically, rather than *increasing* the distance between themselves and a hostile state through annexation, the

Russians have actually *decreased* the distance by eliminating neutral states on their borders, and at the same time *increased* the levels of concern amongst other neighbouring nations.[31] They have built up reservoirs of resentment in those counties/regions that they have either annexed outright, or they control through 'puppet regimes.' Consequently, countries that once might have been considered neutral (or even friendly) and might have opposed any transit through their territory to attack Russia, might instead prove *hostile* to Russia: annexed or subservient states might choose to make common cause with an enemy of Russia in an effort to secure their freedom.[32] This was most apparent during the post-World War II era, when there were uprisings in some of those countries occupied by Russian forces: East Germany in 1953, Hungary (1956), and Czechoslovakia (1968). Historically, the Russians have always done exactly what they allegedly feared other nations might do to them – adding 'hypocrisy' to the charge of paranoia.

Whilst the explanation for territorial expansion might possibly have presented an excuse for Russian enlargement during the reign of the Czars, it was undertaken with a different objective after 1917 as the whole philosophy of Bolshevism/Communism was to convert Europe and the world to this new political philosophy. Lenin wrote to Stalin in July 1920: 'My personal opinion is that to this end, Hungary should be sovietised, and perhaps Czechia and Romania. We have to think it over carefully.'[33] Thus, far from being the victim of potential threats to the Russian motherland, the Bolshevik Revolution officially put the nation on an aggressive footing, at the forefront of the movement to spread Communism throughout the world. The need for land as a means of *defence* against aggressive neighbours cannot be cited by a nation whose key objective is the enforced regime change in those very neighbours. Once again, the charge of hypocrisy weighs heavy on Russian shoulders.

Historical Development

The emergence of Moscow as the capital city of Russia is a convenient point at which to begin this brief synopsis of Russian imperial history; the city was first documented in 1147 as a small town straddling the River Moskva, and expanded over the years into what became known as the Grand Duchy of Moscow. Just under a decade later, in 1156, it had become a fortified city when a moat and wooden defences were constructed, and Moscow's rulers began to annex the territory that surrounded the city. The quest for territory at the expense of neighbouring states typified Russia through its early years of growth as a Grand Duchy, and through the Imperial reigns of various Czars and Czarinas. This expansion continued for centuries, with each Russian emperor adding further to the territories their empire encompassed. A map of 1533 shows just how intertwined were the borders of the various principalities and kingdoms: especially to the East of the continent, where the nascent Russia (or 'Moscovy') appeared squeezed between Ukraine to the south, the Swedish Empire to the north, the Kingdom of Kazakhstan to the south-east, and the vast lands of Siberia to the east, see Map A (below):

The term 'Muscovy' to describe the Grand Duchy of Moscow became the official designation in 1547. The Duchy began an expansion of its borders – principally under Czar Ivan III (who reigned from 1462-1505), and his successor, Vasili III (1505–1533). The Novgorod Republic was annexed in 1478, the Grand Duchy of Tver in 1485, the Pskov Republic in 1510, the Volokolamsk region in 1513, and the principalities of Ryazan (1521), and Novhorod-Siverskyi (1522). Moscow seized control of the Khanate of Kazan (a Tatar Turkic state) to the east in the same year, and in 1526 the Tatar Khanate of Astrakhan to the south: this was centred around the banks of

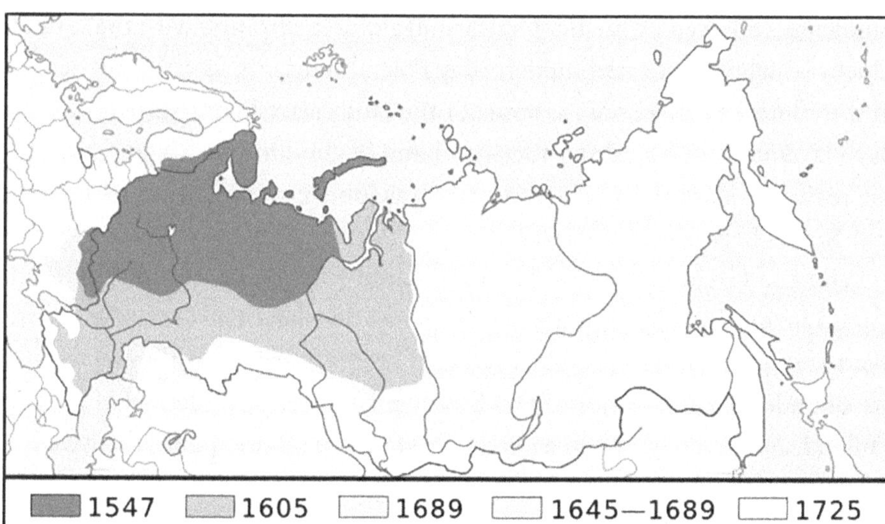

Map A: The growth of Imperial Russia 1547–1725.

the Volga River where it discharges into the Caspian Sea, giving Moscow control of the important Volga trade route and direct access to the Caspian. The annexation of neighbouring states continued against the backdrop of great politico-social instability, which only came to an end in 1613 with the accession to the throne of the Romanov dynasty. The new Czar further increased territorial expansion by focusing on the lands to the east and south and brought thousands of square miles under the control of Moscow. With the accession of Ivan the Terrible to the throne as the first Czar of Russia, there was a renewed push eastwards, leading to the Russo-Crimean Wars (1570–1572), in which the Khanate of Crimea fought against the Russian invaders; in a 1571 reversal of fortunes they pushed the Russians out of Crimea, advanced hundreds of miles north, eventually investing and burning Moscow.

The Russo-Polish War (1609–1618) was fought between Russia (along with its ally Sweden) and the Polish-Lithuanian Commonwealth. In 1610 Sweden withdrew from the Alliance, and this led to the Ingrian War between Russia and the Swedish Empire. The Swedes captured Novogorod, and the war ended with the Treaty of Stolbovo, in which Sweden's intervention in Russian territory was halted, and Russia was blocked from access to the Baltic Sea. In 1634, Czar Michael I initiated a war with the Kingdom of Poland and the Grand Duchy of Lithuania, taking the Voivodship ('Dukedom') of Smolensk, followed by further territory all along the frontier with the Grand Duchy – including most of modern-day Poland. This was a significant period in the context of this book, as some of the lands seized constitute modern-day Ukraine – such as along the west bank of the Dnipro River, Kyiv, and the region of Zaporizhzhia – the latter was jointly administered by Poland and Russia between 1667–1687.

Peter the Great (1682–1725) consolidated Russian control of Kyiv and Zaporizhzhia; in 1700 he went to war against Sweden (The Great Northern War: 1700–1721), and brought Livonia, Estonia, Ingria, and Karelia within the boundaries of his empire. The Swedish Empire controlled what is now Finland, and much of the area encompassed by the Baltic states; the Swedes tried to invade Russia in 1700 but were unsuccessful. Despite Sweden's strong military reputation, it lost much of its territory along the eastern Baltic shoreline, and Czar Peter founded the city of Petrograd on 25 May

1703[34] on the banks of the River Neva, giving Russia an ice-free outlet to the Baltic, and thence to the Atlantic.

The next important monarch in terms of territorial acquisitions was Catherine the Great (1729–1796), and during her reign much more territory was added; her initial focus was on the Caucasus region, but in 1772 she sent Russian forces into Poland to undertake what is now known as the 'First Partition' of Poland. The country was divided between Russia, Austria-Hungary, and Prussia – not only did these countries receive large tracts of Polish territory, but the populations that lived in these areas were forcibly 'transferred' to their new owners, with Russia receiving the largest area (around 36,000 square miles[35] and some 1.3 million people[36]), followed by Austria (32,000 square miles, and 2.65 million), and Prussia (14,000 square miles and around 580,000 people). Poland suffered a second partition in 1793, this time with the country being divided between Russia and Prussia; in this partition, Russia took another large slice of Polish territory, which included Lithuania, Belorussia, and the western part of Ukraine. Prussia received the port city of Gdańsk and other surrounding regions – later to become East Prussia. This was not the final dismemberment of Poland, however, as two years later what remained of the country was divided between the original three aggressors – this time Russia received the Courland region, the remaining Lithuanian territory east of the River Neman, and the Volhyhian region of Ukraine. Prussia gained what remained of the district of Mazoria (which included Warsaw), and Lithuanian territory to the west of the River Neman. Austria took the region of Małopolska (south of the River Vistula), western Podolia, and Galicia. The partitioning of Poland between these three powers was an outright act of aggression, with each claiming territory as a buffer against the others: it showed the inherent instability of Eastern Europe, confirming that the three major powers all harboured expansionist objectives. Subsequent Russian annexations were focused on the south, and took place between 1790 and 1829, concluding with the Treaty of Adrianople. The objective was to annex the territories between the Black and Caspian Seas, and this led to the incorporation of Armenia and Georgia into the Empire.

Possibly the greatest threat to the integrity of Russia had been that posed by Napoleon's invasion of 1812 – the French reached Moscow and burned the city, but were ultimately forced to withdraw – most historians agreeing that this was more a consequence of climate than confrontation. Although the defeat of Napoleon brought some military security to Russia it brought other, more long-term problems, as Russian soldiers had come into contact with European nations and it was feared that they would bring back 'dangerous' Western ideas that might threaten the status quo.[37] Such paranoia was even more apparent with the Communist government.[38] As Alexander Hill explains, this led to 'repressive measures against previously content national minorities' which before long led to 'internal problems' with nations such as the Finns.[39]

The Crimean War (1853-1856) was fought between the Russians and a coalition of three Empires: British, French, and Turkish, in addition to the Kingdom of Sardinia-Piedmonte. The Russians had antagonised the Turks by their advances into the Crimea; the British, French and Sardinians wanted to see the Ottoman Empire preserved as a counterbalance to Russian hegemony in the region. The war resulted in the defeat of the Russians, who also lost the Danube Delta and Bessarabia.

With their continued expansion eastwards and their search for a warm water port, it was inevitable that the Russians would eventually come into conflict with the Japanese, who were also undertaking a programme of territorial expansion, but from east to west: the confrontation between the two powers was known as the Russo-Japanese War (1904–1905). The outcome of which was a surprise as most contemporary observers assumed that Russia would win: however, the Japanese forces were more agile, adaptive, and modern, and their fleet proved excellent. There has been much analysis of this war, and as Richard Connaughton observes, not only were the Japanese superior, but the Russian relied on outdated tactics, which led to huge losses.[40]

The annexation of neighbouring territories took around 350 years and by the time Czar Nicholas II assumed the throne in 1895, the vast Russian Empire stretched from the Arctic and Baltic Seas in the north and northwest, to the Black Sea in the south, from Warsaw in the west to the Pacific Ocean in the east. However, this vast territory brought with it considerable problems of unification, as it encompassed such a range of cultural diversity and language as to make the whole almost ungovernable: Armenians, Finns, Georgians, Latvians, Lithuanians, Mongols, Poles, Russians, Tartars, Ukrainians, and Uzbeks. By the dawn of the twentieth century the Russian Empire constituted the following 'territories': Armenia, Azerbaijan, Belarus, Estonia, Finland, Georgia, Kazakhstan, Kyrgyzstan, Latvia, Lithuania, Moldova, Poland, Tajikistan, Turkmenistan, Ukraine, and Uzbekistan – numerous lands and peoples, most of whom had very little in common culturally and linguistically with Russia, and the majority of whom had no desire to be ruled from Moscow. Such a large area was very difficult to govern, due to the vast distances between the capital and the outlying regions, in addition to the sparse railway and telegraph networks, and the lack of metalled roads throughout the country – all of which made communications (and control) exceedingly difficult. So much so, that it can be argued that the very diversity of ethnic composition of Russia brought into question its viability as a unified country; at that time, and ever since, there was little to suggest that Russia was a *country* in that sense of the word, due to geographical size, and cultural-linguistic diversity. This gave increasing opportunities for dissent and protest, which in turn made for an unstable political entity: the greater the internal dissent, the greater the strain on the existing political systems designed to hold together the corners of such a far-flung disparate empire.

However, the very size of the Empire seemed to blind the world as to its shortcomings: the military might of Russia was generally referred to as the 'Russian steamroller', as it was widely thought that by sheer size and numbers Russia was all but invincible. As Barbara Tuchman, in her epic *The Guns of August* has observed 'on the chessboard of military planning, Russia's size and weight of numbers represented the largest piece.'[41] Despite this, in many respects the country was a 'paper tiger' as there was little to unify the various groupings or cultures within this sprawling empire, and without unification the empire existed on paper only. Whilst Russia could impose its will on neighbours through sheer weight of numbers, in a protracted war against a sophisticated industrial power such as Prussia or France, the country would lack sufficient economic power and politico-social cohesion to present a united front for more than a short time – which is exactly what happened in World War I. This socio-political fragmentation meant that the country was ill-prepared for war: as Peruvian historian Luís Pasará pointed out: 'A country does not win a war simply because it is better armed; firstly, it is essential that it is a country.'[42] Furthermore, in their masterly *Why*

Nations Fail, Daron Acemoglu and James Robinson, suggest that in terms of industrialisation, Russian development had been blocked by the absolutist Romanov monarchy, which had much to lose if there were any major change of the status quo – which explains why the country had fallen behind the level of industrial development of European nations.[43]

Upheaval in Russia

World War I

It is not within the scope of this book to examine the conflict in detail, but to focus on the effect of the war on Russian society and the Russian military. Despite the crucial role of political leaders such as Lenin, it could be argued that the 1917 Revolution might have been contained by the military and would not have succeeded, had the Germans not inflicted such a crushing defeat on the Russians at Tannenberg between 23 and 30 August 1914, and again at Gorlice (2 May–13 July 1915), which resulted in the deaths of thousands, and the capture of thousands more in addition to hundreds of artillery pieces. Of particular significance was the fact that thousands of panicking Russian soldiers fled eastwards, symptomatic of the near-total demoralisation of the Russian army. Robert Asprey comments that once it became obvious to the Russians that they had lost, those remaining surrendered en mass – including units up to brigade size.[44] There were a number of other consequences of this decisive defeat, one of which was that the Russian corps commander, General Samsonov, shot himself. Secondly, the Germans seized considerable quantities of war booty; the final prisoner count exceeded ninety thousand, in addition to thousands of horses killed or captured, the Germans had destroyed two Army Corps, severely mauled another three, and forced those that survived into retreat. Asprey claims that Samsonov lost around ninety per cent of his artillery, and that Russian manpower losses amounted to around thirty thousand.[45] A very good account of the Battle of Tannenberg is also given in Max Hastings' book: *Catastrophe: Europe Goes to War 1914.*[46]

A key consequence for Russian social stability was that many soldiers (including officers) experienced a loss of purpose and morale, and this spilled over into civil society which led to the breakdown of the old order, and helped the Bolsheviks: the opportunity for civil disruption presented itself as the army was too preoccupied with trying to hold what remained of a front line against the Austro-Hungarians and Germans, whilst the police had their hands full dealing with strikes and civil disobedience. In an attempt to halt the revolutionary activities of the Bolsheviks, on 5 November 1914 the government ordered the arrest of some Bolshevik members of the Duma (the Russian parliament), who were then exiled to Siberia, but by then revolutionary thought was too widespread for this to make much difference.

On 2 May 1915 a new combined Austro-German force attacked the Russian 3rd Army at Tarnow and Gorlice in Galicia. After two days of intense artillery bombardment, the Russians finally broke when they were overwhelmed by the attacking force, and they fled eastwards in panic. The Austro-German force halted to regroup, and on 12 June, it resumed its offensive, breaking through the new Russian lines on 17 June: the Russian 3rd and 8th Armies retreated in confusion. General Poplivanov, the Minister for War, reported to the Council of Ministers on 30 July 1915: 'Demoralisation, surrender and desertions are assuming huge proportions. General Headquarters seems to be completely at a loss, and its orders are taking on a hysterical character.'[47] The Austro-German offensive seemed unstoppable: they took Warsaw on 5 August, followed by Ivangorod, Kovno, Brest-Litovsk, Bialystok, Grodno, and Vilna. By the end of September 1915, Russian forces had been driven back 300 miles, as far as their original August 1914 start lines, and to all intents and purpose the Russian military machine ceased to exist, having suffered around 2.5 million casualties, of these around one million had been taken captive.[48] The Germans, feeling that the Russians had been effectively defeated, began to move some units back to the west, to reinforce their move on Paris.

The importance of Tannenberg and the 1915 Galicia disaster that followed cannot be exaggerated – it was the final spark that ignited the slow-burning fuse that exploded into the October Revolution some two years later. It is estimated that, by the autumn of that year, some two million troops had deserted and fled back to their villages.[49] Not only was the majority of Russian troops disillusioned with the war, but crucially they blamed their officers for incompetence – a charge that was undoubtedly grounded in fact – historians such as Norman Stone point to the fact that the Russian officer corps was not like that of Western armies, and as many came from peasant stock, their level of education was very low.[50] There was also a growing backlash against the Czar, his German wife, and senior officers with German names.[51] Whilst the origin of their name did not make them traitorous, the key lay in the *perception* of their loyalties by the mass of peasant soldiers; 'foreigners' were also a convenient scapegoat for the disastrous opening moves of the war, and the blatant corruption associated with the management of the country.[52] There was talk of the German 'stranglehold' on the country, a consequence of the fact that a large number of generals had names of Teutonic or Scandinavian origin.[53]

It would appear that not many observers understood the reason for the calamitous defeat of the Russian army: even with the benefit of hindsight, the British prime minister at the time – David Lloyd George – spectacularly missed the point when he wrote in 1938 attributing the disasters to a lack of munitions, rather than to the rapidly disintegrating morale of the Russians: 'The great retreat of 1915, in which, with unexampled carnage the Russian armies were driven pell-mell out of Poland and the Baltic provinces up to Riga, was entirely due to Russian inferiority in artillery, rifles and ammunition of all kinds.'[54] As he was minister of munitions in the UK War Cabinet between 25 May 1915 and 9 July 1916, it is tempting to conclude that his view of military matters was coloured by his fixation on munitions (especially artillery shells) above all else, obscuring the real causes of defeat: poor leadership, poor conditions of service, and low morale.

The military defeats and subsequent collapse of the Russian army led to Czar Nicolas II taking over as commander in chief on 5 September 1915; this was a bad decision, as any future reverses would now be blamed on him personally, and despite rather than because of his new role as C-in-C, the situation worsened considerably. Those Russian soldiers who had managed to escape death or capture, became a breeding ground for revolution: they were dissatisfied with the way they had been treated in the army, they felt betrayed by their officers, their country, and their monarch. Dominic Lieven, in his study of Czar Nicholas II, describes the mood of the Russian soldiery as 'fickle and unpredictable. In many units the officers were terrified of their men, over whom they had no control.'[55]

Many workers' committees (soviets) were formed, and the end was fast-approaching when troops and sailors mutinied and joined the rioters. Furthermore, as increasingly more men were called up for military service, there remained fewer to farm the land and work in the factories; those who did remain, due to their increasing scarcity, became relatively more important than they had been at any other time – this importance translated into politico-economic power, which was then harnessed by the Bolsheviks. The combination of food shortages, rising prices, and a lack of railway transport for internal food distribution – most railways having been pressed into military service – led to riots breaking out all over the country. Although the Russian armies continued to oppose the Central Powers (the Austro-Hungarians and Germans), it was increasingly obvious that there was no real will to continue the war, and the persistent undermining of the Russian Armed Forces by the Bolsheviks and others served only to further destroy morale and motivation.

Foreign Assistance

In view of the poor performance, lack of stability and dubious loyalty of their Russian ally, it had long been felt by the Western Allies that the Russian monolith was in danger of collapse due to shortages of military equipment and munitions, of competent officers and NCOs,[56] and most importantly, of food. At the Anglo-French Conference in London on 26 December 1916, British Prime Minister Lloyd George advised that there should be serious consideration given to increasing the supply of war materiel to the Russians. He was, however, under no illusions as to how difficult communications and co-ordination were on the Russian Front – in particular he focused on the recent delivery of British field guns to Russia, noting that: 'We think it possible that technical difficulties of communications by sea and rail, lack of communications on the Russian Front, the character of bridges, inadequate personnel training, and the strategic disadvantages of a seriously extended front already alluded to, may possibly be so serious in their cumulative effect as to prevent a full use being put to the guns given to Russia.'[57] With the benefit of hindsight, this might be interpreted as an excuse *not* to supply guns to the Russians, as Britain was unsure as to whether such artillery pieces (and their munitions) would be lost to the Germans – as indeed was the case.

In terms of food supplies, there were two considerations: (1) the production capacity, and (2) the distribution capacity, and related levels of corruption and price inflation. Agriculture in Russia was a highly labour-intensive business, whilst at the same time the Russian army relied on manpower more than technology, which meant that in the millions required by both agriculture and defence, one sector would have to be the loser. After much debate, confusion and procrastination 'partial mobilisation' was declared in 28 July 1914 and then full mobilisation on 31 July;[58] therefore, the first loss to agriculture was the lack of peasant farmers to bring in the September harvests. According to a comprehensive study by Nicholas Golovin, in August 1914 the population of Russia was 65 million, out of which four million were conscripted into the army.[59] If, as is claimed by John Bushnell,[60] '84–88 percent of the Russian soldiers' were peasants, then (even assuming the lower of the two percentages) that would give around 3,360,000 conscripted away from the land. Furthermore, whilst it was true that the Russians had managed to register a slight increase in food production prior to 1914, the rate of population increase had more than overtaken increases in food production.[61]

The second factor relating to food supply was the inadequacy of Russian distribution logistics, and in particular the distribution of grain – principally wheat and maize – throughout the country. As Robert Service[62] points out, food supply had all but collapsed, and this, coupled with rampant inflation meant that there was a real danger of starvation for much of the population. In view of the food riots throughout the country, which grew in number and ferocity as the war progressed, starvation might have been the match that ignited the powder keg of resentment against the war and the government, and this had to be avoided at all costs. Added to these considerations was the fear that, if a separate peace were to be made, the Central Powers would insist on keeping the territory they had won thus far – and which included the rich grain and coalfields of Ukraine. Those parts of Russia that had traditionally supplied agricultural harvests were generally self-sufficient, but as Norman Stone explains, the problem was how to move the grain by overburdened railway from where it was grown, to where it was most needed.[63]

The October Revolution

What has become known as the October 1917 revolution really began on 23 February 1917 in Petrograd (later Leningrad, and now St Petersburg), and when troops from the 181st Infantry Regiment sided with strikers against the police, this heralded the beginning of a widespread breakdown in discipline amongst front-line units, and the beginning of the end for the Czar, who was told by his senior officers that the army would not support him in the event of a revolution. He was forced to abdicate on 15 March 1917, and the government of the country was now in the hands of the Duma, led by the Czar's brother Grand Duke Michael Alexandrovich, although Prince Georgy Yevgenyevich was the *de facto* head of state.

Having seized power, the Bolsheviks formed a new government known as the 'Soviet of People's Commissars' on 26 October, and they quickly established a Bolshevik-Soviet presence as far East as the Ural Mountains, in key cities and regions such as Moscow, Donbass, Baku and the Volga region. The supreme commander of the Russian army, General Dukhonin, was shot along with some of his staff officers on 19 November. The news was received with much consternation abroad: in the British Parliament, Prime Minister Lloyd George announced that:

> The incidents in connection with what I believe will prove to be one of the landmarks in the history of the world have followed each other with such dramatic suddenness that it has not hitherto been possible, and it is not possible to-day, to give to the House of Commons a detailed account of what has actually occurred.[64]

He then admitted that the government had known of the instability in Russia for some time: 'There has for some time been deep discontent in Russia, of which there have been several manifestations, due to the inefficiency of the Government in the conduct of the War. On Friday, the 9th, some riots, due to the scarcity of food, occurred in the streets of Petrograd.'

In that same month the Duma was reconvened, but this semblance of government did nothing to ease the situation, and it was followed by more than a month of strikes at the Putilov Iron Works, near Petrograd – an important centre of production for munitions and armaments. In view of the strategic nature of this factory, the strikers were conscripted and the government oversaw production, but this led to greater discontent and more strikes, the army was used, in conjunction with the police, to crush the strikes. By now, the army had largely lost its sense of purpose and morale: it had suffered defeats on the battlefield, had been forced into major withdrawals, and was increasingly used to oppose (and on occasions kill) striking workers.

Alexander Kerensky – a radical lawyer – was appointed Minister of War in the new provisional government, and insisted that Russia continued to play her part in opposing the Germans and Austrians. In his short time in power, Kerensky had championed some notable causes amongst which were the institution of basic civil liberties, such as the freedom of speech, the right to a free press, political assembly, and religious freedom. He was also a champion of equal rights for women – all of which made him very popular throughout the country. His objective had been two-fold: on the one hand to hold the new government together, whilst simultaneously ensuring that the Bolshevik faction, which was growing in influence, could not seize power. This proved an impossible task, as he had to unite two bitterly divided wings, and unsurprisingly he failed in his efforts: also, one cannot help but surmise that he was considered a threat by Lenin, as if he could give the people what they wanted, (whilst still maintaining the Duma), then the revolution promised by the Bolsheviks might never happen. Notwithstanding the poor morale of the Russian army, Kerensky launched a new offensive between 1 and 4 July 1917, led by General Aleksey A. Brusilov. Despite a promising start, the exhausted Russian troops did not have the stomach for renewed fighting, and there was open rebellion in some sectors of the front line, with troops refusing to leave the relative safety of their trenches to assault enemy positions, and the offensive ground to a halt with heavy losses. The Russian officer corps lost most of its remaining authority, having been compromised by the pervasive influence of Bolshevism amongst the troops.[65] Kerensky lost support from within the government – especially the left-wing elements – and faced downright hostility from the army when he sacked the commander in chief (General Lavr G. Kornilov) on the grounds that the general had been plotting to overthrow the government and replace it with a military dictatorship. There was a glimmer of hope for the government, however, when a revolt at Kronstadt on 15 July was easily put down, and one of the ringleaders – a certain Leon Trotsky – was arrested; the other – Vladimir Lenin – fled into hiding: both had been denounced as 'German agents.'

Even this was not enough to save the government, as it was assaulted from multiple directions simultaneously: the Bolshevik attempts at insurrection, the army's loss of idealism and its growing repugnance at having to shoot strikers, the shortages of food, in addition to weapons, and the growing threat to the economy of inflation. Proclaiming himself prime minister and declaring Russia to be a republic, Kerensky managed to cling to power for another three months, but at least one historian has claimed that it was his fixation with continuing the war that was his downfall.[66] Added to this were the verbal assaults from Russia's erstwhile allies: some of the British press appears to have openly criticised his Cabinet as 'convicts'[67] and on 12 November the Foreign Secretary (Lord Arthur J. Balfour) was accused by Mr Robert Outhwaite, MP for Hanley, of secretly hoping for a return of the Czar – the suspicion being that the Kerensky government was too radical to be trusted to continue the war. Outhwaite asked: 'Are we then to take it that the Government are desirous of seeing these attacks continued for the purpose of restoring the Tsar and of destroying the revolution?'[68] Balfour denied the charge, but in view of later comments made in parliament, it would suggest that (unsurprisingly) the British government did not look favourably on the changes taking place in Russia.

This focus on the conduct of the war, when most Russians were more interested in internal revolution was a major mistake – in modern parlance, Kerensky might be said to have misread the mood of the people. As Peter Hart notes, most Russian soldiers preferred to be observers rather than participants, and voted with their feet, and he claims that by autumn around two million had deserted.[69] Whilst criticism is justified in view of the circumstances, it somewhat misses the point that Kerensky could do little else other than continue with the war for two reasons: the first being that if Russia sought a separate peace with the Central Powers they would be likely to lose all territories captured by the Germans thus far (as indeed did happen at the Treaty of Brest-Litovsk), and would definitely lose all the valuable lend-lease assistance that the allies were currently providing. This included hundreds of artillery pieces and thousands of shells, in addition to over 300,000 infantry rifles supplied by the Winchester company.[70] The

Russians needed Allied weapons as their industrial production was so slow and inefficient that they could not equip all branches of the armed forces: Hew Strachan observes that the rate of Russian industrial production was far behind that of the Western Allies and it lacked a good railway network with which to distribute men and materiel to where it was needed.[71] Lyn MacDonald refers to the scarcity of such basics as infantry rifles, noting that they were so few that many Russian soldiers were forced to retrieve weapons from 'men killed or wounded on the battlefield'.[72]

In addition, the speed of retreat of Russian forces meant that much materiel was left behind, and ultimately captured intact by the Germans. After their hurried retreat from Kovno, for example, the Russian army was found to have left behind 1,300 guns (artillery pieces), in addition to 53,000 new rounds (shells) for heavy artillery pieces, and 800,000 rounds for field artillery pieces.[73] However, despite the paucity of materiel, it was probably the critical situation of grain and other food supplies that caused the greatest worry to the Kerensky government. As has already been noted, to leave the war would almost certainly have meant that no more supplies would be sent by Britain, France, or the USA. A second consideration must have been the state of the Russian army itself: despite the high levels of desertion, there were still millions under arms, and more importantly, under control of the military authorities. If Russia were to agree to an armistice, then these millions would be demobilised and return to their towns and villages – taking their weapons with them. The fear must have been that they would immediately contribute to both food shortages and to the danger of armed uprising.

All of which was very worrying for the Western Allies – the US ambassador in Petrograd telegraphed US Secretary of State, Robert Lansing, in February 1917, pointing out the 'great uneasiness' throughout the city and the strikes and demonstrations were condemned by the governor of Petrograd.[74] A key worry for the Western Allies was whether the Russians would continue to play their part in the war – although they had not officially negotiated a separate peace with the Germans, rumours were growing that this would happen, and great efforts were made to help the Kerensky government, beginning with a congratulatory telegram sent on behalf of the British parliament! Indeed, Lenin was openly talking about halting the war – a clever move as the average Russian soldier was more interested in Lenin's offer of bread, peace and land, than he was in fighting. During the autumn, Kerensky's personal authority and that of his government deteriorated further: by contrast, there was a continued rise in popularity for the Bolsheviks, principally based on two of their promises: (1) to stop Russian involvement in the war, and (2) to undertake a redistribution of land. A further difference between the Bolsheviks and the Russian government, was that the former were well organised and disciplined – partly as a consequence of Trotsky who had taken it upon himself to create a military force (the Red Guards) dedicated to fighting for the revolution. From March 1917 the Bolsheviks were increasingly successful politically – using their superior organisation and discipline, they gradually seized power throughout the country, and by September of that year, soldiers were in revolt against their officers, leading the US ambassador to report 'fighting liable to begin at any moment. Officers naturally timid as their killing continues. Fifteen or twenty reported killed at Viborg and bodies thrown into sea.'[75] Once the Army was in revolt, the process could not be stopped, and this led to the final collapse of government and the proclamation by Lenin of outright revolution in Petrograd on 21 October 1917. As feared in the West, the effective collapse of the Russian war effort allowed the Germans to transfer thousands of troops to the Western Front, sufficient to build up an offensive capability which eventually resulted in the 'Spring Offensive' of 21 March 1918.

The confusion throughout the country was palpable, and some foreign embassies were closed, with diplomatic staff having escaped as best they could. British Foreign Secretary Arthur Balfour appeared to be no better informed than his American counterparts about the general situation in the country: when asked in the House of Commons on 12 November 1917, about the whereabouts of the British ambassador to Russia and the political situation in that country, he replied that whilst he could confirm that the British ambassador was still in Petrograd, he could 'furnish no other information than that which has appeared in the public Press.'[76] It would seem that the political class in the wider world underestimated the seriousness of the situation – perhaps they thought it would soon be contained by the Russian army; what they singularly failed to appreciate, however, was that the Russian army was increasingly siding with the Bolshevik revolutionaries, and that the old order was rapidly disintegrating.

Kerensky fled along with most of his cabinet, leaving the country in turmoil until the Bolsheviks established themselves. There was a multitude of problems they faced, not least of which was foreign recognition of their new government; such recognition was important, as with it came continued financial and military support. In answer to a question about British diplomatic representation with the new post-Kerensky Bolshevik government, Balfour confirmed that 'Since the fall of the Provisional Government no Government has been established in Russia with which His Majesty's Government have found themselves able to enter into relations.'[77] Whilst the world viewed the revolution of October 1917 as the culmination of a long period of uncertainty and instability, Kerensky prophetically announced in 1917: 'The world thinks the Russian Revolution is at an end. Do not be mistaken. The Russian Revolution is just beginning.'[78] His prescient pronouncement was to foreshadow the civil war that tore Russia apart and inflicted lasting damage on the peoples of the various nations of the old Russian Empire.

Perhaps the one saving grace of the whole campaign on the Eastern Front was that it had distracted the Germans who were worried by the initial Russian advance into East Prussia, and rapidly transferred two Army Corps to the Eastern Front – thus weakening the drive on Paris. This, combined with the despatch of another Corps to confront the Belgians, and the change of direction of German attack from an envelopment of Paris from the west to a frontal assault on the capital from the north, meant that the Germans stalled north of Paris, losing the initiative and ultimately the war. The French commander in chief, Marshall Joffre, is reported to have said: 'the Russians had rendered us exactly the service I had expected of them; for, as I learned the next morning…two German Army Corps were leaving our front on their way to East Prussia'.[79]

Throughout his formative years Lenin knew subterfuge, instability and violence but was seemingly too squeamish to become involved in violence himself, whilst being a strong advocate of violence perpetrated by others in the name of the revolution. This rather begs the question whether he was a hypocrite or a coward, or perhaps both? According to Robert Service, in 1905 Lenin 'not only confirmed his commitment to violent methods but gave them a specificity that was more bloodthirsty than anyone thought imaginable. He displayed a virtual lust for violence. While he personally had no ambition to kill or to maim or even to witness any butchery, he took a cruel delight in recommending such mayhem.'[80] Daron Acemoglu and James Robinson, in their analysis of power, prosperity and poverty, summarise the Bolshevik revolution as a 'bloody affair' and note the level of hypocrisy that existed right from the start; they comment that, despite the Bolshevik's exhortations to equality 'the first thing Lenin and his entourage did was to create a new elite, themselves, at the head of the Bolshevik Party. In doing so they purged and murdered not only non-Communist elements, but also other communists who could have threatened their power.'[81] As a part of his new revolution, Lenin seized the banks, factories and mines, in addition to implementing total state regulation of foreign trade; of crucial significance to future international relations was the fact that the Communists cancelled their obligations to service foreign debts, arguing that they were not responsible for agreements made by the previous government. Furthermore, as Service notes, Lenin 'abrogated the rights of the wealthier citizens and established … a class dictatorship'.[82]

Initially when the revolution broke out, the country was divided into factions: despite what Bolshevik propaganda would have the world believe, there was no real unified movement towards revolution, nor did it occur simultaneously throughout the country – in fact in certain areas, there were as many people opposing the Bolsheviks as fighting on their side. Eventually, workers were organised into political units, known as 'Soviets' – basically an elected governmental council. These units initially had a degree of autonomy, but in order to maintain his hold on power, Lenin instituted what has become known as the 'Red Terror', in which he established the internal organisation of a police state, and hundreds of thousands were sent to slave labour camps (Gulags) in Siberia and/or executed.

The Treaty of Brest-Litovsk

The Russian forces, pushed back on all fronts, sought to neutralise the threat from the Central Powers by offering an armistice which came into effect with the Treaty of Brest-Litovsk on 9 February 1918. Whilst the Duma had opposed such a move, the new Bolshevik government felt that it had no option but to concede to German demands – the Bolsheviks needed the army to be under *their* control, not under that of the generals – in order to impose their new philosophy on the country, and were unable to do this whilst millions of men were still at the front line, under military discipline. The Central Powers, already badly stretched and short on manpower, were glad of this cessation of hostilities, as they could then transfer some troops back to the Western Front.

In addition to the cessation of hostilities, there were a number of other outcomes of Brest-Litovsk: the most important being that the Bolsheviks were forced to relinquish their control over a number of ethnically different states that had been subsumed within the Russian Empire. The Germans insisted on keeping most of the territories they had occupied during the war: Belarus, Estonia, Latvia, Lithuania, Poland, and part of Ukraine including the Crimea and territory as far East as Rostov-on-Don. The Bolshevik government was also forced to confirm its recognition (in January 1918) of the independence of Finland, and to halt hostilities against the newly formed Ukrainian People's Republic – the western part of modern-day Ukraine. Thus, Brest-Litovsk ensured that Ukraine became an independent state, and was to provide grain and other foodstuffs which were badly needed in Germany especially, as the British-led blockade had begun to bite – by December 1918 it was claimed that 736,000 German civilians had died from starvation.[83] Whilst military observers at the time might have considered Brest-Litovsk of significance as it ended Russian involvement in World War I, with hindsight it is the loss of territory that is perhaps of greatest relevance to this book – in particular the loss of Ukraine, with its southern coastline and immensely important harbour facilities in Odesa and Sevastopol, in addition to the loss of similar outlets in Latvia and Estonia. Furthermore, with the independence of Ukraine, Russia had lost uninterrupted access to vital agricultural land and mineral deposits (see Map B below: 'Area Lost by Russia Following the Treaty of Brest-Litovsk'). In short, the price that the new Bolshevik government paid for peace was very high – but it allowed them to consolidate their power base; furthermore, viewed from Lenin's perspective, it was only a temporary move, as he fully intended to take back the lost territories in the future – either through military intervention, or subversive activities orchestrated by the Comintern. He commented to his

Map B: Area lost by Russia following the Treaty of Brest-Litovsk.

crony Lev Kamenev: 'Let us, the Great Russians, display caution, patience etc., and gradually we'll get back into our hands all these Ukrainians, Latvians.'[84]

Following the signing of the treaty, the Germans drove the Bolsheviks out of Kyiv, liberating the city on 1 March 1918. Geopolitically, whilst it looked as if Ukraine had managed to secure its freedom from Moscow, it appeared to have exchanged Russian for German control, much to the consternation of the Allies, especially the British, who along with the French, suspected that the German forces in the region would take advantage of the cessation of hostilities to regroup and ship supplies of war material to the Western Front. Whilst Lenin resented the loss of territory as an unavoidable consequence of the peace imposed on Russia by Germany in 1917, there was little he could do about it – he was too busy trying to secure the Revolution against White Russian forces in the Civil War, and foreign military intervention.

An excellent analysis of the extent of lawlessness and confusion at this time is to be found in Antony Beevor's book about the Russian Revolution.[85] The problem was that nobody – including within Russia – was really sure what was going on in such a vast country, and who (if anybody) headed a government capable of making decisions; the situation was admirably illustrated in the House of Commons during a debate relating to the freeing of British subjects held by the Bolsheviks, one Member of Parliament suggested to Lord Robert Cecil (Assistant Secretary of State for Foreign Affairs) that the displeasure of HM Government should be made 'perfectly clear to the Bolshevik Government.' Lord Cecil, his frustration showing even through the normally bland pages of *Hansard* replied at length that the situation was not as straightforward as the MP had suggested, pointing out that:

> it really is very misleading to talk of a central government in Russia at the present moment. If you have a quarrel with an ordinary civilised country you can approach the Central Government...in the present condition of Russia, the amount of connection between the Central Government, if it may be so called, sitting in Moscow, and the outside of Russia is of the slightest possible description. It would be almost true to say that each town has a Government of its own, with a very slight connection with the Central Government, if any...a situation which is exceedingly difficult to deal with; a situation in which, for all practical purposes, the bonds of ordinary society have been absolutely destroyed, and you have something very like anarchy existing throughout Russia.[86]

Revolution and Retribution

Famine

By 1918 it had become obvious that land ownership would have to be the first objective of the new government in its 'collectivisation' programme – in particular those landowners who held more than eight acres of land, and who were denigrated as 'Kulaks'[87] and were a particular target and deemed worthy of punishment. A major problem for the Communists was their need for grain – this would enable them to secure their power base by feeding the population. Of the ten goals of Communism, that of land ownership *('Abolition of property in land and application of all rents of land to public purposes')* was directly responsible for a famine that killed millions. This resulted in a lasting hatred for Russia and Communism within Ukraine, explaining why the country welcomed what it thought were German liberators in July 1941.

The major source of grain production was Ukraine, and production quotas were imposed on Ukrainian farmers who were obliged to produce for the greater good of society through these arbitrary (and impossible) quotas. Newly imposed Soviet legislation prohibited the peasants from keeping any of the grain they had grown until they had met their quotas; Soviet officials then resorted to confiscating as much grain as they could find, and left the peasants to starve. As might have been expected, however, farmers tried to hide their grain from the Bolshevik officials sent to check that each farm was fulfilling its required quota. From being enthusiastic supporters of the revolution, the peasant farmers became hostile to the government; Nicolas Werth points out that, ironically, it was the armed groups of Red Army soldiers that had been sent to enforce the grain collections, that 'alienated the same peasant producers who had helped bring down the old tsarist order with their violent rebelliousness.'[88] This resulted in 'pitched battles between peasants and the new representatives of Soviet power. Peasant uprisings broke out in Ukraine, in the Tambov region, along the Volga'. Lenin had a savage approach to all landowners – in a telegram to Penza communists (south-east of Moscow) on 11 August 1918, he urged that at least 100 Kulaks be hanged in public (see Box A):

Box A

Lenin's Call to Hang the Kulaks

'Comrades! The insurrection of five kulak districts should be *pitilessly* suppressed . The interests of the *whole* revolution requires this because 'the last decisive battle' with the kulaks is now underway *everywhere*. An example must be demonstrated:

1. Hang (and make sure that the hanging takes place *in full view of the people) no fewer than one hundred* known kulaks, rich men, bloodsuckers.
2. Publish their names.
3. Seize *all* their grain from them.
4. Designate hostages in accordance with yesterday's telegram. Do it in such a fashion that for hundreds of kilometres around the people might see, tremble'.

(Quoted from: Robert Service, *Lenin: A Biography*, p.365)

Yuri Shapoval and Marta Olynyk, in an extensively researched article on the famine, quoted one Soviet official who, in trying to justify the persecution in Ukraine, told his staff of 'the categorical existence in Ukraine of an organized, counterrevolutionary, insurgent underground, which is linked to foreign countries and foreign intelligence services, mainly in the Polish General Staff'.[89] Needless to say, he offered no evidence of such a serious claim.

The sheer magnitude of policing such a policy led to a massive expansion of the police force, and a refocusing of police objectives away from fighting crime, to ensuring that people were not keeping back any part of that demanded by the government. The Bolsheviks' answer to internal control, was to recruit a force of political police – and thus began the terror inflicted on the newly Sovietised citizens.

The Red Terror

Before seizing power in 1917, Lenin had publicly stated that the new Russian state would not even need a traditional police force, as crime would be unnecessary in the new utopia – why should anyone steal, for example, when all their needs would be met? However, as Gill Bennet notes, Lenin had privately concluded that 'a coercive organisation would be needed to ensure the success of the revolution and neutralise political opposition'.[90]

The solution was the 'Cheka'[91] which Lenin founded on 20 December 1917. It was based loosely on the old Czarist secret police organisation (the 'Okrana') and comprised many former Okrana officers, many of whom brought with them their brutal methods. The first head of the Cheka was Feliks Dzerzhinsky, who set up his headquarters in Lubyanka Square, Moscow; the Cheka was formed ostensibly to combat foreign interference, in reality the organisation was predominately used to terrorise citizens to ensure no internal opposition to the Bolsheviks – a function that it carried out with zeal, due to the number of fanatics and psychopaths in its ranks. From the outset, the Cheka used intimidation, torture, and extrajudicial murder to frighten the population into submission, leaving the security services to concentrate their activities on real (or imagined) threats from outside the country. In February 1918 Lenin officially authorised the Cheka to torture and kill without trial any arrested person deemed guilty: as Antony Beevor notes, the backlog of cases to be investigated prior to any trial meant that it had become quicker and easier 'to execute prisoners rather than undertake extensive investigations as to any presumed guilt'.[92] Let loose from any legal restrictions on their activities, the Cheka instituted a period commonly known as the 'Red Terror', in which people were arrested, tortured and executed, generally without trial. The Bolsheviks admitted that the Cheka had carried out some 8,500 executions in the first year of the 'Terror', and it is estimated that ten times that number were arrested and sent to labour or prison camps. One source suggests that the true number of 'extra-legal' killings was nearer to six figures;[93] in addition, many deaths were classified as 'shot whilst attempting to escape' – as reported in the Marxist newspaper *Novaia zhizn* (New Life) on 19 April 1918.[94] An eyewitness reported that, in Petrograd, the numbers executed in 1918 were around 1300, even though the Bolsheviks only admitted to around 500. The same eyewitness suggested that in the naval base of Kronstadt, there were some 400 shot in one night alone.[95]

Lenin established total control over the state by terror; he admonished his old revolutionary crony Lev Kamenev who wished to see an end to capital punishment: 'How can you make a revolution without firing squads? ... What other means of repression do we have?'[96] By far the most comprehensive analysis of Cheka atrocities is that given by Sergey Melgunov, in his book *"Red Terror" in Russia*, in which he lists the abuses the Cheka meted out to ordinary Russians on a daily basis. People were arrested, tortured and then generally executed on the merest suspicion of being what were variously described as 'bandits', 'counter-revolutionaries', 'bourgeoisie', or 'dangerous intellectuals.' He cites the Cheka of Tsaritsin and Kamishin who used to 'saw their victim's bones apart' (whilst the victims were still alive) and at Poltava and Kremenchug they 'made it their speciality to impale clergy.'[97] In a comprehensive study of Cheka's atrocities, George Leggett describes some of the various torture methods that they employed, such as tying White Russian officers to planks, before slowly feeding them alive into furnaces or boiling water. He also claims that the tortures varied according to region: the Kharkiv Cheka liked to peel the skin from victim's hands 'to produce "gloves"'; in Voronezh they studded barrels internally with nails, and then rolled their naked victims around in these; the Dnipropetrovsk Cheka preferred to crucify or stone their victims to death; in Orel, naked prisoners were forced to stand in the street (in temperatures well below zero), while they had cold water poured on them. Perhaps most horrifyingly, there are reports of Chinese Cheka who forced rats into a metal tube, one end of which was attached to the victim's stomach – heat was applied to the other end of the tube, and the rats gnawed their way through the victim (who was still alive) in an attempt to escape the gradually increasing heat at the other end of the tube.[98]

The horror and terror inflicted on the population stemmed not just from the barbaric methods of torture and execution that the Cheka employed, but also from the constant uncertainty that anyone could be denounced as belonging to what were classified as 'dangerous' categories. Following the attempt on Lenin's life by Fanya Kaplan on 30 August 1918, the Cheka went berserk, and killed all 500 prisoners held in jail in Petrograd – described by

Bolshevik authorities as 'hostages' – and another forty-one were executed in the afternoon of the same day in Nizhny Novgorod. An additional 300 were killed the following month – amongst whom were 'former Tsarist officials and Socialist Revolutionaries'[99] and who were all shot in public. Anna Reid claims that in the two months following the assassination attempt, some 'six thousand death sentences were issued, but the actual number of killings was much higher.'[100] The number murdered by the Cheka was only just beginning to filter to the outside world, when the Conservative MP for Marylebone West, Sir Samuel E. Scott, told the UK parliament that the Cheka had issued a warning that 'to every murder of a Communist or an attempt at such a murder we shall reply by shooting bourgeois hostages.'[101] It is interesting to note that much the same rationale was given by German occupation forces during World War II – a number of hostages were shot for every German soldier killed; yet although the Russians denounced this as German barbarism, they had been content to commit atrocities on a similar basis, some thirty years earlier.

The Civil War

The immediate post-war period was a mass of contradictions: allied aid to the Russian governments of the Czar and Kerensky turned into armed opposition to the Bolsheviks; there were 'Red Russians' fighting 'White Russians' in uncoordinated campaigns throughout the geographical length and breadth of the country – each force seemingly commanded by a general of varying capabilities and each with a different agenda. Allied troops found themselves fighting the very people who had previously been praised as their ally, and ethnic groups that had fought with the Russians against the Central Powers later fought each other and the Russians – and in some instances (such as the Finns and Czechs), created great problems for the new Bolshevik government. As the authority of the Provisional government collapsed, there emerged growing independence movements that challenged the authority of control from Moscow – in particular from Finland and Ukraine. Both were to prove problematic for the Bolsheviks under Lenin, and later, the Soviets under Stalin. Neither leader wished to see them go, as both Ukraine and Finland were of significant value to the Russian (later Soviet) Empire: Finland provided a maritime outlet to the Baltic, and from there to the Atlantic, whilst the value of Ukraine lay in its geostrategic location containing warm water ports on the Black Sea, and as a centre of mining and agriculture. The two Russian leaders used armed intervention in an attempt to prevent the cessation of both: Ukraine was forced to fight for its independence between 1917 and 1921, but ultimately lost the struggle and was subsumed within the Soviet Empire. The early attempts at independence by Finland resulted in a Civil War that began in 1918, and which was based around two power groupings – those Finns (the 'Reds') who backed the new Soviet government, and those (the 'Whites') who saw their future as lying with Germany. The 'Whites' won, and Finland moved out of the Soviet orbit into that of Germany – the Russians, however, would not accept this for long, and some twenty years later, in 1939, manufactured an excuse to invade the country once more, leading to what is generally referred to as 'The Winter War'.

The new Bolshevik government, through the Red Army, controlled most of central Russia, but its authority was threatened by a number of rebel armies – known collectively as 'The White Russians'. Fighting between the two groups began in late 1917 and lasted until 1920: it was another two years, however, before the Bolsheviks could crush all opposition, and establish themselves as the new government of what was called the Union of Soviet Socialist Republics. It is also instructive to note that, according to Russian military historian Mikhail Khvostov in Central Asia, in Russia itself, and in Ukraine there were 'local independence movements' that continued to present armed opposition to Moscow until as late as 1926.[102] Despite what Bolshevik propaganda would have the world believe, there was no real unified movement towards revolution, nor did it occur simultaneously throughout the country – in fact in certain areas, there were as many people opposing the Bolsheviks as fighting on their side.

The war raged throughout the country, and initially it seemed as if the 'whites' would emerge victorious as the Red forces were stretched to breaking point. Between August and November 1918, for example, the various units of the Red Army held a front from the Caspian Sea (approximately 200 miles east of Astrakhan), to the north-east of Ykaterinburg – facing them to the east was the Czech Legion, the People's Army, Orenburg Cossacks, and the Ural Cossacks. To the southwest there was another front line, held by five Red Armies (8th, 9th, 10th, 11th and 12th), which extended from the Black Sea to encompass the Donbass region, and was anchored on the sea of Azov, to the west of Taganrog – these armies faced the Don Army, and two Volunteer Army units. Suffice it to say that between the defeat of the Czar's armies, the establishment of Kerensky's interim government and the seizure of power by the Bolsheviks, the country was in total chaos – split between various power factions, and loyalties to different leaders. One strategic advantage that the 'Reds' had was that their forces, by and large were in the centre of the country, which meant that inter-army communications were not as difficult as between the various 'White' armies, which were generally centred around the coastal ports – Archangelsk, Murmansk, Vladivostok, Kherson, and Odesa.

Whilst all were ostensibly fighting the Bolsheviks, the 'Whites' had differing objectives and it was the lack of communication between these various groups and lack of unifying purpose, that more than anything else, ensured the failure of these anti-Bolshevik forces. There were 'national' armies from the various republics – such as Poland, Latvia, Finland and Ukraine – some were fighting for independence, some for the Bolsheviks, and some for the restauration of the old Russian Empire, and (initially) the Czar. There was even a Ukrainian pro-Bolshevik force led by General Ataman Grigoriev.[103] Some forces were basically armed groups that were little more than opportunists or outlaws. Thus, the Russian 'civil war' was unlike any that had preceded it, explaining why it dragged on for so long, and the legacy of resentment and bitterness that it left in its wake.

It is difficult to sum up the Civil War, other than to say it was a confusion of a number of nationalities, conflicting geopolitical objectives, different armies and tactics, thrown together over a diverse number of battlefields ranging from Poland in the west to Siberia in the east, and from Murmansk in the north to the Crimea in the south. One writer has noted that, in Ukraine for example, there were many armed groups that were motivated by various factors, such as 'nationalism, political ideology, or simply local aspirations'.[104] The basic problem was the question of internal stability and control, and the jockeying for power between the various 'Red' and 'White' factions within the country.

Foreign Intervention

Foreign intervention in the Russian Civil War was the outcome of a series of threats engendered by actual events, and by yet more threats (perceived or anticipated) to the stability of the West. The first moves towards intervention had already been taken, albeit inadvertently, with the allied aid to Russia programme, and the British and French in particular already had military personnel in parts of the country to distribute incoming aid – of both a military and a humanitarian nature. Even after the new revolutionary government of Kerensky took over following the fall of the Czar, it was still hoped that the Russians could be persuaded to continue fighting against the Central Powers – the Germans in the north, and the Austro-Hungarians in the south. However, following the fall of Kerensky, and the seizure of power by the Bolsheviks in November 1917, there was no appetite to continue, and by early 1918, Western intelligence sources were forecasting that Russia was rapidly deteriorating into anarchy and that very soon they would not be able to field any resistance to the Central Powers: allowing the Germans to transfer more troops and munitions from the Russian Front to the Western Front. In addition, it was feared that the vast quantities of weapons and munitions that the Allies had supplied to the Russian would fall into German hands. All this changed however, when the new Bolshevik government signed the Treaty of Brest-Litovsk, agreeing a separate peace with Germany, thus at a stroke of the pen eliminating the main reasons for allied intervention – what had been feared was now reality. From this point, Allied intervention was spurred by a combination of three new objectives: the imposition of debt repayment schedules on the new Communist government, the establishment of independent states, and preventing the spread of Bolshevism. Even before the war had officially ended the British sent a contingent of Royal Marines to secure the northern port of Murmansk on 6 March 1918; ironically, the British military presence had been requested by the Bolsheviks, as they were afraid of the Finns, based on the rumours of military co-operation between Finnish and German forces. Indeed, on 10 May the shore party of marines from the destroyer HMS *Cochrane*, found itself surrounded and fired upon by a reported two hundred Finnish ski-troops.[105]

The armistice that brought World War I to a close came into effect on 11 November 1918; the Western Allies moved fast, firstly agreeing spheres of influence within Russian territory, and then sending military contingents to their respective spheres. Various forces from outside the borders of the old Russian Empire were sent to Russia on the pretence of 'keeping the peace' – but they were really there to ensure that the Bolshevik revolution did not spread beyond the old borders, and to ensure that the German and Austro-Hungarian troops did not avail themselves of any Russian munitions, weapons, or vehicles. Probably the best account of the confusion accompanying foreign intervention, is to be found in the book by Anna Reid – *A Nasty Little War*.[106] Following the November 1918 Armistice, the occupying German forces retreated from Ukraine leaving a power vacuum in the South, especially around the key port of Odesa, and a mixed Allied force was landed there and at Sevastopol in the Crimea in mid-December. Once the German forces had left, the Bolsheviks reneged on the Brest-Litovsk Treaty, and invaded Ukraine; by now the country was effectively split into two regions: the Western Ukrainian People's Republic (WUNR) and the Ukrainian People's Republic (UNR), and these two united on 22 January 1919, with an 'Act of Union' signed at Kyiv. Despite this apparent unity, chaos reigned in Ukraine, and foreign governments were unsure as to what was happening: on 5 March 1919 in the House of Commons, Lieutenant Colonel Cecil Malone asked the foreign secretary 'whether, in the Ukraine, the British Government are supporting the Petlura or the Ataman of the Ukraine; whether their war aims are identical; and, if so, on what policy the British Government decides to whom its support should be accredited?'[107] The foreign secretary was absent from the debate, and so it fell to the Under Secretary of State, Mr Cecil Harmsworth, to answer this question. His reply suggested that HM Government was no better informed than Colonel Malone, perhaps explaining why the foreign secretary himself was absent:

> As regards the first and third parts of the honourable and gallant Member's question, no negotiations have been entered into by His Majesty's Government with any authorities in the Ukraine, nor have they decided to support any particular party in that territory. As regards the war aims of General Petlura, it is understood that he is aiming at the establishment of an independent Ukraine. General Skoropadski, the Hetman of the Ukraine, fled from Kiev last November, and is not at present in Russia.[108]

Despite the conflict lasting another year, the eventual outcome was never really in doubt: the Bolsheviks controlled most of Ukraine by mid-1919, and the country was eventually annexed into the new Soviet Union. The importance of this first military 'adventure' by the Bolsheviks shows that Ukraine has been, since its inception, subject to aggression and occupation by Russia – small wonder then, that the Ukrainians of today are prepared to fight in defence of their homeland, as they know the history of occupation by the Russians.

The intervention of Britain, Czechoslovakia, France, Japan, Italy, the USA and other nations appears to have had little impact on the outcome of the war for the same reason that plagued the 'White' armies: there was very little co-ordination between the constituent parts of this Foreign/White Russian force. For example, when asked in the UK parliament whether 'any discussion has taken place between the Allies co-operating in the Murmansk, Archangel, and Vladivostok (Siberian) expeditions as to the objectives to be gained?' Mr Bonar Law, the chancellor of the exchequer replying on behalf of the prime minister, said: 'This is a kind of question which I must decline to answer.'[109] It is unclear whether his refusal to answer was based on the grounds of security – he did not want the Bolsheviks to know the extent of inter-Allied co-operation, or on ignorance – that he simply did not know, but did not want anyone to know that he did not know. In view of the muddle in which the Allies found themselves, the most likely explanation is that there was no co-ordination between the various forces, a consequence of geography as much as anything else, with the port of Murmansk at the northern coast of Russia, around 100 miles from the Finnish border. Archangel lay around 300 miles further east, on an inlet in the White Sea, and the port of Vladivostok (where an American force had landed) was on the Sea of Japan, near the border with China – some 2,500 miles to the east. Added to the distances between the forces, were communication problems caused by the weather, a lack of landlines, little or no radio communication, poor flying conditions, and at least four languages!

The 'White' Forces

Whilst it is difficult to be precise as to the numbers and nationalities of foreign soldiers who were present in the various regions of Russia the following countries supplied various numbers and types of forces at one time or another: Australia, Britain, Canada, China, Czechoslovakia, Estonia, France, Greece, Italy, Japan, Romania, and the USA, although the majority of interventionist forces were supplied by Britain, Czechoslovakia, France, and the USA. Rather than go into detail regarding all the interventionist forces sent by each nation, it is sufficient to give a 'flavour' of the confused and divided campaign by highlighting the various forces commanded by four different 'White' generals, the geographical areas in which they conducted anti-Communist operations and the support they received from their Western Allies.

General Denikin and the Armed Forces of Southern Russia

Probably the most successful of all the 'White' generals was Anton Denikin, who assumed command of the armies of the Crimea following the death of General Kornilov in April 1918. His forces included the Crimea-Azov Army, the Turkestan Army, and various units from the northern Caucasus region. Denikin's forces were amongst the most effective in the fight against Bolshevism, partly because he managed to bring various units/armies under his command, allowing the force to act cohesively, rather than as various separate units. On 8 January 1919, Denikin brought together various existing formations: the Volunteer Army in Ukraine, led by General Mikhail Alexyev; in the southern centre of the country, there was the Army of the Don (named after the river), which was led by a succession of generals, the first being General K.S. Poliakov (from April 1917), then a month later by Major General Pyotr Popov. Under Denikin's overall command, these units eventually formed into the Armed Forces of Southern Russia (AFSR), which at its height counted on some 270,000 soldiers (including 48,000 cavalry), and was supplied by the British with just under 380,000 rifles, over 4,000 machine guns, 917 cannons, 102 tanks, 1,335 cars/lorries, and 112 tractors.[110] In addition, Denikin received a valuable air contingent from the British: 277 aircraft, 101 RAF officers, and 300 airmen, all of whom were anti-Bolshevik volunteers.[111] He also received a contingent of 15,000 troops from the disputed Polish-Ukrainian province of Galicia[112] – confirmed by Winston Churchill, in the House of Commons, on 2 December 1919.[113] There was also the strongest naval flotilla in Russia, all of which had been crewed by professional sailors in the Czar's navy. It was an anti-Bolshevik force, but crucially one that also wished to preserve the borders of the old Russian Empire, and did not therefore, look favourably on independence movements.

General Pyotr Wrangel (Crimea)

'Wrangel's Russian Army' was a formation raised by General Pyotr N. Wrangel to defend the Crimea – which by the time of its formation in May 1920 – was the last stronghold of the White armies in the south of the country.[114] His forces were driven steadily south into the Crimean Peninsula, where they managed to hold out against the Bolshevik armies for just under six months, allowing time for the bulk of his force to be evacuated from the port of Sevastopol and others. In all, they managed to evacuate around 150,000 military personnel and civilians, effectively bringing the Civil War to an end in November 1920. Of those people that remained, the Bolshevik forces promised them amnesty if they would surrender: all did, but instead of being treated honourably as prisoners of war, thousands were executed.[115]

General Yudenich and the Northern Army

To the northwest of the country, the Northern Army consisted of the Northern Corps commanded by General Nicolai Yudenich, and the 'Russian' Corps (General Bermont-Avalov), plus a number of other units.[116] Yudenich had been a successful Tsarist general and assumed command of the White forces in the Baltic region. The Northern Army received great encouragement and practical support from the British. There was an allied expeditionary force at Archangel, which (in conjunction with some White Russian forces), had pushed as far east as Pinega and as far south as Troitskaya. The Royal Navy was represented by a flotilla of some twenty ships, including the seaplane carriers HMS *Pegasus* and HMS *Nairana.* The British forces in Russia were by far the most numerous and well-equipped, and included both naval and air forces. Geoffrey Best suggests that there were 14,378 British troops in North Russia.[117] Charlotte Alston claims that there were another 1,800 in Siberia,[118] and Damien Wright gives the number (including Commonwealth troops) in the Caucasus region as 40,000 just prior to the British withdrawal.[119] In addition to British forces, the Commonwealth (Canada, Australia and others) provided a number of troops: there were some 4,000 Canadians in

Siberia, and around 600 in Arkhangelsk.[120] As the British and French were short of troops to achieve their objectives, their governments requested that President Wilson provide American forces to help with the campaign in the North. In July 1918, after much discussion, Wilson agreed to the strictly limited participation of 5,000 US army troops in the campaign. This force, which became known as the 'Polar Bear Expedition' was sent to Arkhangelsk while another 8,000 soldiers – the American Expeditionary Force (Siberia) – were landed at Vladivostok.

General Alezander Kolchak (Siberia)

One more general of note was Alezander Kolchak, an ex-naval officer who commanded the White Russian forces in Siberia. His was an unfortunate appointment, as in addition to engaging with Bolshevik forces, his troops reportedly indulged in massacres of civilians and those who were fighting for the independence of their own country-regions. His forces moved westwards towards the Bolshevik stronghold of Moscow, but at Kazan and Samara his advance was halted, and he was forced back east. As the war had progressed, Kolchak had begun to assume authoritarian powers, and as a measure of the distaste in which he was increasingly held, he was betrayed to the Bolsheviks by his own forces, captured, and executed.

Czech Forces

The Czech Legion consisted of a mixture of peoples, ranging from soldiers who had formally (and reluctantly) served in the Austro-Hungarian (AH) army, in addition to a large number of Czechs who lived in Russia, principally around the western Ukrainian region of Volhynia, and the city of Kiev. At the outbreak of war, they had asked Czar Nicholas to be allowed to form a separate Czech Legion (rather than remain under Russian control), in order to fight the Central Powers (principally AH). In their early beginnings, the Czechs were known as the *Druzhina.*[121] On 2 February 1916, the various Czech units were officially amalgamated to form the Czechoslovak Rifle Regiment, which was brought up to brigade strength in May of that same year. However, as with many other ethnic minorities within Russia, the abdication of the Czar and the fall of the Kerensky government spurred them on to seek independent nation status – this was proclaimed after the

Armistice of November 1918. With the formation of the Ukrainian Peoples' Republic (UNR), and the fact that there were a number of Czech troops stationed near Kyiv, they were eventually drawn into fighting attempts by the Bolsheviks to re-incorporate the region into Russia.

What happened next embodied the tragedy of most of Eastern European ethnic groupings: the Bolshevik government decided that, rather than have these POWs sitting in camps in Russia, they would encourage them to fight against their former 'masters', the Austro-Hungarians. At the Treaty of Brest-Litovsk, it had been agreed that all POWs held by the Soviets would be repatriated on the condition that they did not take up arms against the Russians: in return, the Bolsheviks promised the Czech contingent that they would be allowed safe passage through Siberia to Vladivostok, from where they could be shipped to France, and from there to the newly formed Czechoslovakia. It was hoped that they would then help knock AH out of the war, and establish an independent Czech state, free from AH control. Whilst the principal seemed sound, the way in which the local Bolshevik factions operated left much to be desired, as they appeared to be beyond the control of the Bolshevik leadership. The end result was a relatively large Czech contingent (David Bullock gives it as 70,000 men)[122], that effectively took control of the Trans-Siberian Railway, and immediately adjacent lands for a distance of some 6,000 miles as they made their way east to Vladivostok. Had they been allowed to proceed uninterrupted, the plan might have worked, but due to excessive interference by local Bolshevik groups along the way, fighting eventually broke out between the Czech Legion and the Russians, negating any advantage that the Bolsheviks might have accrued through this imaginative plan.

On 9 March 1918, the new Bolshevik government formally changed its name to the 'All-Russian' Communist Party, and declared the country a Union of Soviet Socialist Republics from 30 December 1922, with Lenin as its leader. On 31 December 1925, the Party underwent yet another change of name, becoming the 'All-Union' Communist Party', in an attempt to play down the imbalance that Russia had in its dominant relationships with the other Soviet republics. At the same time, the new structure envisaged a union of all the various geographical entities ('Soviet republics'), ostensibly an equal confederation, but in reality, it had already been decided to bring these various 'republics' under the direct control of Moscow. In this respect, the only real difference between Lenin and his successor Josef Stalin, was in the degree of autonomy the 'republics' were allowed: Lenin wanted more self-determination so as not to be compared to the old Empire of the Czars. Whether his view would have prevailed will never be known as there was an attempt made on Lenin's life, after which he was confined to a wheelchair and he died on 24 January 1924 from a stroke. He was succeeded by Josef Stalin, his deputy, who from the outset made no pretence of his intentions: he wanted total control from Moscow, and used the various secret police organisations – from the Cheka onwards – to ensure no challenge to his authority.

The involvement of foreign forces in the Russian Civil War is an area that has been hotly debated for a number of years, and is relevant to the theme of this book. The Communists have always claimed that these foreign armies should never have intervened in what was a purely domestic Russian affair, and cited the involvement of other nations as justification for their suspicion that the Western powers had the destruction of Bolshevism as their ultimate aim; this gave them an apparently legitimate excuse for the formation and activities of the Cheka. However, it is also argued that Allied intervention was justified for a number of reasons: one being the repudiation of all foreign debt by the Bolshevik government on 10 February 1918. Up to the late 1870s, the Czar had relied on loans from British banks; these had been gradually replaced by German banks from 1871 when the new German Empire was formed under Bismark. This source of funding was reflected in the trading arrangements as Germany gradually assumed the role of major trading partner with Russia, and French banks began to increase their loans to the Czar's government. It has been estimated that by the outbreak of World War I, around eighty per cent of Russian external debt was held by French investors,[123] who not unnaturally were most concerned when the Bolsheviks reneged on their obligations. The Bolsheviks claimed that they were under no obligation to honour the debts incurred by the Czar.

The second, and perhaps more important concern, was with the stated objective of the Bolsheviks to incite revolution throughout Europe – which, not surprisingly, alarmed all European governments, and many outside Europe, such as the USA and Japan. Ever since the Bolsheviks had taken control, they had cited their fear of attack from the West as the reason for their constant vigilance, espionage networks, and attempted destabilisation of neighbouring governments. What they ignored, however, was that this so-called threat from the West was one that the Russians themselves had created: the stated long-term objective of Communism is world revolution, leading the West to understandably fear aggression and destabilisation from Moscow. Therefore, the intervention of foreign forces should have come as no surprise to the Bolshevik/Communists as the danger they posed to Western democracies (and to the wider world) was made very clear by Lenin. Winston Churchill famously said of the Bolshevik revolution: 'I think the day will come when it will be recognised without doubt… that the strangling of Bolshevism at its birth would have been an untold blessing to the human race.'[124]

Summary

The analysis of Imperial Russia shows an empire driven by insecurity and paranoia, which sought to conquer as much neighbouring territory as possible. This empire was dysfunctional and disorganised, it lacked any cohesive culture, structure and order, and the internal contradictions that plagued it ultimately led to its fall. The replacement, a dictatorship of the proletariat was even worse; domestically the new Bolshevik government instituted a reign of terror far in excess of that of the Czar; internationally the new Bolshevik (later Communist) government simply continued the seizure and annexation of neighbouring states, the only real difference being that the Communist agenda included the destruction of socio-political systems, and the fomenting of revolution throughout Europe and the world. Thus, from its earliest beginnings, Russia sought to destabilise and annex its near neighbours, and Ukraine has always been a particularly attractive target, as a consequence of its geostrategic position, and its great agricultural and extractive (coal, gas, oil) production.

Chapter 2

Communist Russia – The Subversive State

'The Red Army will consider its Bolshevik mission complete when it achieves control of the entire globe.'

Jakov Tzudikovich Gamarnik,
Chief of the Political Directorate of the Red Army, 15 March 1937

Lenin chose violence as the means of overthrowing the government, and in order to maintain control, he and his successors encouraged this violence to continue long after the new government was firmly established; key figures from the Czar's government were executed, and others fled. The Czar and his family – including children – were shot in a squalid cellar in the town of Yekaterinburg.[125] Doubtless apologists for the revolution would argue that killing them was necessary to eliminate the possibility of an organised counter-revolution, and to send a message to those who were wavering in their support for the revolution. The real question, however, is whether it is morally acceptable to overthrow one regime citing the regime's use of violence and tyranny as the reason for its overthrow, yet use the same to punish members of that regime, and to persecute those who were simply getting on with their lives? From a purely practical point of view, all people see is that the new government is behaving in much the same way as the old government, so what has been achieved? The irony is that a revolution, ostensibly started to give people freedom from oppression, should find itself terrorising, torturing, and executing its citizens, putting down movements for independence, and paving the way for forceful inclusion into a new regime.

Lenin realised that if Russia were to become an international force with which to spread Communism throughout the world, it needed access to the outside. The old Imperial Russia had just this – its borders were shared with

East European countries in Prussian and in the Austro-Hungarian Empire, and it could access the Baltic through the Baltic states and Finland; to the south, there was the strategically important Ukraine and the ports of Odesa and Sevastopol. Following the collapse of the Imperial government, all the countries on the fringes of Russia pushed for independence and had they been successful, then the land borders and sea ports might have become inaccessible to the new Bolshevik government. This could not be allowed to happen, so regardless of the principles that Lenin and others may have first espoused, these were overtaken by practical concerns: the new Soviet Union could not allow these countries to achieve their independence.

Uprisings Against the New Government

Even before the civil war had finished the Bolsheviks were faced with a series of internal revolts against their authority, predominately from amongst the very people Lenin had said that the revolution would make free. The reasons for rebellion were many, but principally hatred of the collectivisation of agriculture with its accompanying imposed quotas, seizure of grain and subsequent famine. As if that were not bad enough, rather than address the root cause of such disquiet, the authorities employed very heavy-handed means of suppressing dissent – often sending in the Cheka, the Joint State Political Directive (OGPU) or Cossacks to quell rebellion by killing protestors, or exiling them to the Gulag camps. The disruption began in 1921, and outbreaks of rebellion occurred throughout the decade, with some semblance of stability only being achieved by the authorities in 1930; many revolts took place in the Soviet Asian Republic of Kazakhstan.

1921: Anti-Bolshevik revolt (North Kazakhstan)

This was triggered by the demands from Moscow that the Kazak farmers give far more grain and other foodstuffs than they could supply. After the revolt had been suppressed, 232 rebels who had surrendered were shot by the Bolshevik authorities.

1928–1930: Sary-Sozak revolt (South Kazakhstan)

This was another uprising in response to the 'collectivisation' programme and the seizure of a number of farms by the government. Estimates as to the numbers involved vary between 2,000–4,500, and this presented a serious problem for the Bolshevik administration. A number of peasants were deported away from the area, and an unknown number were executed – ostensibly because they had murdered Bolshevik Party officials who had been overseeing the transfer of grain and property.

1929: Bostandyk

As with the previous two uprisings, this was sparked by the grain seizures, and the heavy-handed response of Bolshevik officials, and the uprising was undertaken by around 500 people. An OGPU unit suppressed the uprising, with fifty civilians killed, and two sentenced to death; around fifty-eight were given prison sentences in the Gulags, of between seven and ten years.

1930: Sarbaz

This was yet another uprising in the Kazakhstan Soviet Republic, once again in protest at the enforced collectivisation of agriculture, and the activities of Communist officials. Interestingly, the other grievance that was expressed was against the attempted interference with religious rights in the area – religion was anathema to the Communists, who saw it as a direct (and largely organised) challenge to their authority. This was all the more ironic, as the repressions ordered from the mid-1920s were orchestrated by Stalin – who in his youth had trained to be a priest. The rebellion in Sarbaz was possibly the greatest threat to the early Communist regime, as the threat to the people's religion was something that affected the entire population, and not just the farming community. Added to this, the population was well-armed and order was only restored with heavy loss of life.

Rebellions and uprisings continued into the 1930s, and Moscow was forced to employ thousands of security troops to contain the dissent. This must have been a worrying situation for the new government, as it showed the extent to which their policies were opposed from within the country; whilst attacks against the regime had been expected from foreign governments, what had *not* been expected was the level of domestic opposition – something that worried the Bolsheviks considerably, so much so, that they used excessive violence in combatting these uprisings which were put down with great savagery.

'Peaceful Coexistence'

The term 'peaceful coexistence' is generally attributed to Karl Marx, but in fact it was coined by a Prussian-born American officer, Joseph A. Weydemeyer[126] who was a follower of Marx and Engels. There is some debate[127] as to whether the term 'dictatorship' meant the same then as it does now; it is suggested that the original meaning was one of a temporary assumption of absolute power in times of crisis – as first used in the Roman Empire. As the only real difference in meaning was to be found in the definition of 'temporary' – it can be dismissed as an argument over lexical semantics more than anything else. Thus, the objective of the early Bolsheviks was an administration in which they alone exercised absolute power – in essence no different to any other dictatorship that had preceded it.

The ex-GRU[128] operative turned defector Viktor Suvorov, grew up in the Communist system, and understood its global goals. In his analysis of the early phase of Bolshevism, he noted that Lenin had declared that one world war might not be sufficient to bring about the world Communist revolution, and that a second major might be needed. Lenin had reasoned that as war is the 'mother of invention' 'world war is the mother of world revolution.' He postulated that the 'longer the war lasts, the more bloodshed and destruction it brings, the sooner revolution takes place'.[129]

Lenin identified three key objectives that pose a major threat to Western civilisation and society:

1) The old world must be destroyed, and a new one built in its place
2) To destroy the old world and build a new one it is necessary to gain political power. Gaining political power requires using all measures, ranging from the most peaceful to the most violent, from the most open to the most secretive
3) The struggle for a new world must unfold not on a national scale, but on a world scale.[130]

Lenin could not wait for the collapse of society to happen 'naturally', and advocated revolution as the catalyst for this momentous social change – 'world Communism.' In 1919, he founded the 'Third International' (also known as 'The Communist International' or 'Comintern'), which was an association of national Communist parties, each working under the direction of Moscow to impose Communism throughout the world. Authors such as Harold Fisher have described the Comintern as the 'General Staff of World Revolution', noting that the executive committee of Comintern had one single broad objective behind its formation which was the overthrow of 'the international bourgeoisie' which would be accomplished through struggle 'by all available means, including armed force'. The objective was 'the creation of the international Soviet republic as a transition stage to the complete abolition of the state'.[131] Thus, Communism is incompatible with individual nation states. It is described as 'a tool or weapon such as no other country possessed, and the Soviet Union never hesitated to use it when the occasion demanded. Masquerading as a political party in a country permitting it to operate openly, a Communist party was in fact a fifth column'.[132] As Suvorov claims: 'The goal of the Comintern was the creation of a "World Soviet Socialist Republic"'[133] This means that Communism can never 'peacefully co-exist'[134] with the rest of the world, and especially with the Western democracies as its very existence poses a threat to world stability; through its own admission, its objective is to 'destroy the old world' and replace it not by a new democratic state, but by the 'dictatorship of the proletariat'.

In order to achieve this 'world revolution', Lenin needed to have links outside Russia, and this presented a major challenge: on the one hand to provoke world revolution, the Bolsheviks had to communicate with the rest of the world. However, as communication channels are generally two-way, there was a danger that those whom the Bolsheviks were trying to convert might end up converting the Bolsheviks. The answer was to maintain channels for propaganda and subversion, whilst at the same time ensure that the population of Russia had no access to information from the outside. To do this required the two fundamentals of any totalitarian state: censorship and internal control and of the two, the most immediately important was control.

The Bolsheviks vowed not to rest until they had 'destroyed the old world and built a new one in its place': they viewed this as the ultimate goal of Communism and were prepared to use all means at their disposal to achieve it – including violence and subterfuge. Small wonder that the major world powers took fright, and tried to 'strangle Bolshevism at birth.' It is essential that democracies throughout the world understand this threat: for too long they have been manipulated into thinking that Communism is simply a more radical form of socialism, and as most democracies contain varying shades of socialism, it would appear that the threat posed by Communism is exaggerated. The key question that democracies should ask themselves, however, is why has no country ever voted for Communism, and why has it always been necessary to impose it on people? By contrast, there are very many countries that have moved from Communism to democracy as soon as they were allowed to do so.[135] As US President Reagan pointed out in a speech to the British parliament in 1982: 'From Stettin on the Baltic to Varna on the Black Sea, the regimes planted by totalitarianism have had more than thirty years to establish their legitimacy. But none – not one regime – has yet been able to risk free elections. Regimes planted by bayonets do not take root.'[136]

Covert Strategies

In order to achieve this destruction of the old world, the Soviet Union and more recently Russia, has targeted the West in a number of ways – both covert and overt – to sow confusion and division and incite anarchy, leading to the collapse of governments. However, rather than launch full-out military assaults on their perceived enemies, the Communists were generally far more subtle. In 1946, when the Communist threat was arguably at its most severe, Winston Churchill highlighted the danger:

> in a great number of countries, far from the Russian frontiers and throughout the world, Communist fifth columns are established and work in complete unity and absolute obedience to the directions they receive from the Communist centre... the Communist parties or fifth columns constitute a growing challenge and peril to Christian civilization.[137]

As this strategy is of a very long-term nature it is likely to remain largely undetected by defence security services: a KGB defector, Yuri Bezmenov, explained in 1984 that the Communists think very long term, and generally in some form of 'covert' operation. Bezmenov said that around 85 per cent of KBG activities were aimed at the long-term 'brainwashing' of the populace: 'a slow process which we call either ideological subversion, active measures, or psychological warfare.'[138] This brainwashing is designed, in his words, to 'change the perception of reality of every American to such an extent that despite of the abundance of information no one is able to come to sensible conclusions in the interest of defending themselves, their families, their community, and their country'. He identified three stages in this process: (1) demoralisation (which takes around 15–20 years, i.e. a generation); destabilisation (2–5 years); and crisis (1–6 weeks) – and in total could take up to thirty years to achieve.

In addition to being more difficult to identify and challenge, covert actions have proven effective as a consequence of the naïve attitudes throughout the West: always trying to see the Russian point of view, striving for impartiality and compromise, and a determination to avoid conflict – admirable traits in themselves, but of little use when dealing with an enemy who views these as signs of weakness. Winston Churchill – a wartime ally of the Russians, and someone who knew what Stalin was really like – explained in his famous 'Iron Curtain' speech at Westminster College, in Fulton, Missouri, on 5 March 1946:

> From what I have seen of our Russian friends and Allies during the war, I am convinced that there is nothing they admire so much as strength, and there is nothing for which they have less respect than weakness, especially military weakness. For that reason the old doctrine of a balance of power is unsound.[139]

The danger was highlighted by US President Ronald Reagan in 1983, in an address he gave to the National Association of Evangelicals, Orlando, Florida, on the subject of the arms race; he warned the West against adopting a complacent attitude to what he termed the 'evil empire', and the tendency of Western liberal intellectuals discount the dangers posed by the Russians:

> Let us be aware that while they [the Russians] preach the supremacy of the State, declare its omnipotence over individual man, and predict its eventual domination of all peoples on the earth, they are the focus of evil in the modern world ....I urge you to beware the temptation of pride – the temptation of blithely declaring yourselves above it all and label both sides equally at fault, to ignore the facts of history and the aggressive impulses of an evil empire, to simply call the arms race a giant misunderstanding and thereby remove yourself from the struggle between right and wrong and good and evil.[140]

The West suffers from complacency – there is a prevailing view held largely by socialists, liberals, and fellow-travellers that, as the Russians have not attacked Western democracies so far, nor is it in their interests to do so in the future one should give them the benefit of the doubt and seek to develop open friendly relations. There is a school of thought that insists that the West is equally to blame for international tensions and standoffs. It is this complacency and a desire to be impartial on the part of the West, that makes Communism in the twenty-first century far more dangerous than any possible resurgent Fascism or Nazism. Stephen Ambrose observes that both the Nazis and the Communists had world domination as their overall objective, but that the 'Soviet method, however, differed from Hitler's and was potentially more dangerous…the Russians would not inaugurate large-scale war but would rather avoid armed conflict while advancing their aims through internal subversion'.[141] This is more difficult to identify and counter, whilst an outright attack against a neighbouring country – such as the Russian attack on Ukraine in 2014, even if preceded by a 'false-flag' operation – is obvious to the whole world. Conversely, the 'salami tactics'[142] employed by the Communists are far more difficult to identify and challenge. People tend not to see the slow but inexorable eating away at democracy by the combined efforts of the organs of the various Communist parties – eroding Western values and defences inch by inch: never taking so much at once as to cause alarm. To be most effective, each 'slice' should be justified where necessary, so there is unlikely to be a backlash against this slow incursion. When challenged directly, there has been a marked tendency to back down, such as in Berlin in 1961 and the Cuban Missile Crisis (1962). There are six broad methods employed by the Russians, and whilst their use was probably at its height during the Communist era, they are still used by Putin's forces.

Propaganda

There are two main streams of propaganda: one is aimed at the domestic population (generally a long-term operation), and another is aimed at foreign audiences (generally short-term). For the domestic targets, the idea is to inculcate the younger generations with the values and standards of the current regime in the hope that a whole new generation of children would grow up as committed Communists/nationalists. To this end, a number of Communist youth organisations such as the *Komsomol* (the 'All-Union Leninist Young Communist League') – were formed, with the express intention of developing young communists. There is not the space to go into a detailed examination of the Komsomol or any of its similar organisations – suffice it to say that, in accordance with the long-term Communist objective of imposing a Communist revolution throughout the world, the Communist youth organisations prepared their citizens for a life of Communist servitude, and the 'future progress of mankind'. To Lenin, this subjugation of the youth was essential, and just as Hitler did some fifteen years later, the cadres of young that were to be indoctrinated proved to be the most fanatical fighters when it came to their turn to pick up a rifle.

The second strand of this propaganda offensive was directed against those regarded as external enemies – basically the whole non-Communist world! The Russians have made repeated efforts to spread propaganda as an effective means of destabilising Western powers, and attempting to sow discord, using a variety of communications ranging from word of mouth to sophisticated print media, and radio broadcasts. As early as 1937, in view of the growing political uncertainties within Europe, these broadcasts were worrying, as they were a vehicle through which listeners could submit questions on politics, which would be answered with a Soviet slant. In the House of Commons, on 1 March, the Conservative MP, Mr Marcus Samuel, asked a question to the Foreign Secretary (Mr Anthony Eden), whether Mr Eden,

> is aware that the Russian wireless station known as Radio Moscow is broadcasting messages in English and expressed as being for English listeners, inviting them to send questions upon political matters to which a reply is promised, and asking that such listeners should communicate with Radio Moscow any criticisms they may have of the programmes; and, in view of the fact that when these broadcasts in English were first instituted it was stated that their purpose was solely to instruct Russians in the use of the English language, whether any assurance to this effect was given to His Majesty's Government; and if so, whether he will take up this matter with the Government of the Union of Soviet Socialist Republics?[143]

Mr Eden replied with his usual smooth self-assured ambiguity:

> According to my information, the Moscow station extends a general invitation to listeners to communicate to the office of the station any criticisms or observations they may have to make on any item in the programmes. These programmes, however, are not specifically political in character. As regards the second part of the question, I am not aware that, when these broadcasts were instituted, it was definitely stated that their purpose was solely to instruct Soviet citizens in the English language. No assurance to that effect has been given by the Soviet Government. As regards the last part of the question, if my hon. Friend can furnish me with evidence showing that any particular broadcast contained a direct attack on the Government or institutions of this country, I will certainly undertake to consider the question of representations.[144]

The Communists have traditionally made heavy use of Western media through which they reach millions of people with their messages; they can do this as democracies allow freedom of speech, and do not censor their media outlets – the increased use of the internet and social media has made it even easier for Moscow to speak directly to people, and they know how to turn this to their advantage. As the majority of communication nowadays is through the television or the internet, Moscow has broadcasts beamed through the RT channel, which was established in 2000 as Russia Today, and rebranded 'RT' in 2005 in an attempt to disguise its origins.

Censorship

At the same time as broadcasting propaganda abroad, the Russians have always imposed strict controls on the information available to their own population, which is basically a mixture of state censorship, lies, and disinformation. For example, on 29 September 1958 there was an explosion at the nuclear waste disposal site, near Blagoveshensk, in the Republic of Bashkortostan, near the Ural Mountains, some 1,400 kilometres east of Moscow. Despite the fact that around 200 people died, and some 10,000 were evacuated from the immediate vicinity, the Soviet censors managed to keep the disaster secret until 1976 when the Soviet dissident Zhores Medvedev announced it to the world in an article in *The New Scientist*[145]. Medvedev claimed that: 'Tens of thousands of people were affected, hundreds dying, though the real figures have never been made public.'

More recently, within four days of Putin's invasion of Ukraine, the organisation Human Rights Watch announced that the Russian authorities had threatened 'to fine or block 10 Russian independent media outlets if they do not delete publications about the war in Ukraine'. The state media and communications regulator accused these independent outlets of publishing 'false information' about the war, such as the 'information that the Russian military is shelling Ukrainian cities and causing civilian casualties'.[146] All this despite the fact that the Russian constitution explicitly bans censorship. Chapter 2, Article 29 'Rights and Freedoms of Man and Citizen' of the Russian constitution states: 'The freedom of mass communication shall be guaranteed. Censorship shall be banned.'[147] There is, however, a caveat to this, which allows state censorship under certain circumstances, one of which is 'during war,' which rather begs the question why Putin persisted in the pretence of labelling his invasion a 'Special Military Operation'? Calling it a war would have allowed him total censorship of all media. The most likely explanation is a miscalculation as to the speed with which he hoped to have defeated Ukraine: call it a 'war' and everybody looks at operations critically, in addition to which all sorts of other considerations have to be taken into account, such as diplomatic positioning, placing the economy on a war footing, conscription, and implementing internal security measures. If, however, the military subjugation of Ukraine could be achieved within a matter of days (as Putin initially hoped) or even a matter of weeks, then calling it a 'Special Military Operation' would have avoided the inevitable refocusing of the economy, diplomacy, international trade, and so forth.

Discreditation

The objective behind Communist propaganda and disinformation campaigns is to make people believe that Communism poses no threat, whilst at the same time, to 'talk up' the potential threat posed by any conservative or right-of-centre party;[148] to this end, they exaggerate the right-wing credentials of individuals, organisations, and political parties that oppose Communism, and try to link them to Fascism and/or Nazism – just as Putin did as his excuse for attacking Ukraine. It is worrying to note that Communism appears to have succeeded in brainwashing vast swathes of the populations of the world into believing that whilst Nazism/Fascism were evil creeds (which indeed they were), people have nothing to fear from Communism. This message has been pumped out *ad nauseum* from a number of sources —consistency and repetition are the key measures by which such messages are judged; as Winston Churchill famously said: 'The Russian Bolsheviks have discovered that truth does not matter so long as there is reiteration. They have no difficulty whatever in countering a fact by a lie which, if repeated often enough and loudly enough, becomes accepted by the people.'[149] The Soviet Union did exactly the same as the Nazis: both forbad internal dissent, instituted a regime of secret police, divided populations, invaded other countries, and practised genocide. This, however, appears to have escaped the notice of most people, who have been subtly brainwashed into thinking that there was only one evil political regime in the world – Nazism. As Suvorov observes, there has always been an inequality of historical comparison between the Communist and Nazi systems, even though they were and still are basically the same: 'The world hated Hitler and commiserated with Stalin. Hitler conquered half of Europe, and the rest of the world declared war against him. Stalin conquered half of Europe, and the world sent him greetings.'[150] This double standard is testimony to the skilful use of propaganda by the Communists, who have for years tried to persuade people that their objective is to save people from evil dictators such as Hitler, and to give freedom to the workers.

However, what many media commentators seem to forget is that when they seek to discredit an individual or a political grouping by referring to them as 'right wing', such parties participate in the democratic process – which is more than can be said for Communist administrations.[151] In this respect, the key to their success is that they get others to front the accusations and condemnations, whist they remain in the background. The mainstream media (including the BBC in the UK) appears to delight in denigrating 'right-of-centre' political parties and individuals and equate them – directly or by association – with Nazism/Fascism. They shy away, however, from making a similar link between 'left-of-centre' parties and Communism. For example, in the September 2022 Italian presidential elections, Giorgia Meloni won power as head of the *Fratelli d'Italia* (Brothers of Italy) party; her victory was reported by the left-leaning BBC as: 'Italy's most right-wing government since World War Two'.[152] To this was added the curious claim that this administration: 'will alarm much of Europe as Italy is the EU's third-biggest economy' without explaining the supposed link between the size of Italian economy and the alleged 'alarm' felt at the election of Meloni. She was also labelled a 'far-right leader'[153] in another BBC report. Her success as the head of a populist government was commented on spitefully in the UK left-leaning newspaper *The Guardian* that she represented a 'danger' to European democracy[154] without giving any hard evidence for this claim, other than to say that her party is descended from that of Mussolini, and that she recently espoused certain values which, for a Christian country are perfectly acceptable. She said: 'I am Giorgia, I am a woman, I am a mother, I am Italian, I am a Christian' and gave 'God, homeland, family' as her slogan in 2019 – which as is pointed out *ad nauseum*, was the same slogan that Benito Mussolini used. It is this constant 'drip-drip' that eventually undermines the ability of people to make judgements based on the facts. By contrast, the same BBC made no political positioning link on the decidedly left-wing Luiz Inácio Lula da Silva when he won the presidency of Brazil on 31 October 2022.[155]

Subversion

Subversion generally manifests itself in the slow but inexorable eating away at democracy by the combined efforts of the various Communist Party organs – it is also referred to as 'salami tactics' and it is difficult to identify and challenge. The American Communist John T. Pace, in his testimony to the Committee on Un-American Activities in 1948, explained how Moscow recruited members of the American Communist Party: 'for the purpose of organizing the youth and indoctrinating them with the Communist ideology and philosophy' and 'that they would be prepared to carry out acts of sabotage and espionage and acts of mutiny within our Armed Forces.'[156]

Within the UK, Communist subversion has been a 'stock-in-trade' of the Russians for years. The fear that the government and/or security services had been infiltrated remained real; according to the website of the British Security Service (MI5) however: 'Whitehall sometimes adopted a broader definition of subversion than its own.'[157] The most probable explanation for this paranoia is the be found in the extensive Russian infiltration of the UK Foreign Office and Intelligences service – MI6 – by people who were Russian agents – see below, 'Betrayal'.

'Useful Idiots'

The Communists have traditionally relied on a great number of people in the West to further their cause: some have done so as they are committed 'fellow-travellers', whilst others do not realise they are being manipulated – these people are generally termed: 'useful idiots.' Owen Matthews, writing in *The Spectator* pointed out that:

> In the 1930s brilliant operatives like Willi Muenzenberg convinced 'useful idiots' to join anti-fascist organisations that were really fronts for the Soviet-backed Communist International. Even in the twilight years of the Soviet Union the KGB was highly successful at orchestrating nuclear disarmament movements and trade unionism across the West.[158]

The Russians set up the World Congress of Intellectuals for Peace, later renamed the World Peace Council (WPC), with the first meeting being held in Wroclaw, Poland, in August 1948. The stated aims of which were 'universal disarmament' and 'peaceful coexistence' with all states. It also wished to see an 'end to imperialism', 'weapons of mass destruction', and 'all forms of discrimination'. This was a very clever move, as nobody could publicly oppose these aims without running the risk of being labelled a 'warmonger.' It is interesting to note the date on which the WPC was founded – some two months after the Russians tried to starve the population of occupied Berlin, by cutting all links with the outside world on 24 June 1948, leading to the Berlin Airlift: 24 June 1948 to 12 May 1949. The foundation of the WPC and the isolation of Berlin are classic examples of the Russian 'carrot and stick' strategy of dealing with the West. The WPC was undoubtedly attractive to many people with a genuine belief in peace, and whilst many might have been aware of the Russian ulterior objectives, felt that it was step in the right direction. Within the umbrella of the WPC, the Russians also encouraged the formation in 1957, of a new, anti-nuclear group called CND – the Campaign for Nuclear Disarmament. This was another clever move by Moscow, which although they had tested their first nuclear bomb in 1949, they still lacked the quantity and sophistication of nuclear weapons held by the West, and so sought to neutralise these advantages held by, in particular, the USA and the UK.[159] CND was a useful tool for the Russians, as it attracted genuine people who were afraid of the proliferation of nuclear weapons; the CND website claims that as multinational nuclear disarmament was not working, its policy of *unilateral* nuclear disarmament had 'caught the imagination of many'.[160]

Some cheerleaders for the anti-Western cause go to great pains to put their highly partial point of view across: the UK MP Jeremy Corbyn was the vice-chairman of CND, and rather than condemning the Russian invasion of Ukraine in 2022, he urged the West to stop arming Ukraine: 'Pouring arms in isn't going to bring about a solution; it's only going to prolong and exaggerate this war' and he called for the disbandment of NATO.[161] Just under a year earlier as vice-president of the 'Stop the War' coalition, he signed a letter in which the group sought to justify the Russian invasion of Ukraine, saying that the invasion was 'the product of 30 years of failed policies, including the expansion of NATO and US hegemony at the expense of other countries as well as major wars of aggression by the USA, Britain and other NATO powers which have undermined international law and the United Nations'.[162] The tone of the letter suggests that the blame for the invasion of Ukraine lies with the West and NATO!

In his book *Hidden Agendas*, the journalist John Pilger claimed to be writing about 'power, propaganda and censorship',[163] yet in the index to this book neither 'Communism' not 'Soviets' are mentioned at all – instead he seems to be content to list the 'crimes' of the West, charging that it has, 'invaded, stolen land and resources, subverted local culture and abused and enslaved indigenous populations'. [164] That the Soviet Union (and latterly Russia) has done the same, does not seem to bother him at all.[165] His comment that: 'The end of the old Cold War and the collapse of the Soviet Union have removed the most important restraint on Western terrorism.'[166] shows his anti-Western attitude. Not only would it appear that he is against certain Western powers (in particular the USA and the UK), but he goes out of his way to excuse Russian atrocities: on 13 May 2014, he appeared to support Putin's first invasion of Ukraine by placing the blame on the USA and NATO, claiming that Ukraine is 'being torn apart by fascist forces unleashed by the US and the EU. We in the West are now backing neo-Nazis in a country where Ukrainian Nazis backed Hitler.' He concluded, without presenting any evidence, that 'Washington's planned seizure of Russia's historic, legitimate warm-water naval base in Crimea failed'.[167]

As with most of Pilger's hysterical hyperbole, there is little or no evidence presented for his wild accusations – such as in an interview he did for Russian television on 18 March 2018, in which he described the poisoning of the Russian defector Sergei Skripal, and his daughter Yulia as 'part of the propaganda campaign that has been building now for several years in order to justify the actions of NATO, Britain the United States, towards Russia. That's a fact.'[168] Unfortunately he did not provide any evidence to support this 'fact'. Despite his vitriolic condemnation of the West, Pilger is not prevented from voicing his opinion; it is interesting to speculate whether he would he be allowed to express his views if they were anti-Russian, and he were based in Moscow?

Betrayal

Spying on one's enemies or potential enemies is widely practiced by all nations to a greater or lesser degree. However, there is a difference between straightforward espionage against one's enemies, and the betrayal of ones' allies. During World War II, when Russia was supposed to be an ally of the West, there were those who actively sought to further the Soviet cause clandestinely, and in order to achieve their objectives were told to show no pro-Soviet inclinations, but to work their way as far up the 'ladder' of the establishment as they could, and pass Allied intelligence on to their Soviet handlers. Whilst many countries had their traitors, the four most notorious of these were British: two who achieved influential positions in the UK Foreign Office (which controls overseas espionage activities), Donald Maclean and Guy Burgess[169], and in the security services – Kim Philby and Anthony Blunt. The most important was Kim Philby, who by September 1941 was working in Section 5 (Offensive Counter Intelligence) of the British Secret Intelligence Service (SIS), also known as MI6. He later became head of that same unit, and in February 1947, he was appointed deputy head of British intelligence in Turkey. He did incalculable damage in his various roles. Larry Holzwarth claims that assessing the extent of the damage was difficult as it covered a number of areas: 'classified data, information about atomic and thermonuclear weapons, troops deployments, and much more. Agents formerly working for the Americans vanished.'[170] Another infamous British traitor was George Blake, whose activities did considerable damage to the UK's defence capability from the mid-1950s; his betrayal is presented in the book by Steve Vogel, *Betrayal in Berlin.*[171] Perhaps of greatest importance was the long-term damage done by the 'Cambridge Spies' as they were collectively known; once they had been unmasked, the Americans were understandably reticent to trust British intelligence for decades – thus at a stroke, the Soviets had managed to drive a wedge between two key allies.

Overt Strategies

Preventative War/Pre-emptive Action

In a study of pre-emptive actions, Barry Strauss explained the difference between the two sub-classifications: preventive war and pre-emptive strike: 'A preventive war is a military, diplomatic, and strategic endeavour, aimed at an enemy whom one expects to grow so strong that delay would cause defeat. A pre-emptive strike is a military operation or series of operations to pre-empt an enemy's ability to attack you.'[172] The two options could equally be referred to as 'strategic' or 'tactical, with the first (preventative) taking place at the strategic (country) level and the second (pre-emptive) at a tactical (battlefield) level. The Russians practice both – and justify their use by citing so-called intelligence received by their security services – intelligence that may well have been fabricated by those same Security Services. Needless to say, these sources are never identified, nor are transcripts of intelligence reports available to the world press to show justification for their actions. Russia claims it has evidence that a country (usually a neighbour) was about to attack them, so they attacked first to disrupt the enemy's invasion/attack plans.

From the mid-1980s, there was considerable controversy aroused by the publication of the book by Victor Suvorov, a former Russian GRU (military intelligence) officer, who claimed that contrary to received wisdom, Stalin had been planning to attack Germany for a long time – a preventive war – as he saw Germany as the only power capable of resisting the inexorable westward march of Communism. It was said that Lenin had proclaimed that if there was no worldwide Communist revolution after 1917, then another world war would be necessary to achieve it. Rather than suggesting that the Soviet Union was a victim of Nazi aggression, Suvorov claims (based on an examination of declassified Soviet documents) that had Hitler not pre-empted him, Stalin would have launched the Red Army westwards much sooner than he did.[173] Such strategic considerations still exercise the Russian military mind today: Alexander Velez-Green, a research associate at the Centre for a New American Security explains that there has long been a debate within the Russian military, as to what to do in the face of a surprise NATO attack. One group believe that 'defensive operations alone will be unable to stop such an attack; consequently, they are arguing for Russia to adopt a doctrine of pre-emption to protect its territorial integrity and vital interests. This doctrine would authorize the first use of strategic non-nuclear or limited nuclear attacks on NATO military or civilian targets once an attack on vital Russian interests seemed imminent'.[174] The idea that Russia is under constant threat is an old excuse that is trotted out periodically as justification for Russo-Soviet military expenditure.

Retaliatory Action

Most people would agree that to retaliate militarily against an aggressor nation is a legitimate use of force: for example, the USA declared war on Japan in 1941 as a consequence of the Japanese attack on Pearl Harbour. Indeed, Article 51 of the United Nations' Charter states that:

> Nothing in the present Charter shall impair the inherent right of individual or collective self-defence if an armed attack occurs against a Member of the United Nations, until the Security Council has taken measures necessary to maintain international peace and security. Measures taken by Members in the exercise of this right of self-defence shall be immediately reported to the Security Council and shall not in any way affect the authority and responsibility of the Security Council under the present Charter to take at any time such action as it deems necessary in order to maintain or restore international peace and security.[175]

Following the end of World War II, in answer to the growing hostility of the Soviet Union, NATO (the North Atlantic Treaty Organisation) was formed on 4 April 1949, with the explicit objective of mutual self-defence (also known as 'collective defence'), as expressed in Article 5:

> The Parties agree that an armed attack against one or more of them in Europe or North America shall be considered an attack against them all and consequently they agree that, if such an armed attack occurs, each of them, in exercise of the right of individual or collective self-defence recognised by Article 51 of the Charter of the United Nations, will assist the Party or Parties so attacked by taking forthwith, individually and in concert with the other Parties, such action as it deems necessary, including the use of armed force, to restore and maintain the security of the North Atlantic area.[176]

Therefore, at first sight the concept of individual or collective defence would appear straightforward, and indeed obviates the need for a nation to declare war on its aggressor: it is sufficient to meet the aggression with sufficient force to repel the invader, just as the UK government did in response to the Argentine attack on the British Falkland Islands and South Georgia, in April 1982.

The ambiguity, however, lies in the way in which an 'aggressive action' can be interpreted. If there is nothing against which to retaliate, Russia (as with all totalitarian regimes) will manufacture a reason – the 'false flag' strategy. This is designed to provide an immediate excuse for intervention in another country: for example, forces from Country A – masquerading as forces from Country B, attack an establishment in their own country (A): targets generally include military outposts, ammunition depots, border control posts, infrastructure or communications hubs, but nothing crucial, and that could not be repaired within a matter of days. The damage inflicted by the 'enemy' is shown to the world, and this is the justification needed to 'retaliate'. It is a very effective device and has been used frequently to provide a pretext for intervention – perhaps most famously when the Nazis used a false-flag operation to provide an excuse for attacking Poland, on the night of 31 August 1939. The operation, known in German as *Überfall auf den Sender Gleiwitz* was when German SS troops dressed as Polish military, attacked the German border radio station at Gleiwitz, and took with them some concentration camp inmates, who were shot and left there as 'evidence' of Polish involvement. Using this pretext of Polish hostilities, Hitler attacked Poland the next day – 1 September 1939.

Stalin also relied on false flag activities to provide the final excuse for his assault on Finland – which had gained its independence from Russia in 1918.

Initially Stalin had supported the idea of Finnish independence, doubtless feeling that Finland, with its warm relations with the Soviet Union, would become an ally on the international stage. However, as the Finns appeared more interested in developing relations with the West, Stalin changed his mind, and began to regard an independent Finland as a threat, and one that had to be neutralised as the Soviet-Finnish border was only some fifty miles from Leningrad at its nearest point: the Soviet leadership felt this to be too close, and wished to push the frontier further north back into Finnish territory. Their suggestion was rejected, and Stalin realised that he would have to use force to deal with the Finns. On 26 November 1939, Russian forces fired a mortar at a Russian border outpost, allegedly killing three privates and an NCO, and left two officers and seven privates wounded – this took place near the village of Mainila. As a Finnish border guard testified later: 'I heard a shot fired crosswise from the east and in a matter of twenty seconds a shell exploded…the shot was succeeded by six more, all shells exploding in the same field. The last shell exploded at 3.05 pm. Ten minutes later six men arrived on the spot where the shells had fallen, stayed three minutes in inspecting the ground…No dead or wounded were taken away.'[177] The Soviet government immediately accused the Finns of attacking Russian territory and killing Russian servicemen. The Finnish ambassador to Moscow was summoned to the Kremlin, and handed a note, in which it was claimed that as a consequence of the aggression of Finnish forces, the Soviet Union insisted that the Finns de-militarise the Karelian frontier, by withdrawing their forces 'twenty to twenty-five kilometres, thus eliminating the possibility of fresh provocations'.[178] The Finns denied culpability, and in response the Soviets then revealed their real intentions behind the incident, saying (untruly) that 'attacks by units of the Finnish armed forces against Soviet forces continue not only on the Karelian Isthmus but also at other points on the Soviet-Finnish frontier'. They concluded that the Finnish government was to blame for this, and that, consequently, 'the Soviet government can no longer maintain normal relations with Finland'.[179]

Two days later, the Soviet Union mobilised its forces and on 30 November 1939, they launched attacks along the length of the Soviet-Finnish frontier, from Petsamo and Salla in the north, in the centre and south-east towards Suomussalmi, Raate, Khumo, Leiksa, Illomantsi, Tolvajärvi, Kollaa, and

Sortavala. Simultaneously, an assault was launched along the Karelian Usthmus, aimed at taking the towns of Viipuri and Käkisalmi. The very extent of the assault confirms that the Russians had been concentrating their forces for some time – such an extensive invasion could not have been organised and executed in a matter of days. Stalin was ready to invade – all he needed was an excuse, and the false flag attack provided this.

In the current Russian war on Ukraine, the initial 'reason' for invasion was the false claim that the Kyiv government was Nazi-controlled – a clever move by Putin, as even in today's Russia, calling a government 'Nazi' and moving against it, is certain to elicit a high level of Russian public approval, such is the strength of collective memory of the Nazi-Soviet conflict, even amongst those who were born years after the war ended. By late October 2022, Vladimir Saldo, the Russian-installed governor of Kherson city in southern Ukraine, had claimed that Ukrainian forces were plotting to blow up the Nova Kakhovka power station and river dam to the north of the city,[180] as a means of attacking the Russian troops entrenched around the strategic communications hub. As with most Russian pronouncements, whatever they claim that the enemy is going to do is generally what they themselves intend to do. Were the dam to have been destroyed, then the resulting floodwaters would have hit the citizens of the downstream city of Kherson, and devastated miles of farmland and Ukrainian villages on both sides of the Dnipro River. By contrast, the Russians would have benefitted from just such an operation as any subsequent flooded areas would have given their forces a protective barrier against the Ukrainian forces that were by then counter-attacking; objectively, Ukraine had nothing to gain from such an action, whilst Russia had much to gain. As a 'bonus' the Russian occupiers would be able to blame the resulting humanitarian crisis on the Kyiv government and the Ukrainian military. The river dam with its road atop, and the nearby city of Kherson are all of strategic significance, as they are basically the gateway to the Crimea. As expected, the threat that the Ukrainians were going to destroy the dam was a precursor to what happened in reality, but some eight months later than expected, when the dam was destroyed in the first week of June 2023. Reports claimed that Ukrainian officials were warning of the potentially serious long-term consequences for agriculture should the area be flooded – not only would the vast waves of water (estimated at around four cubic miles) damage houses, infrastructure and agriculture in the area, but it would deprive those fields further upstream of vital water for their crops, turning the land 'into deserts'.[181] To date there is no conclusive proof as to which side was responsible, but all indicators point to Russian culpability for a number of reasons:

1) Explosives Required. In his comprehensive study of the famous Dambusters Raid of World War II, Max Hastings comments on the difficulties of breaching a dam by bombs, noting that an assessment by the UK government research department claimed that the amount of explosives needed would be more than any aircraft of the time could carry, although it was acknowledged that a relatively small explosive 'might achieve a wholly disproportionate result if it were detonated sub-aqueously: it could harness the power of the water mass to channel the force of the blast'.[182] The key factor is where exactly the charge were placed. As the dam was controlled by the Russians, and as the Ukrainians did not have rockets capable of carrying sufficiently quantities of explosive, these can be ruled out. The destruction of the dams is nothing new to the Russians – on 18 August 1941, Soviet forces retreating eastwards from the advance of the German army, blew up the power plant and dam at Zaporizhzhia, very close to the site of the modern-day Kakhovka dam, as a part of their 'scorched earth' policy of leaving nothing to the advancing Germans. To achieve this destruction, the Red Army needed 20,000 tons of explosive, and once the dam has been breached there were some 100,000 people (mostly Russians) who died in the resulting floodwaters.

2) Timing. Why was the dam was not blown when the water level would have been higher, and the level of destruction caused by the floodwaters would have been even higher, rather than in June? There are a number of reasons for this: perhaps the Russians wanted the dam intact as it provided the major water supply for the Crimea peninsular, currently occupied (illegally) by Russian forces. To cut off the water supply to the strategically important Crimea would have been highly counter-productive and would have weakened their hold on the peninsular. Alternatively, they may have hoped to use the dam's road access as a means of crossing the Dnipro River in a renewed offensive in the summer of 2023: to destroy it would not have been conducive to such operations.

3) Ukrainian Counteroffensive. As previously noted, at the time of the dam's destruction (6 June 2023), it was not the Russians, but the Ukrainians who had launched a strategic counter-offensive; having retaken the city of Kherson, Ukrainian forces were now poised to cross the Dnipro. Rather than providing a road bridge for a Russian east-west attack, it could now be used by the Ukrainians to strike west-east. It is safe to assume that by this stage of the war, with losses of occupied territory, mass desertions from their armed forces, and heavy losses of both military personnel and equipment, the Russian General Staff had ruled out any counterattack in this region. In addition, they may well have concluded that they might have to withdraw from the Crimea. Consequently, if the dam were to be destroyed Ukrainian forces would be faced with a mass of fast-moving water, effectively preventing them from launching an attack on Russian occupation forces, and allowing the Russians to redeploy some of their units to the Bakhmut area, which was the scene of intense fighting.

4) Point of Explosion. Following extensive investigations, the *New York Times* reported that evidence pointed to 'an explosive charge in a passageway running through the dam's concrete base' which was the cause of the dam's destruction. The report added: 'The evidence clearly suggests the dam was crippled by an explosion set off by the side that controls it: Russia.' This assessment was agreed with by a team of international investigators, who concluded that it was 'highly likely' that the collapse of the dam was caused by explosives planted by Russians.[183]

In another example of cynical manipulation of the facts, on 25 October 2022, Russia delivered a letter to the UN in which it claimed that Ukraine was developing a 'dirty bomb'[184] – a combination of conventional explosives, with radioactive materials. It is designed to have a limited explosive range of around a few miles, and to deny the contaminated area to the enemy. As noted by Hamish de Bretton-Gordon there was a confusing element of 'double bluff' in the letter, as the Russians also claimed that Ukraine had intended the bomb to 'be a false-flag operation, in which the Ukrainians would claim it was a Russian low-yield nuclear weapon containing highly enriched uranium, which would be detected in the atmosphere'.[185] This worried Western military analysts: not that they really believed that Ukraine was about to detonate a 'dirty bomb' on Ukrainian territory, but that in view of previous deceptions, they suspected that the Russians might be about to do just that; Ukrainian and Western officials suspected that Moscow was making such allegations so that it would be able to explode its own dirty bomb, and blame Kyiv. US Secretary of State, Anthony Blinken, suggested that 'the world would see through any attempt by Russia to use this allegation as a pretext for escalation'.[186] Ukraine further demolished this Russian disinformation strategy by inviting UN Atomic Agency inspectors to investigate all their nuclear sites, and the UN team found 'no sign of undeclared nuclear activity after inspecting three sites at Ukraine's request in response to Russian allegations that work was being done on a "dirty bomb"'.[187]

Defence of Ethnic Minorities

The basis of this justification for military intervention is that members of an ethnic grouping, living outside their native country (sometimes referred to as 'diaspora') are being persecuted and that their mother country is forced into military intervention to protect the rights of this group. The beauty of using such an excuse is that it is very difficult to quantify what exactly constitutes a sufficiently high level of 'persecution' to justify intervention. Furthermore, it is not always clear as to whether the 'persecution' is a reality, or has been manufactured as an excuse for intervention – a variation on the false-flag strategy.

There are a number of stages through which such a charade generally progresses: this is the classic Russian *modus operandi*, and has featured in Putin's wars on both Georgia (2008) and Ukraine (both in 2014 and 2022):

(1) Establish the presence of an ethnic Russian minority in the country to be targeted; to date, there is no minimum percentage of the population that represents 'a presence' sufficient to warrant Russian interest – in any case this is merely a pretext for invasion and annexation.
(2) Claim that this minority is suffering persecution – no actual evidence of this is required
(3) Encourage the formation of a separatist faction that claims independence from central government, and wishes to re-unite with Russia. This separatist faction need not be very big, but must be vociferous.
(4) If no political solution is forthcoming, then use this inactivity as an excuse for invasion.

The 'abuse of ethnic minorities' was used by Adolf Hitler as an excuse to seize the border area between Germany and Czechoslovakia in 1938. The region, known in Germany as the *Sudetenland*, contained many ethnic Germans, and Hitler claimed that they wished to be 'reunited' with Germany as a consequence of their 'persecution' by the Czech government – taken at face value, this appeared reasonable. In a speech he made to the German NSDAP Conference in Nuremberg, on 12 September 1938, he claimed: 'I am simply demanding that the oppression of three and a half million Germans in Czechoslovakia cease and that the inalienable right to self-determination take its place.'[188] Looking at this from the point of view of Putin's invasion of Ukraine, there are many similarities:

> In both cases, a carefully stage-managed popular referendum was held and, in both cases, its outcome was strongly in favor of annexation. It almost seems that Putin took a page out of Hitler's book when he described Crimea's annexation as a 'homecoming'.' Hitler had welcomed Austria 'home' in the same way (*Heim ins Reich*).[189]

After sending his troops into Crimea in 2014, Putin justified this flagrant breach of international law on the grounds that he was protecting ethnic Russians from 'far-right' extremists.[190] Based on his activities thus far in this respect, there is a clear danger that he could use similar reasons for the seizure of the Baltic republics, citing the numbers of ethnic Russians living in these states who have been 'persecuted': there are around 300,000 Russians living in Estonia, and in Latvia they comprise around 30 per cent of the population (around 540,000), and around 25 per cent (707,536) in Lithuania. Within the old 'client states' of Eastern Europe, there are significant numbers of Russians: 31,000 in Bulgaria, 30,000 in Romania, and 20,000 in Hungary. All of whom could be used by Putin as an excuse for invasion and annexation of territory. An important question is, therefore, what would NATO do if the Russians were to invade a member state such as Latvia, Estonia, or Romania?

The difference between Hitler and Putin is that, whilst the United Nations (UN) did not exist when Hitler launched his assault on Europe, Putin has been forced to accept that his actions are now measurable against the Articles of the UN Charter. Article 2 (4) of this charter states that: 'All Members shall refrain in their international relations from the threat or use of force against the territorial integrity or political independence of any State, or in any other manner inconsistent with the Purposes of the United Nations';[191] this article outlaws the use of force against another member state. Given this, how could Putin possibly justify his attack on Ukraine? The answer lies in his 'interpretation' of a subsequent article – Article 51 of the same charter – in which it states that:

> Nothing in the present Charter shall impair the inherent right of individual or collective self-defence if an armed attack occurs against a Member of the United Nations until the Security Council has taken the measures necessary to maintain international peace and security.[192]

In other words, if a member state is attacked, then it has the right to use force of arms to defend itself. Again, this appears logical, but has been twisted by Putin as he maintains that the eastern regions of Ukraine – Luhansk, Donetsk and the Crimea (due to their percentage of ethnic Russians) are part of Russia, so an attack on any of these is an attack on Russia, and the UN charter therefore gives him the right to defend himself under these circumstances. Putin sought to justify his 'Special Military Operation' on the grounds that Ukraine was a 'hotbed' of Nazis: in a televised speech[193] he announced that he wanted to 'protect people who have been abused by the genocide of the Kyiv regime for eight years' and that his objective was the 'bringing to justice those who committed numerous bloody crimes against civilians'. Putin has changed the terms of reference to suit his own agenda, as the definition of an 'attack' on the state in now taken to include citizens (civilians) who are placed under political and/or physical danger as a consequence of the actions of another state. By expanding the concept of self-defence of *territory* to include self-defence of *people* (*ethnic* self-defence), the state can legitimately employ force to 'emancipate expatriate citizens or ethnic groups in foreign countries'.[194] Putin has very cleverly turned the UN Charter on its head and employed it to his advantage.

Invitation

There are occasions on which the Russians have been 'invited' into a country – ostensibly to keep order when the national government has failed, or when its continued existence is under threat from rebel insurgent forces. Such invitations are generally issued by friendly governments which fear they are likely to toppled by a popular revolution, which then allows the Russians to claim that they are not 'invading' but are responding to calls to help maintain the peace. For example, at the start of January 2022, the Central Asian Republic of Kazakhstan was in turmoil – the unpopular government of President Kassym-Jomart Tokarev was besieged by a wave of strikes and violent demonstrations, mostly as a consequence of the high price of domestic gas. As the country is one of the largest oil and gas producers in the world, there was a suspicion that certain people in positions of power were making money at the expense of ordinary consumers. The strikes spread, enveloping much of the country, and the Presidential palace was burned to the ground. Tokarev appealed for assistance to the Eurasian military alliance – the Collective Security Treaty Organisation (CSTO), and troops from Russia, Belarus, Armenia, Tajikistan, and Kyrgystan were sent to the country,[195] with orders to 'open fire to kill terrorists without warning'.[196] The CSTO is basically a front to allow the Russians to intervene in other countries when they perceive that their interests might be threatened. Russian paratroopers were sent to Kazakhstan at the request of its president to help 'stabilise the country': it is claimed that they are there as part of a peacekeeping force to protect civilian and military installations such as gas pipelines, and military bases, and the Cosmodrome complex from which Russian space activities – such as rocket launching facilities for crewed spaceflights – are coordinated, and which is located in the Baikonur enclave. By involving troops from so many nations, Putin obviously thought that the move would not be construed internationally as a Russian invasion. However, as the US Secretary of State Antony Blinken observed: 'It would seem to me that the Kazakh authorities in government certainly have the capacity to deal appropriately with protests, to do so in a way that respects the rights of protesters while maintaining law and order. So it's not clear why they feel the need for any outside assistance.' As he joked to the assembled reporters: 'I think one lesson in recent history is that once Russians are in your house, it's sometimes very difficult to get them to leave.'[197]

The 'Russian Defence'

The Russian leadership has never liked their actions being challenged; if this happens, they resort to a script based on what this author calls the the 'Russian Defence'. It comprises three stages – ideally dragged out as long as possible in the hope that the world will have either lost interest, and/or events will have overtaken the situation; it is generally the first response to condemnation, and is usually employed when Russian aggression, subterfuge or hostility is unmasked, prior to any admission of guilt, and generally before any armed response. It has been widely used by every Soviet leader since Lenin and in its latest iteration has been perfected by Putin. The 'Russian Defence' is summarised as: Deny, Counter-accuse, Blame – 'DeCaB':

Stage 1: Deny

The instinct of the Russians is to lie and deny having done whatever they are accused of having done; thus a denial of culpability is generally the first step. This is admirably illustrated in Vladimir Putin's flat denial that the Russian troops amassing on the Ukrainian border, were there for any reason other than training purposes,[198] and were not a threat to any other country – six days later on 24 February 2022 his forces invaded Ukraine. Alternatively, they may simply ignore any accusations, presumably in the hope that those levelling such accusations will give up after a while. Generally, there is little or no evidence offered to support this denial of culpability.

Stage 2: Counter-accuse

The second stage is to turn any accusation on its head, levelling the same charge against the accuser. This is generally sufficient to prolong the course of any independent investigation by 'muddying the waters' to the extent that impartial observers/commentators, are forced to examine the Russian counterclaims with equal diligence. At the start of Putin's 2022 invasion of Ukraine, Sergey Lavrov, the Russian foreign minister tried to lay the blame for the war on NATO, when he wrote in *TASS* on 25 February:

> The West was silently encouraging the rise of neo-Nazism and Russophobia in Ukraine and covering up the crimes of the Kiev regime in Donbass, which in the end led to the country's tragedy... During this entire period, the population...was subjected to abuse, perennial shelling on the part of the Kiev

> regime that openly adopted a course towards Russophobia and genocide... All these years, our Western colleagues were consistently covering up for the Ukrainian regime, turning a blind eye to military crimes against civilians, to the murders of women, children, seniors, to the destruction of civilian infrastructure and silently encouraging the rapid rise of neo-Nazism and Russophobia which in the end led to the country's tragedy. And, of course, the West fully supported the Kiev regime in its attempts to sabotage and finally destroy the Minsk Accords.[199]

From the Russian point of view, a counter-accusation has the advantage of presenting both accused and accuser as equals whilst the accusations are being investigated. It may even be that the investigation takes so long to reach a conclusion that the environment has changed drastically, making any findings irrelevant.

Stage 3: Blame

If the accusation cannot be dealt with by ignoring, denying, or fabricating a counter charge, then the next stage is to find a scapegoat; someone (preferably dead and/or disgraced) is held up as being responsible, and it is suggested that they acted independently, and had they not died, they would have been severely punished by the government. A classic example of this is Khruschev's denunciation of Stalin, in which he laid all the blame for Russian atrocities in the 1940s–1950s at the feet of the dead dictator. To be fair to the Russians, this defence has been adopted by many regimes throughout the world, such as the post-war attempt by the German establishment to blame the Waffen-SS for all atrocities committed by German forces on the battlefield.[200] If all else fails, a standard fallback position is to blame the dead.[201]

Whilst there are variations to this progression depending on specific circumstances, these stages generally represent the standard Russian response to accusations of atrocities and there are numerous examples that illustrate this cynical defence, some of which are examined below. Two examples suffice to illustrate the progression and show that the Russians were prepared to lie to so-called Allies even before the end of the war: the Russian massacre of Polish POWs in 1940, and the denials they issued over their capture of US POWs, previously held by the Germans, and 'liberated' as the Red Army moved westwards.

The Katyn Wood Massacre (1940)

Background

Near Smolensk is the forest of Katyn[202], which had been under German occupation since the invasion of the USSR in June 1941; on 13 April 1943, Berlin Radio announced that German forces in the area had uncovered 'a ditch…28 meters long and 16 meters wide, in which the bodies of 3,000 Polish officers were piled up in twelve layers.'[203] Berlin Radio accused the Soviets of having murdered these officers, and claimed that there was evidence of other graves nearby, which would likely result in more bodies being found. Based on the dimensions of the other pits, they estimated that there might be up to an additional 10,000 bodies yet to be discovered.[204] Benjamin Fisher claims that 'In all, the NKVD executed almost half the Polish officer corps'[205] By the time further excavations had finished, there were just under 22,000 bodies discovered by the German authorities, including more Polish prisoners of war, politicians, and members of the Polish intelligentsia; it was claimed that the murders had been carried out between April and May of 1940 by the Soviet NKVD, on the orders of Stalin. Robert Service, in his masterly biography of Stalin, claims that the Soviet dictator was 'determined that whatever Polish state emerged from the debris of the war would stay under the hegemony of the USSR'.[206] As Robert Service notes, Stalin ordered the execution of these prisoners as: 'He no more wanted the survival of Poland's political and military elite than he aimed to preserve the elites in Estonia, Latvia and Lithuania – and he was long practised in the art of solving public problems by means of the physical liquidation of those who embodied them.'[207]

Although the bodies were found buried in the Katyn Woods, it was determined that the POWs had been murdered by the NKVD at various locations – generally in prisons or POW camps. The online historical information resource Timenote gives a graphic description of the process by which these unfortunate individuals were murdered by the Soviets inside Kalinin prison. The account is based on detailed information provided by Dmitri Tokarev, the former head of the board of the district NKVD in Kalinin:

> The executions were usually performed with German-made 7.65 x 17mm Walter PPK pistols supplied by Moscow, but 7.62 x 38mm Nagant M1895 revolvers were also used. The executioners used German weapons rather than the standard Soviet revolvers, as the latter were said to offer too much recoil, which made shooting painful after the first dozen executions.... The killings were methodical. After the personal information of the condemned was checked, he was handcuffed and led to a cell insulated with stacks of sandbags along the walls and a felt-lined, heavy door. The victim was told to kneel in the middle of the cell, was then approached from behind by the executioner and immediately shot in the back of the head. The body was carried out through the opposite door and laid in one of the five or six waiting trucks.[208]

Denial and counter-accusation

The bodies presented a problem for the Soviets, as their existence could not be ignored. Stalin moved quickly, denied Soviet culpability, and launched a counter-accusation on 15 April, claiming that the dead were, in the words of the official Soviet communique 'former Polish prisoners of war, who... fell into the hands of the German-fascist hangmen in the summer of 1941'.[209] The obvious conclusion that they wished people to draw was that these unfortunates had been taken prisoner and subsequently murdered by the Nazis during their invasion of the USSR in Operation Barbarossa, on 22 June 1941. The astute German Minister for Propaganda, Dr Josef Goebbels, made full use of the propaganda value of this find.[210] However, at the time, and in view of the various reports of German atrocities that were emerging, it seemed logical to conclude that this was just another example of Nazi barbarity. The problem for the Soviets, however, was that closer investigation proved their culpability for a number of reasons:

Number of Poles captured by the Soviets following the invasion of Poland

The Germans and Soviets had invaded Poland on 1 September 1939 and 17 September, respectively, and had defeated Poland militarily by the time the Poles surrendered on 6 October. The Polish army had undertaken a strategic withdrawal towards the east, away from the invading Germans, and so when the Soviets stabbed them in the back by invading Poland on 17 September, the majority of the Polish Armed Forces were captured by the Soviets, not the Germans. Authors such as George Sanford[211] point out that the Soviets captured large numbers of Poles in 1939, whilst Steven Zaloga puts it as the more precise figure of '15,000 Polish officers captured by the Red Army in 1939'.[212] His estimate is close to that of the online publication *World War 2 Gravestone*, which puts the number at 14,500.[213]

The date at which the Germans had first occupied that region

The German army only entered Smolensk on 15 July 1941 – nearly one month after the invasion. On some bodies, documentation was found indicating that they had been killed no later than April 1940 – in other words, over a year before the German invasion. This would also be indicative of when they had been murdered; as further evidence to place the responsibility with the Soviets, the Germans allowed the Polish Red Cross to visit to examine the bodies; they concluded that the bodies had been buried for a number of years.

Polish government-in-exile

The Polish government-in-exile in London had been making enquiries about the fate of its captured officers for over a year: they asked for an official investigation by the International Red Cross, based in Switzerland. Rather than agreeing to this, Stalin immediately cut all diplomatic links with the Poles and accused them of siding with the Nazis.

Methods of execution typical of the NKVD

Typical execution methods of the NKVD were a close range shot through the back of the skull.

It was later determined that those killed had been executed in various prisons, including Kalinin and Kharkiv, where thousands of Polish prisoners had been incarcerated after their surrender. The only survivor was Major Eugenjusz Komorowski, who wrote a book about the massacre.[214]

US POWs in Russian Hands

Towards the end of World War II, there were many POWs held by the German army who had been 'liberated' from their POW camps by the Soviets as they advanced westwards. Rather than assisting these POWs to return home to the USA or UK via the US airbase at Poltava in Ukraine or via another route such as Persia, they were detained by the Soviets as a cynical way of holding a 'bargaining chip' in order to put pressure on the British and American governments. All Allied efforts to locate these POWs and bring them back home were met by the standard DeCaB responses: initially, the Soviets denied that they held any allied soldiers against their will. US Ambassador Harriman wrote that: 'It seems obvious that the Soviets have been attempting to stall us off by misinformation.'[215] It was only when he was directly accused by President Roosevelt of mistreating US ex-Wehrmacht captives currently in Russian hands that Stalin moved to stage two – 'counter-accuse'- claiming that 'conditions for American ex-POWs were better than those for Soviet ex-POWs in the American camps',[216] obviously forgetting that he had previously denied having any ex-Wehrmacht US POWs! Later in the war (May 1945), Stalin threatened that if the West did not give him back those Russians who had been captured by the Germans and who were now in Allied hands, there would be grave consequences, including the retention of British and American POWs 'liberated' from the Germans, and held in the Soviet Union.

Summary

The previous chapter showed how the thirst for territory was a constant in the development of the Russian Empire: either through a desire to acquire agricultural and/or mineral wealth, or to maintain a *cordon sanitaire* around the growing Empire. This chapter continued the narrative in a similar vein, but with the additional and highly important consideration that the country now sought to export the Soviet revolution to as many countries as possible; Soviet aggressive expansion showed that the push for territory was possibly more important than ever before, driven by the ideological underpinning of Communism.

Chapter 3

Relations with Neighbours

'Whether you like it or not, history is on our side. We will bury you!'

Soviet Premier Nikita Khrushchev, to Western ambassadors at a reception given at the Polish Embassy in Moscow, 18 November 1956.

This chapter summarises the geographical scope, scale, and frequency with which Moscow has intervened in neighbouring countries since the formation of the Soviet Union – generally such interventions are preceded by one or more of the excuses detailed in 'Overt Strategies' in the previous chapter. Rather than go into details over each and every incident of Soviet interference, only the more significant are addressed in depth: a full list can be found in Appendix B.

Once under the 'protection' of Communism, there is huge reluctance to allow any country its independence. Whether the period is one of Bolshevism under Lenin, Communism under Stalin, Revisionism under Khrushchev, or Nationalism under Putin, the driving motivation behind Moscow's foreign policy has always been one of land seizure, and the suppression of opposition. Lenin, Stalin, and more recently, Putin have all adhered to this concept of a Western shift of Moscow's influence, generally through territorial conquest. Stalin was concerned with reinstating the old Tsarist frontiers, although he claimed to observe 'equality of nations and the integrity of their territories, liberation of enslaved nations and restoration of their sovereign rights, the right of every nation to arrange its affairs as it wishes', which is hardly consistent with a desire to reimpose rule from Moscow.

A Chronology of Soviet Aggression

The Lenin Years (1917–1921)

The main driving force behind the Bolshevik movement was Vladimir Lenin – real name Vladimir Ilich Ulyanov – born on 10 April 1870, to an upper middle-class family living in Simbirsk. He described himself as a 'revolutionary socialist' in his formative years and involved in street demonstrations from an early age. He was arrested for sedition in 1897, and was sentenced to three years' exile in Shushenskoye in Siberia. Returning from exile, he moved to Europe, where he became an intellectual theorist as a member of the Marxist Russian Social Democratic Labour Party (RSDLP), leaving some six years later to lead the Bolshevik faction following an ideological split with the mainstream Marxists.

The fact that Lenin's elder brother (Aleksandr) was hanged for being part of a terrorist faction and the attempted assassination of the Czar was almost certainly a major factor in pushing him towards opposition to the state and to the formation of the Bolshevik Party. Added to this was the injustice of the old Russian system, which starved peasants and rewarded corruption and greed. As Robert Service has noted with regard to the early influences on Lenin: 'Environment was immensely significant'[217] and it helped him formulated his early ideas. Service suggests that it was this environment that was the catalyst for the revolution:

> The political and economic structure was offensive to him; the social hierarchy disgusted him. The opportunities for consensual development held no appeal for him. He hated the Romanovs and Old Russia. He wanted a New Russia, a European Russia, a Westernised Russia…But Lenin's approval of 'the West' was selective. He admired Marx, the German Marxist movement and contemporary German industry and technology. But he wanted the West too to change.[218]

From all accounts, it would appear that Lenin could be cold and clinical when it came to making decisions, including those involving life or death; Geoffrey Jukes points out the dichotomy of deliberation that was Lenin, when he notes that whilst Lenin and the Bolsheviks were opposed to World War I, they were not opposed 'to war as such. They believed that those socialists who supported their national war efforts had betrayed socialism'.[219] Whilst the importance of Lenin lay in his guidance of the Revolution in the early years, he was subsequently remembered for his involvement in torture, repression, death, the formation of the Cheka, the collectivisation of agriculture (leading to famine) and persecution of the Kulaks.

Ukrainian War of Independence (1917–1921)

Following the confusion and disruption of World War I and the collapse of the Imperial Russian Empire, the region of Ukrainian sought to secure its independence from what had been Russia; this met with opposition from the newly installed Bolshevik government, which wanted Ukraine for its strategic position on the southern flank or Russia and provided a number of 'warm water' outlets to the sea for the Russian navy. Moscow helped in the formation of various Ukrainian Bolshevik parties and encouraged them to rise up against the new Ukrainian government; they achieved some success in the Kyiv district, where they defeated the forces of the new Ukrainian People's Republic, declaring the capital city under Bolshevik control. At the same time as Lenin and others were encouraging Ukrainian Bolsheviks to rebel against the forces of the Russian Republic (led by Kerensky), there was an upsurge in Ukrainian nationalism, demanding independence from both the old Russian Empire, and the newly formed Russian Soviet Republic.

The Bolsheviks, in conjunction with their Soviet Polish allies beat the Ukrainian nationalists after what can be justifiably considered as the start of Ukrainian attempts to achieve independence from the Soviet Union. The importance of this first military 'adventure' by the Bolsheviks showed that, ever since its first declaration of independence, Ukraine has been subject to aggression and occupation by Russia – small wonder then, that the Ukrainians of today are prepared to fight in defence of their homeland, as they know the history of occupation by the Russians.

Following the Armistice, the occupying German forces retreated from Ukraine in November 1918, which left a power vacuum in the south, especially around the key port of Odessa, and a mixed Allied force was landed there and at Sevastopol in mid-December. A more detailed account of this first attempt at independence is given in Chapter 4: Ukraine – The Sunflower State.

Polish War of Independence (1919–1921)

Following the Armistice (11 November 1918), the Poles declared their independence from the Soviets; there were still considerable German forces in the area, and as they retreated west the Soviets tried to seize parts of Poland. In their campaign to oust the occupying Russian forces, the Poles were assisted by Ukrainian and Lithuanian allies, and beat back the Soviet invaders, until an eventual peace was signed. The conflict had been a particularly vicious one, driven by a Communist ideology on one side, and a sense of defence of the homeland on the other. Predictably, numbers of casualties vary according to the source consulted, but it is generally accepted that the Russians lost some 60,000 killed, and around 80,000 taken prisoner. Figures for wounded or those who died as a consequence of wounds are almost non-existent, as the Soviet authorities were unwilling to disclose the final total. The Allied forces suffered around 17,000 dead, with another 30,000 dying of wounds, and around 50,000 taken prisoner or missing.[220] Lenin's attempt to spread the revolution further westwards failed, and the Poles enjoyed a period of peace and independence until the next invasion of their territory in 1939.

The Stalin Years (1921–1953)

Joseph Stalin – real name Joseph Vissarionovich Dzhughasvili – was born on 21 December 1879, in the small town of Gori, in the province of Tiflis. There was an early religious influence in his life, as he attended a seminary, but soon decided that formalised religion was not for him. In his early years he suffered an accident when he was knocked over in the street by a horse and cart, leaving him with a permanently damaged left arm and leg – which meant that he was declared unfit for military service – which probably saved his life. His early political career is rather sketchy but appears to have been based on radicalised student opposition: the problem is that, as commented on earlier, Stalin was so involved in altering history – especially as it related to himself – that it is questionable whether one can really rely on the voracity of anything published in Russia during his era. Of those writings that mentioned Stalin, none were published without his approval leaving him the option to re-write history to a certain degree[221] – something that increasingly became a feature of his dictatorship. It would appear that he operated on the fringes of the Bolshevik party for over a decade before the October 1917 Revolution. It was Stalin's aggressive and combative (rather than his intellectual) attitude to politics that distinguished him from other students. He became a member of the Bolshevik faction within the Russian Social Democratic Party, and after proving himself an outspoken player in the local party factions, he was eventually elected their leader. At the end of the Revolution, he entered politics full-time, working closely with Lenin; Stalin used his position to play a decisive role in engineering the 1921 Red Army invasion of Georgia, adopting a hardline nationalistic approach to opposition, including severe repression of any dissent.

Stalin's early years were a complex mix of deceit, disinformation, persecution, aggression, self-aggrandisement, violence, and paranoia. Thus, it is perhaps no surprise that he turned out the way he did, and his level of violence may have stemmed from his personal insecurity – hence the numerous purges he instituted. Despite his attitude to other countries, Stalin described himself as a 'nationalist' not an 'imperialist', but his distinct brand of nationalism was an eclectic mix of many influences. Robert Service describes Stalin's interpretation of nationalism as 'a Russian nationalism of the state, of technology and intolerance, of atheism, of cities, of military power. It was so idiosyncratic a compilation as to be virtually his own invention'.[222] His brand of nationalism became apparent in his relations with bordering states; despite his avowed support of democracy and independence – he is quoted as having once said of World War II that it was fought for the 'abolition of racial exclusiveness; equality of nations and inviolability of their territories; liberation of the enslaved nations and restoration of their sovereign rights; the right of every nation to manage its affairs in its own way; economic aid to war-ravaged nations and assistance in establishing their material welfare; restoration of democratic liberties; destruction of the Hitler regime'.[223] Whether he believed this, is another matter, as authors such as Robert Edwards define Stalin's foreign policy as comprising two 'clear imperatives': the 'recovery' of Czarist territories that had been lost as a consequence of the Brest-Litovsk Treaty, and the second from an eventual 'realization that the Tsarist state had been a perfectly viable nation and that these carefully assembled western frontiers reflected an optimum balance between security and territory'.[224]

Stalin, more than Lenin, is remembered for the atrocities committed in his name; extra-judicial murder worsened under Stalin, and by the mid-1930s it was the subject of debate in the UK House of Commons,[225] between the Foreign Secretary (Sir Anthony Eden) and Captain Archibald Ramsay MP (Member of Parliament), who asked the foreign secretary: 'whether he is aware that over 80 persons have been executed without any trial in Moscow and Petrograd during the last two weeks; and will he make immediate representations to the League of Nations, with a view to organising a combined protest against this infringement of Article IX of the League of Nations Covenant?' Eden balanced his reply on linguistic niceties, without touching on the main principles at issue: 'According to my information it does not appear that these persons were executed without trial. The terms of the Covenant provide the League of Nations with no *locus standi* for intervention with the Soviet Government in such a matter.' Ramsay countered by pointing out that whilst 'accepting the statement of the hon. Gentleman that there is some form of trial… it is the essential duty of the League to protest if any signatory of the Covenant fails to carry out in the letter and the spirit the ordinary course of Justice such as civilised nations understand; are we to understand that the right hon. Gentleman is satisfied that the spirit and the letter of the Covenant have been fulfilled and if not, does he still propose to do nothing about the matter?' Eden then sidestepped the issue: 'Article IX which the hon. and gallant Member quotes has nothing whatever to do with the matter. So far as I am aware, the League has no *locus standi* in the matter.' His reluctance to give any useful reply was probably because he had no wish to upset Stalin, who at the time (late 1934) was beginning to be perceived as a useful potential counterbalance to the rising threat of Hitler.

The Georgian historian, Roy Aleksandrovich Medvedev, estimated that the death toll directly attributable to Stalin's regime was many millions – this was in addition to millions of battlefield deaths during World War II. According to Palash R. Ghosh, writing in the *International Business Times,* Medvedev broke down his estimates of the seven to eight million who died as follows: six to seven million killed by an artificial famine in 1932–1934, and one million executed during the 'Great Terror' of 1936–1938. In addition, there were between four and six million people sent to forced labour camps, and between 1946–1953, there was at least one million people arrested and sentenced for what were described as 'political crimes.' In 1935 alone, there were one million people exiled from Moscow and Leningrad. Later, during World War II, there was another ten to twelve million forcibly relocated – some due to their doubtful political loyalty. The peasantry, who provided that they continued to produce food and steer clear of politics, generally escaped death or imprisonment, as they could be useful to the regime: they tended to be dealt with by relocation (they were sent far away from their family and friends – a fate that befell between nine and eleven million who were forced off their land), millions of peasants who suffered 'relocation' (generally to Siberia), and some two to three million who were arrested or exiled during the first mass collectivisation programme.[226]

In his book *Unnatural Deaths in the U.S.S.R.: 1928–1954*[227] Iosef Dyadkin estimated that the USSR suffered 56 to 62 million 'unnatural deaths' during that period, with 34 to 49 million directly linked to Stalin. In a similar vein, British historian Norman Davies calculated that there were some 50 million killed between 1924–53, excluding wartime casualties[228]. In Latvia alone, it has been estimated that one per cent of all Latvians (around 15,000 people) were sent to their deaths in Siberia, during the night of 14 June 1941; the author of this claim, Augustinas Zemaitis, also says that: 'The brutality of First Soviet occupation (1940–1941) was such that it has been named the 'Year of Terror.' All Latvian property was nationalized. Some 35,000 were arrested, murdered or expelled to inhospitably cold Siberia – most never to return. So terrible was the Soviet occupation that many Latvians welcomed the new occupation by the German forces in 1941 as a relief.'[229]

A major difference between Lenin and Stalin was in their attitudes towards independence for the provinces – whilst Lenin wished them to be subservient to Moscow, he also recognised that they needed a degree of independence; ironically, as a Georgian, Stalin was in favour of far less independence and wanted direct and total control from Moscow. Lenin and Stalin were diametrically opposed in their attitudes towards independence for the provinces; the future relationship between Moscow and the newly independent autonomous Soviet republics and Russia, was to prove a major area of disagreement: Stalin wanted to adopt a hardline nationalistic approach to opposition, including severe repression of any dissent, and felt that this was best achieved via direct control from Moscow. Lenin, by contrast, felt that such an arrangement would be little better than the Russian Empire under the last Czar.

There was another major difference – that of the concentration of power: Lenin wished it to be held by a group (the 'Supreme Soviet') whilst Stalin wished it to be held by one man – himself. In his lust for power, Stalin clashed frequently with the other main revolutionary leader – Leon Trotsky – so much so that it appeared to threaten the unity of purpose of the governing Soviet: Lenin recommended that Stalin be removed from his position as secretary-general of the party, as he regarded Stalin as a threat to the unity of the Central Committee, due to the 'strained relationship between Stalin and Trotsky'. Following Lenin's death, Stalin, changed the party's name on 31 December 1925, to the All-Union Communist Party, in an attempt to play down the imbalance that Russia had in its relationships with the other Soviet republics. In an attempt to ingratiate himself with Lenin's supporters and to present himself as a loyal servant of the people and one of Lenin's most fervent admirers and followers, Stalin published a letter in Pravda on 24 January after Lenin's death, in which he lauded Lenin and his achievements, and he proposed that the name of the second city of Russia (Petrograd) be changed to Leningrad.[230] Stalin's connections helped him to gain influential positions behind the scenes in the Soviet-Russian government; he was the General Secretary of the Central Committee of the Communist Party of the Soviet Union from 1922 until his death in 1953. In such a position he could exert considerable influence on all aspects of Soviet society, whilst not apparently being responsible for the daily running of operations: power without accountability.

There have been many comparisons between Hitler and Stalin, yet Stalin, despite being feared by the population, despite having murdered hundreds of thousands, and despite having sent millions to the Gulags, achieved a national unity of purpose by harnessing patriotism. Hitler from the outset focused on economic prosperity for the Germans, and the promise to right the 'wrongs' inflicted on the German nation by the Treaty of Versailles: according to many historians, this explained the level of popular support that his regime commanded in its initial stages.[231] However, despite initial success, he failed to inculcate unity of purpose amongst the wider population, and once the military tide had turned against the Axis forces, there appears to have been little or no attempt to appeal to patriotism to unite the nation – great efforts were made to highlight the barbarity of the Soviet regime, and what it would mean to suffer Soviet occupation, but little else. The end of Nazi Germany witnessed a vehement out-pouring of political posturing, far detached from reality, and more akin to a Wagnerian *Götterdämmerung* than to any organised last-ditch defence. By contrast, at the most dangerous period for the Soviets – the defence of Moscow in December 1941 – Stalin had appealed for patriotic unity, with far greater success.

Georgian War of Independence (1921–1924)

Following the Russian Revolution, Georgia declared its independence from Moscow on 7 May 1920, at the Treaty of Moscow, when it became the Democratic Republic of Georgia, and installed its own social democratic government. During Lenin's convalescence he remained wheelchair bound, and his duties were taken over by Stalin, who used his new power to persuade a sick Lenin to agree to the agree to the invasion of Georgia – in response to pleas from Georgian workers and peasants – on 14 February 1921. By 25 February the Red Army had captured the Georgian capital Tbilisi and declared the country to be the Georgian Soviet Socialist Republic and installed a puppet government – a blueprint for what was to happen throughout Eastern Europe over the following sixty years or more. Georgians continued to resist the Russian invaders and this widespread insurrection was put down with great brutality by the Russians, who resorted to killing whole families in their desperate attempts to wipe out the anti-Communist elements in Georgian society. Casualty figures are difficult to confirm, but most sources appear to accept that the Russians lost around 5,500 killed, 2,500 captured and an unknown number of wounded; figures for Georgia were 3,500 killed or captured and an unknown number wounded.

Occupation of Eastern Poland (1939–1941)

The Soviet Union and Nazi Germany signed a non-aggression pact on 23 August 1939, a week before Germany unleashed its blitzkrieg on Poland, heralding the start of World War II in Europe. The pact contained a secret provision for spheres of influence in Eastern Europe that both sides would accept after Germany had defeated Poland; the dividing line was to be roughly along the River Bug, with the Soviets taking everything to the east, and the Germans everything to the West. It was also agreed that the Soviet Union would acquire Lithuania, Estonia and Latvia. On 17 September, just over two weeks after Germany invaded Poland, the Soviet Union attacked from the east, effectively stabbing the Poles in the back as the bulk of Polish forces were facing West, trying to halt the German advance. Worn down after fighting with the Germans, the Poles offered little resistance to the Soviet incursion. German and Soviet soldiers met in the middle of Poland, and the Soviet Union took control of their part of the country. Whilst the world remembers the Nazi attack on Poland in September 1939, far fewer people are aware of the Soviet attack – Communist propaganda sought to downplay this blatant opportunism, and Communist parties throughout the West chose to remain silent.

The Attack on Finland (1939–1940)

The so-called 'Winter War' was a conflict fought between Finland and the Soviet Union that began in the winter of 1939. Stalin had made a series of unreasonable demands on Finland, which were rejected by the Finnish government. The Soviets manufactured an excuse to attack (refer back to false-flag activities in 'Overt Strategies'), then launched a major assault against Finland in three places. The Finns fought desperately, and inflicted horrendous casualties on the Red Army, which was poorly led and inadequately prepared to fight in winter conditions. The smaller Finnish army dealt the Soviet troops a bitter defeat, especially at Suomussalmi. The Red Army regrouped and changed leadership, eventually overpowering the Finns who lost 11 per cent of their territory. The poor performance of the Soviet military emboldened Hitler to invade the Soviet Union in 1941. Following the end of the war, in the peace imposed on Finland, there was a significant border zone retained by Moscow, in addition to some strategic islands to the south; these losses were confirmed as permanent following the end of World War II. A good account of the war is given in *White Death* by Robert Edwards.[232]

The Occupation of the Baltic States (1940–1941)

Following the treaty with Nazi Germany, and the invasion and occupation of Poland, Stalin sought to annex the Baltic republics of Lithuania, Latvia, and

Estonia; he forced the three states to sign a mutual assistance pact with the USSR in October 1939, which included Moscow's right to establish military bases in the countries. The reason – from Moscow's point of view – was that they were pre-empting German attempts to do the same, and to threaten Leningrad. Stalin sent the Red Army into occupy the three countries in the summer of 1940, and forced the governments to resign – the presidents of Estonia and Latvia were sent to Gulags where they were subsequently held until their deaths: they were replaced by puppet governments controlled by Moscow. To give a veneer of legitimacy, elections were held, but were rigged by Moscow, and the result was never in doubt; the outcome was that the new 'governments' passed resolutions 'requesting' that their respective countries be allowed into the Soviet Union. Their request, of course, was granted.

In between being absorbed into the USSR, and the German invasion of 1941, the Soviet authorities – led by the NKVD – rounded up thousands of citizens (some sources say 130,000) and deported them to the gulags in June 1941. The deportations were carried out under the instructions of KBG General Ivan Serov and became known as the 'Serov Instructions': these gave detailed instructions as to how the deportations were to be carried out between 13 and 14 June 1941. What the Soviets had not appreciated, however, was that their brutal occupation, executions, and mass deportations would turn the citizens of these countries against them, and that within a matter of weeks of the repressive measures being enacted, the German forces invading these countries would be greeted as liberators by the local populations. Following the defeat of the Axis forces, and the re-occupation of Latvia by the Red Army, there was another wave of deportations: an estimated 42,000 people were rounded up and sent to the gulags on the night of 24–25 March 1949.[233] Most were never seen again.

The Occupation of Bessarabia, Northern Bukovina and Herta (1940–1991)

The Soviet Union had not recognised the sovereign claim of Romania to the province of Bessarabia since the union of 1918; on 28 June 1940, Moscow issued an ultimatum to the Romanians, demanding the evacuation of their military and administrative personnel from the territory, in addition to the removal of all Romanians from the northern part of the Romanian province of Bukovina. The Romanian government caved in to these demands under threats of military intervention from Moscow and from Berlin. The three regions were occupied by Axis forces from July 1941, but once retaken by the USSR in 1944, they remained under Soviet control until 1991 – after which they were rejoined with Moldova and Ukraine.

The Occupation of Eastern Europe (from 1944)

Many might disagree with the inclusion of this section as an example of Soviet aggression, claiming that this was a geographical consequence of the Red Army's push west in pursuit of the defeated Axis forces that had invaded the Soviet Union in June 1941. There is undoubtedly a strong basis for such an argument, but what it fails to address is the fact that the Soviets, having ejected Axis forces in the countries they entered, replaced the previous pro-Axis administrations with pro-Soviet administrations. In some instances, such as the Warsaw uprising against German occupation, the Red Army even waited on the east bank of the Vistula until the revolt had been put down before they entered the city – Stalin was doubtless thankful that the Germans had destroyed the Polish resistance, as it saved him having to do the same later; politically the Red Army – and not Polish patriots – had to be seen to 'liberate' Warsaw, thus preparing the ground for the Soviet imposition of a pro-Moscow government shortly afterwards. In such manner, Stalin was able to reconquer those territories that had been lost following World War I and the Treaty of Brest-Litovsk.

Had the Soviets been true liberators they would have pulled out of the countries from which they had ejected the Axis forces, and allowed these countries the freedom to rebuild their democracies; however, as history has shown, the opposite happened, as all the countries of Eastern Europe and the Baltic states that the Soviet Union 'liberated' from Axis control, were subsequently occupied by Soviet forces until they were recalled – many in the late 1940s, but some remained in occupation until the death of Stalin in 1953. Before leaving, the Russians installed puppet Communist governments, that, whilst ostensibly independent, took their orders from Moscow. The rationale behind this was twofold: firstly, letting these countries 'govern' themselves would obviate the potential criticism from the West that the USSR had occupied the countries. Secondly, it was much cheaper to let these countries police themselves – any criticism could be handled by their own governments, leaving Moscow to focus on other priorities. In most countries, the Russians maintained some form of politico-military presence until 1991, in particular in the newly formed state of East Germany. States that fell under Soviet control were: Austria (from 1945–1955), Bulgaria, Czechoslovakia, East Germany, Estonia, Hungary, The Kuril Islands, Japan (from 1945), Latvia, Lithuania, Moldova, Northern Norway (1944–1946), Poland, and Romania. In addition to the control of Eastern Europe, Moscow sent forces to eject the Japanese occupiers from Manchuria in northern China, in 1945. These forces remained in occupation until 1946: they only left when it became apparent that the then pro-Russian Communist forces led by Mao Tse Tung would take over the country. In conjunction with the Chinese Communist forces, the Russians sought to confront the West by supporting the new North Korean Communist government, formed in 1945; they eventually persuaded the North Koreans to attempt to take over the southern half of the country, resulting in the Korean War (1950–1953).

Post-World War II Partisan Resistance to Soviet Occupation (1945–1960)
As previously explained, Soviet control of Eastern Europe was initially established through a series of puppet states, each of which had a Moscow-installed and approved Communist government; whilst theoretically, each was an independent nation, they were tightly controlled by secret police forces and hosted large numbers of Russian military personnel – including armoured units – usually stationed in barracks near the capital city. For evidence of the resentment this Soviet control caused, one only has to look at the number of anti-Communist insurgency movements that sprang up from the last days of World War II, and lasted well after the war had ended:

1. The Ukranian Insurgent Army (UPA) actively opposed Soviet Russian occupation for over ten years following the end of the war, disbanding only in 1956. Through their brutal treatment of the civilian population, the Russians created a situation in which the partisan armies received civilian support in many forms, with many citizens actively joining the partisans. The only way the Russians felt they could counter growing Ukrainian resistance was though deportations and executions: these continued after the war, and in October 1947, there were 76,192 civilians arrested in Western Ukraine and deported to the gulag.[234] What the Russian occupiers forgot (or cared

not to remember) was that similar tactics by Axis occupation forces earlier had acted as a 'recruiting sergeant' for the Ukrainian partisan units that had resisted the invaders.

2. Widespread opposition to the Russians in the Baltic states led to the formation of a series of resistance armies, estimated to comprise up to 50,000, who fought the Soviet occupiers from their forest bases until 1956.[235]
3. In Romania, there were two major armed anti-Communist groups, both of which were based in mountainous regions, and which became active from early 1948: the group based in the Făgăras Mountains, and led by Ion Gavrilă, and the group based in the Apuseni Mountains, and led by Leon Şuşman. Both groups fought until the early 1960s.
4. In Poland and in Bulgaria, resistance began in 1944 and lasted until around the mid-1950s and early 1960s respectively.

The Korean War (1950–1953)

Whilst most direct military support for the North Koreans was provided by the Chinese, the Russians did occasionally become involved in air combat but avoided putting 'boots on the ground' as they were afraid that if become known it might escalate the conflict into a nuclear exchange, and they were not prepared for that. Having said this, some estimates have put Russian involvement as up to 72,000 personnel – a figure that was kept secret by both the US and Soviet governments, as they had no desire to widen the conflict.[236] The largest contribution that the Soviets made was in terms of medical supplies and weaponry.

The Malenkov Year (1953)

Suppression of the Berlin Uprising (June 1953)

After the end of World War II, the defeated German nation was divided into three zones of occupation, with the victorious Allies controlling a zone each: the British in the north, the French along the Franco-German border, and the Americans in the south. The Russians were also allotted a zone to the east – which ultimately became East Germany (or the ironically named German Democratic Republic). The tough conditions under which Germans in this Russian-occupied zone were forced to live was one of deprivation, physical abuse – including rape and murder – by their Russian occupiers, and the shipment of thousands of tons of goods back to Russia. Goods ranged from the household possessions of individual German civilians to capital goods, such as factories, rolling stock, and power plants. The erstwhile capital, Berlin, was also divided into zones of occupation, but the problem was that the city of Berlin and its suburbs lay inside East Germany – and whilst there were both land and air corridors to the city from the West, these were subject to sudden closure by the Russians. Within East Berlin the workforce suffered greatly, and the imposition of production quotas without an increase in living standards finally proved too much and on 16 June 1953 workers in East Berlin went on strike: the strike quickly spread throughout the country until an estimated one million East Germans were in revolt against Soviet control. Stalin had died just three months earlier, and this coupled with the perceived weakness of the new Malenkov administration, was the catalyst that had led to the revolt. This presented the Russians with both an ideological and a practical problem: ideologically, these workers should have been satisfied with their existence in the 'worker's paradise' of Communism, but they were not. Practically, the Russians were faced with putting down a widespread insurrection without too much bloodshed as the eyes of the world were on them. The authorities had to be careful how they suppressed the riots – the East German workers were the most productive of the whole Soviet Bloc, and the Red Army was instructed not to shoot more than absolutely necessary – after all, a dead worker produces nothing. The Soviets eventually put down the revolt in October of the same year, using armoured forces: the East German administration refused to confirm the number of deaths, but sources have put fatalities at 55, although some estimates go as high as 125, with more protestors being arrested and executed soon after, and thousands arrested and sent to gulag penal camps.[237] A short but informative account of the uprising is provided in Steve Vogel's book *Betrayal in Berlin*.[238]

The Khrushchev Years (1953–1964)

Khrushchev was born on 15 April 1894 in Kalinovka, Russia, and later moved to Ukraine. His first job was in mines in the Donbas region, where he became a pipe fitter – a job that exempted him from military service in

World War I. He joined the Communist Party after the revolution, and also joined the Red Army as a commissar, a position that he also held during World War II. He rose in the ranks of the party, and eventually became first secretary – basically president under the Communist regime – from 14 September 1953–14 October 1964. The British PM Harold Macmillan had meetings with Khrushchev, whom he described as: 'Impulsive, sensitive of his own dignity and insensitive of anyone else's feelings; quick in argument, never missing or overlooking a point; with an extraordinary memory and encyclopaedic information at his command; vulgar, and yet capable of a certain dignity when he is simple and forgets to 'show off'; ruthless, but sentimental'.[239] In the West, Khrushchev is best remembered for two incidents (1) the denunciation of Stalin for his crimes, and (2) confronting the USA over the Cuban Missile Crisis.

His attacks on Stalin were a deliberate ploy, designed to give the impression that the USSR was no longer the enemy of the West, and bearing in mind the DeCaB strategy outlined earlier, enabled him to distance himself from the numerous atrocities committed during the Stalin era. Khrushchev tried to scapegoat Stalin, just as some sixty years later, Putin tried to scapegoat Communism: neither succeeded, as their message was lost in the military adventures that followed. Whilst appearing to 'soften' his attitude towards the West, Khrushchev's actions did not mirror his proclamations. He authorised the suppression of the Hungarian uprising in 1956, the building of the 'Iron Curtain' and Berlin Wall in 1961, and in the same year, he supported the newly installed regime of Fidel Castro on the Caribbean island of Cuba, following the overthrow of the Cuban dictator, Fulgencio Batista.

Suppression of the Hungarian Uprising (1956)

Following the death of Stalin, there were expectations that the Soviet control over Hungary would be relaxed, and when nothing happened, rebellion broke out throughout the country in October 1956. There were some successes achieved early on, and the Premier Imre Nagy was forced to concede to the establishment of a multiparty system, and that the country would become neutral in any East-West dispute. This was anathema to Moscow, which made its displeasure clear, and threatened armed intervention. Nagy appealed to the West for help, but nothing was forthcoming as NATO was afraid of antagonising the Russians. The Russians sent their tanks into Budapest on 4 November, put down the rebellion with great brutality, and took Nagy back to Moscow where he was executed.

The Bay of Pigs (1961)

Cuban exiles in Miami, financed, armed, and trained by the CIA[240], attempted a military landing at the Bay of Pigs on the island of Cuba to regain their homeland, but were repulsed by the Cuban forces: heavily armed with Russian-supplied weapons and vehicles. Khrushchev acknowledged the rising level of discontent with the new regime in his 'memoirs':

> Castro's policies...were earning him many enemies. The President whom he'd appointed when he first came to power fled to America, and many of the men who had fought at his side during the struggle for independence were turning away from him...They had been fed up with Batista and eager to overthrow the corrupt old regime, but they were against Castro's nationalization of all businesses, his restrictive policies against the landowners...[241]

The Berlin Wall and the 'Iron Curtain' (1961)

The Soviet-controlled countries of Europe had been beset by problems ever since the end of the war, and they faced a major crisis in terms of the numbers of citizens who fled to the West every year in search of better economic prospects and political freedom. Rather than make it more attractive to people to stay, it was decided to make it more difficult to leave. Within the divided city of Berlin, the East German administration built a wall overnight, cutting the city in half and preventing escapes. All along the frontier where Soviet-controlled countries shared a common border with democratic countries, they constructed a continuous fence line, with armed guard posts, barbed wire, and extensive minefields – ostensibly to keep out illegal Western incursions, but as most of the weapons faced eastwards, the real purpose was obvious. It was Winston Churchill who first drew the world's attention to what was happening in a speech at Westminster College, Fulton, Missouri, USA, on 5 March 1946:

> From Stettin in the Baltic to Trieste in the Adriatic, an iron curtain has descended across the Continent. Behind that line lie all the capitals of the

> ancient states of Central and Eastern Europe. Warsaw, Berlin, Prague, Vienna, Budapest, Belgrade, Bucharest and Sofia; all these famous cities and the populations around them lie in what I must call the Soviet sphere, and all are subject, in one form or another, not only to Soviet influence but to a very high and in some cases increasing measure of control from Moscow.[242]

The Cuban Missile Crisis (1962)

Once the Cuban rebels in the Bay of Pigs invasion had been defeated, the Soviet Union set about arming the Castro regime to counter any further threats. The Cubans were supplied with a variety of weapons – some offensive in nature, some defensive: Khrushchev claims that the Cubans were sent 'tanks, artillery, fighter planes and instructors'[243] while Max Hastings is more precise, saying that 650 Russian military advisors and trainers were sent to Cuba.[244] However, Khrushchev also let slip the real reason for the arming of Cuba by the Soviet Union, which was perfectly in line with the Communist doctrine of 'exporting' what he referred to as 'Socialism' throughout the world: 'We had an obligation to do everything in our power to protect Cuba's existence as a Socialist country and as a working example to the other countries of Latin America. It was clear to me that we might very well lose Cuba if we didn't take some decisive steps in her defence.'[245] In other words, the arming of Cuba by the Russians had little if anything to do with the defence of Cuba, but more with the maintenance of a Communist stronghold in the Americas. It was in this aspect that Khrushchev made a big mistake, and one that was to haunt him for the remainder of his premiership. He decided that the only way to defend Cuba was to station intermediate ballistic missiles on the island, aimed at the USA. Whilst the positioning of short-range, tactical missiles might have been legitimately accepted as a defensive measure against any further US-sponsored attacks from Florida, to install offensive long-range missiles was totally different, and had only one explanation – that the USSR was contemplating using Cuba as a missile base for attacks on the USA. Yet Khrushchev still protested that these were for defensive purposes only: 'I want to make one thing absolutely clear: when we put our ballistic missiles in Cuba, we had no desire to start a war.'[246]

The problem with such a claim is twofold: firstly, as a deterrent the missiles were useless as they had been emplaced covertly: for a deterrent to be effective, a potential enemy has to be aware of its existence. The launch sites had only been discovered by US photo-reconnaissance aircraft, and once their presence on the island had been confirmed, this led to intense speculation in Washington this suggested that they were to be used in a secret attack on US territory: if they were of a purely defensive nature, then why not advertise their presence? Secondly, the type of missile used was an R-16 liquid fuel rocket[247] which could carry a five-megaton thermonuclear warhead up to a distance of some 11,000 kilometres (just over 6,000 miles). This meant that, from their bases in Cuba, these rockets – equipped with thermonuclear warheads – could hit any major city in the USA: New York is some 1,200 miles away from Cuba, Los Angeles 2,300 miles, San Francisco 2,600 miles, and Washington D.C. 2,700. Unless the Russians wished to start a nuclear war, then this level of nuclear armament was unnecessarily provocative – far cheaper, and more effective, would have been to supply the Cubans with naval protection in the form of destroyers, fast patrol boats or submarines; these would have defended Cuban shores against any invasion. As it was, his actions nearly led to World War III. On being briefed about the missiles in Cuba, the US President, John F. Kennedy sent Khrushchev an ultimatum that Russian ships carrying more missiles would be sunk unless they turned back, as he had put the island in 'quarantine', vowing that the US would prevent the arrival and emplacement of any further military hardware. Any attempt to break the quarantine would be considered an act of war, and the Americans would respond appropriately. There followed a 35-day stand-off (16 October–20 November 1962), until Khrushchev backed down, and ordered the ships to turn back. It is generally accepted that this is the closest the world has come to nuclear war. The reply Kennedy received from Khrushchev is interesting, as he tried to turn the ultimatum back on Kennedy, initially by asking him to see things from the Russian point of view. See Box B (opposite):

Khrushchev makes some blatantly hypocritical accusations: 'It would mean for us to conduct our relations with other countries not by reason, but by yielding to tyranny... You want to force us to renounce the rights enjoyed by every sovereign state; you are attempting to legislate questions of international law; you are violating the generally accepted standards of this law.' The violation of the rights of sovereign states through military action

Box B

Khrushchev's Response to Kennedy's Ultimatum

Imagine, Mr. President, what if we were to present to you such an ultimatum as you have presented to us by your actions. How would you react to it? I think you would be outraged at such a move on our part. And this we would understand.

Having presented these conditions to us, Mr. President, you have thrown down the gauntlet. Who asked you to do this? By what right have you done this? Our ties with the Republic of Cuba, as well as our relations with other nations, regardless of their political system, concern only the two countries between which these relations exist....

You, Mr. President, are not declaring a quarantine, but rather issuing an ultimatum, and you are threatening that if we do not obey your orders, you will then use force. Think about what you are saying! And you want to persuade me to agree to this! What does it mean to agree to these demands? It would mean for us to conduct our relations with other countries not by reason, but by yielding to tyranny. You are not appealing to reason; you want to intimidate us ... You want to force us to renounce the rights enjoyed by every sovereign state; you are attempting to legislate questions of international law; you are violating the generally accepted standards of this law. All this is due not only to hatred for the Cuban people and their government, but also for reasons having to do with the election campaign in the USA. What morals, what laws can justify such an approach by the American government to international affairs? .... Unfortunately, people of all nations, and not least the American people themselves, could suffer heavily from madness such as this, since with the appearance of modern types of weapons, the USA has completely lost its former inaccessibility. (24 October 1962)

Source: 'Khrushchev letter to President Kennedy', *Exhibitions: Revelations from the Russian Archives.* (Translation of letter held in the US Library of Congress); https://www.loc.gov./exhibits/archives/trans-x2jfk.html

was used by the Russians when they sent their tanks into East Germany (in 1953), and into Hungary (1956), none of which were threatening the USSR at the time, only seeking their independence from unelected Communist rule.[248] The irony is, of course, that the Soviet Union had always conducted its foreign relations by force, as is apparent in this chapter.

The Brezhnev Years (1964–1982)

Involvement in the Vietnam War (1965–1975)

Leonid Brezhnev wanted to please the more hardline members of the Politburo, so he began military aid to the Communist North Vietnamese.[249] When the Soviet Union broke up in 1991, previously classified documents revealed that at the time, and despite their protestations to the contrary, the Soviets had stationed up to 3,000 Red Army personnel in Vietnam in a training role, in addition to a number of special forces units. The Russians supplied military equipment to the Communist Vietnamese, in addition to providing them with intelligence as to US actions and force locations. One source, writing in the state-controlled *Rossiyskaya Gazeta* even makes the claim that Russian military supplies 'completely transformed the nature of the war' and that this enabled the Vietnamese to fight not just with 'with just cunning and camouflage, they hit the Americans with firepower on a staggering scale. Their arsenal included 2,000 tanks, 7,000 artillery guns, over 5,000 anti-aircraft guns and 158 surface-to-air rocket launchers.'[250]

Suppression of the 'Czech Spring' (August 1968)

The General Secretary of the Czech Communist Party – Alexander Dubček – replaced the unpopular President Antonín Novotnýas on 5 January 1968, and set in motion a series of reforms that held wide appeal for the Czechs, but not for their Russian masters. Leonid Brezhnev was a hardliner who thought that deviation by any Soviet State would ultimately bring about the collapse of the whole empire: he was afraid that the reforms initiated in Czechoslovakia would soon be demanded throughout the rest of the Soviet Union. At a meeting in Dresden on 23 March 1968, the representatives of five nations (Bulgaria, East Germany, Hungary, Poland, and Russia) accused the Czech delegation of criticising the USSR, and complained that the attitude of the Czech Press was similar to that of Hungary in 1956. Recently released files provided by the KGB defector Vasiliy Mitrokhin, show that Russia did not initially wish to replace Dubček's government as this would signal more problems in the Soviet Bloc to the West. They tried the covert approach first, launching Operation Progress – in which the KGB tried to infiltrate a number of Czech organisations, including the Charles University in Prague, and the Czech Socialist and Christian Democrat parties; their objective was threefold: to identify ringleaders and opinion-makers, to try to dissuade further 'liberalisation', and to prepare for invasion by the armed forces of other Soviet nations. Ultimately, the covert attempts at suppressing the 'Czech Spring' as it became known failed and true to form, Dubček's government was overthrown when the forces of Russia, Poland, Bulgaria, and Hungary invaded during the night of 20–21 August 1968. The initial invasion force consisted of 200,000 troops and around 2,000 tanks, which first seized the airport, and then major communication centres. The Russian press published a copy of a letter purporting to come from some members of the Czech government, in which the Czechs pleaded for immediate help, including assistance with armed forces.[251] This is a classic example of the strategy referred to earlier as 'Invitation'. There was little resistance as the invaders had occupied the country quickly, and put down any attempts at resistance with great brutality. There are thought to have been 108[252] civilian victims, with another 400 the following year – killed by the Czech security services when they rounded up others who had been involved in the riots. An estimated 300,000 Czechs fled across the border into West Germany or Austria. In their extensively researched book on the invasion, Czech historians Prokop Tomek and Ivo Pejčoch quoted from eyewitnesses who said that 'the invaders shot more than 50 people dead already on the first day of the occupation' and that a 91-year-old Czech man was deliberately run over by a Soviet tank. They found no evidence of any Soviet troops being killed by Czech civilians – a claim made by Moscow to justify the retaliatory shooting of Czechs who, it was suggested, had attacked the Warsaw Pact invasion force.[253]

The Invasion of Afghanistan (1979)

Although never part of the Soviet Union, Afghanistan had always formed an important part of Moscow's geopolitical considerations, due to its strategic location along the southern flank of the USSR. In late 1979, it appeared that Afghanistan might be slipping into the Western orbit of influence, or would go the way of Iran, where the Shah had been overthrown and been replaced by an Islamic republic. This could not be allowed to happen in a neighbouring state, and it was this real fear of the possibility of an unstable and fanatical Islamic neighbour on its southern flank, that pushed the Soviet Union into invasion with the ultimate goal of regime change. Brezhnev decided to launch a cross-border invasion, ostensibly under the doctrine which allowed for support for any Soviet state if it felt threatened by an external power, one of mutual defence – this came under the auspices of the Warsaw Pact. Afghans were subjected to atrocities and many forms of inhuman treatment, including the mass killing of civilians in the summer of 1980. In their research for a report commissioned for the Helsinki Watch organisation[254], authors Jeri Laker and Barnett Rubin interviewed hundreds of Afghan refugees who had fled across the border into Pakistan. The experiences of these people make harrowing reading, such as the fate of two elderly and infirm Afghans who could not escape the Russians, so their captors 'tied dynamite to their backs and blew them up'.[255] Or the more general account of the ways in which the Russians dealt with the populations of rural villages:

> We visited hospitals where we met paraplegics and amputees, victims of anti-personnel mines ... or of the camouflaged plastic 'butterfly' mines that are dropped from helicopters and intended to maim, not kill, the children and their flocks... From our interviews, it soon became clear that just about every conceivable human rights violation is occurring in Afghanistan, and on an enormous scale.[256]

The occupation lasted over ten years, and cost 125,000 Russian military lives, and the lives of over one million Afghan civilians.

The Andropov Years (1982–1984)

Continued occupations of Eastern Europe, the Baltic States, Bessarabia, Northern Bukovina, Hertsa and Afghanistan.

The Chernenko Years (1984–1985)

Continued occupations of Eastern Europe, the Baltic States, Bessarabia, Northern Bukovina, Hertsa and Afghanistan.

The Gorbachev Years (1985–1991)

This period saw a slew of states proclaiming their independence from Moscow: whilst they declared their independence, this was not recognised by Moscow until some months after the event; finally, however, Gorbachev agreed, and the Russian Parliament gave its consent, with independence for Estonia, Latvia, and Lithuania being declared on 6 September 1991. Despite this, Moscow continued to station some military forces in the three countries until their eventual withdrawal in August 1993 (from Lithuania). Even with Gorbachev at the helm, the process did not go smoothly, as many nationalist politicians (backed by the military) wished to retain a Russian presence, claiming that their forces were necessary to protect the 'human rights' of ethnic Russians living in the Baltic republics. This is a well-worn Russian tactic, and was used in 2022 by Vladimir Putin to justify his reinvasion of Ukraine, which had declared its independence on 16 July 1990.[257] Independence for the other States was recognised by Moscow on 26 December 1991: Azerbaijan, Georgia, The Russian Federation, Uzbeckistan, Moldova, Ukraine, Belarus, Armenia, Turkmenistan, Tajikistan, Kazakhstan, Chechnya, Kyrgyzstan, and South Ossetia (since 2008). There were growing tensions between the USSR and the Soviet republics until, on 26 December 1990, Gorbachev formally dissolved the Soviet Union. In addition to the independence of the old Soviet states, there was a freedom movement in Eastern Europe, and the East European puppet (satellite) states that had been militarily occupied by the Soviet Union also declared their independence: the German Democratic Republic officially ceased to exist on 3 October 1990 with the Reunification Treaty, and the country was officially merged with what was then West Germany on 15 March 1991. The Velvet Revolution saw the peaceful independence of Czechoslovakia on 29 December 1989, Bulgaria in June 1990, Hungary in June 1991, Ukraine on 24 August 1991, and Poland on 27 October 1991. The remainder had all declared their independence by the end of 1991.

Some Russians, however, felt that Gorbachev's reforms had gone too far too quickly, and this resulted in an attempted coup in Moscow on 19 August 1991: this was put down after only two days, but one of the stated objective of the plotters – to forcibly bring the states back into the USSR – sent a strong message to many, including Ukraine, that the danger of re-incorporation into the USSR was very real; as one of the more economically powerful states in the old Soviet Union, Ukraine was considered a prime target for reincorporation.

The Collapse of the Soviet Union

Before proceeding to analyse the role played by the men who assumed the leadership of Russia post-USSR (Yeltsin, Medvedev, and Putin), it is important to analyse why the Soviet Union, once thought of as the second most powerful state in the world, disintegrated into its constituent countries; the effect this had on the nation as a whole and on Vladimir Putin in particular is crucial, as it accounts for the level of discontent that exists within Russia, and the ease with which Putin is able to suggest that the post-USSR chaos is a direct consequence of malignant interference from the West in general, and from the USA in particular. Putin is on record as having said that the collapse of the USSR was the 'greatest geopolitical catastrophe of the century',[258] allowing for a degree of hyperbole in his assessment, it has to be admitted that the loss of prestige and order that was felt by ordinary Russians after December 1991 was real. Unemployment rose dramatically, as did inflation and corruption, and just as Hitler had managed to convince the German people that Germany's economic woes of the 1920s were a direct consequence of the Treaty of Versailles, Putin has managed to convince Russians that the Soviet Union gave them a century of politico-economic stability.[259] Such a link is, of course, patent nonsense, yet people believe what they want to believe, and nostalgia tends to paint the past in warm colours. A more factual assessment of why the Soviet Union collapsed is necessary – there are a number of key reasons why the Soviet Union collapsed, and these are examined below.

Cultural Differences

As with the Imperial Russian state, the new Soviet Union suffered from the problem of trying to integrate widely different cultures, languages and religions within one country. From the more European of the Soviet states such as Russia or Ukraine, to the more Asiatic such as Azerbaijan, or Chechnya, or Georgia, there was little common ground – the artificial union created by Communism was the only thing that really held these states together, and, as with Yugoslavia, once centralised control had gone, they began to fall apart of their own volition.

Political Differences

It is perhaps not surprising to learn that hundreds of thousands of Soviet citizens had no wish to remain under the centralised Communist control of Moscow – this was especially true in those states that had suffered most under Communist economic policies such as the collectivisation of agriculture. This desire for political independence manifested itself most strongly in those countries that had been within the Comecon sphere, but on the fringes of Soviet rule: Bulgaria, Czechoslovakia, Estonia, Hungary, Latvia, Lithuania, Poland, and Romania.

Corruption

Corruption was found in all sectors of society but was probably greatest in politics. An analysis of political corruption within the USSR undertaken on behalf of the national Criminal Justice System and published in the *Western Political Quarterly* in 1977 found: 'Most corruption in the Soviet Union falls within two broad categories: (1) corruption for bureaucratic gain and (2) corruption for private gain.' The same report identified economic crimes as accounting for 'almost one-quarter of all crime in the country' and that there is a tendency for public officials 'to use illegal means to acquire housing in a nation with a serious shortage'. The report also identified 'widespread shortages of consumer goods and agricultural products' which contributed to corruption 'for private gain'.[260]

The Economy

The real question relating to the break-up of the USSR, however, is whether one factor was more important than the others? Was there an initial catalyst that prompted the break-up? Unsurprisingly, there are many opinions, but all appear to cite the declining economic power of the USSR as *the* major contributor, generally for a number of reasons. The economy of the whole USSR and the separate economies of the states within the greater union of the USSR were both weak – they were inefficiently managed, over-staffed, heavily subsidised, and riddled with waste and corruption. The basic problem was that Moscow could not or would not understand that collectivisation of agriculture and state ownership of businesses were destroying the economy and taking away any motivation from the workforce to increase quality standards. In addition, there was a disproportionately high percentage of GDP spent on the military, police, and secret services. British Prime Minister Margaret Thatcher commented that at the time she took office (May 1979), Soviet military expenditure stood at between 12 and 14 per cent of GDP, rising to around 25–30 per cent by the end of the 1980s – this was far in excess of expenditure in Europe, the USA, and Canada.

The system suffered from an overall lack of efficiency – specifically in terms of resource distribution channels and from a lack of economic stability. In his memoirs, President Nikita Khrushchev tried to put a political 'spin' on the economic hardships of the immediate post-war period, commenting that in Ukraine there was a 'widespread feeling of responsibility for contributing to the security of the rest of the country by providing the necessary agricultural products'.[261] This, of course, is errant nonsense: if anything, one can imagine a widespread feeling of *resentment* on the part of Ukrainian farmers, who had been forced to live through one of the worst famines in history – and one that was directly attributable to Communist collectivisation policies, and then forced to feed a regime into which they had been co-opted against their will.

Post-Stalin, the economy of the USSR was typified by the decentralisation of economic decision-making to the various republics of the USSR. This was not always a good idea, as various national leaders had differing opinions as to the best economic policy. For example, in East Germany, the Soviet-appointed leader Walter Ulbricht continued with the implementation of a Communist economic policy of state ownership of business and collectivisation of farms. In his study of the Berlin Wall, and the reasons leading to its erection, Frederick Taylor comments on the dire economic situation in which Ulbricht found himself with a deficit of 700 million *Ostmarks* in 1952,[262] and a negative trade balance of around 600 million with other Communist countries. Despite this grim outlook, Ulbrich continued with his collectivisation programme and the seizure of businesses, and thousands of people fled abroad to West Germany.[263] To prevent this continued 'brain drain' of skilled Germans to the West, which exacerbated the economic difficulties in which the puppet state found itself, it was decided to restrict the movement of ordinary Germans living in the Russian-occupied zone, and this led to the construction of the Berlin Wall.

The final stage of economic decline related to President Gorbachev's *Perestroika* initiative, in which the frailties of the Communist economic philosophy were finally acknowledged, and attempts were made to open up the economy to competition and foreign investment. By then it was too late, and all that Gorbachev really achieved was to open the inefficient, sluggish, and corrupt Soviet economy to direct competition from the West; the result was a forgone conclusion.

The Cracks in the Wall

The old Soviet Union collapsed internally from an accumulation of all these factors, with the increasingly rapid disintegration of the political structure in which the Soviet republics were subservient to Moscow. Once this had begun, it developed a momentum of its own, and soon became an unstoppable force, as one republic after another declared their independence. The first to do so was the Estonian Soviet Socialist Republic (ESSR) on 16 November 1988, even before the official break-up of the Soviet Union. The cracks really began to appear in the Communist alliance when the Hungarian authorities tore down their section of the 'Iron Curtain' on 2 May 1989, and allowed Hungarians to travel abroad. Madsen Pirie, writing on the thirtieth anniversary of the Berlin Wall's collapse, observed that, even before its official demise, the Hungarian portion of the Wall had become a victim of corruption, as the Hungarian army had been busy dismantling it, to be sold for scrap! 'When Hungary's Foreign Minister, Gyula Horn, and his Austrian counterpart, Alois Mock, held a symbolic fence-cutting ceremony at the crossing, both armed with heavy bolt cutters, and filmed by Western TV crews, much of the barbed wire had already gone, sold for scrap by the Hungarian army.'[264]

A Chronology of Post-Soviet Aggression

The Yeltsin Years (1991–1999)

Post break-up of the USSR, Russia continued to display the tendencies that had characterised the previous Communist administrations. Instead of taking advantage of this radical shift in political statehood, and curtailing all forms of interference and intervention abroad, it seemed as if it were 'business as usual' with interventions abroad, although not on the scale practiced by Stalin.

Intervention in the Tajikistan Civil War (1992–1997)

In 1991 the autonomous Soviet state of Tajikistan sought its independence from Moscow. The state had always been highly unstable as it was culturally, ethnically, and politically diverse, and had only been held together by the iron fist of Moscow. Not surprisingly, fighting soon broke out between different ethnic groups, and between some of these groups and the government led by President Rahmon Nabiyev, whose government was propped up by Uzbeki forces. Initially it seemed as if the rebels were winning, and they captured Nabiyev and forced him to resign his position. Conscious of the dangers should the conflict spill over the border into Uzbekistan, President Islam Karimov ordered his military into Tajikistan to 'restore order', which only resulted in further chao. Eventually the conflict was ended when a UN-backed armistice ended the war in 1997, and a tenuous power-sharing agreement was reached; the death toll was around 100,000. Whilst the invaders in this instance came from Uzbekistan, not Russia, there is speculation that Moscow had considered sending in Russian troops, but was afraid that this might be interpreted as an 'anti-Muslim' crusade (most Tajikis are Sunni Muslims): instead, they left intervention to the Uzbekis (another predominately Muslim nation), which allowed Moscow to exercise control over events at arm's length.

The First Chechen War (1994–1996)

Taking advantage of the turbulence caused by the disintegration of the USSR, Chechen Major-General Dzhokhar Dudayev launched a military coup against the Communist government and proclaimed the country's independence as the Chechen Republic of Ichkeria, on 6 September 1991. The problem was that the country existed in name only, as it had always been considered a republic within the Soviet Union/Russian Federation, and as such, Moscow would not permit any ceding of control – doubtless fearing that this would signal the loss of the other republics. The country degenerated into lawlessness; and President Boris Yeltsin felt obliged to act. His first move was to encourage (through the supply of weapons and funding) the emergence of a series of groups opposed to the new Chechen government. This proved unsuccessful, so eventually Yeltsin gave orders for a full-scale military intervention on 11 December 1994, to install a puppet administration in Grozny the capital city. Initially the invasion seemed successful, as the Russian forces pushed towards Grozny, but in the battle for the capital – which lasted from 22 December 1994 to 6 March 1995 – the Chechens gave the Russians a bloody nose. Despite the Russian great superiority in modern sophisticated weaponry, the Chechens were able to fight a prolonged and successful guerrilla campaign from the mountainous and heavily wooded terrain that covered most of the country. As in Ukraine, nearly thirty years later, the Russian army was taken by surprise by the tenacity and skill of the defenders, and the invasion bogged down for nearly two years whilst the Russian invaders were subjected to continued guerrilla fighting that caused them thousands of casualties,[265] making the war unpopular in the extreme. The guerrilla resistance and consequent instability continued for just under another two years, with Chechen guerrillas harassing the Russian occupation forces, and attacking government installations, power supplies, oil fields and troop depots. The end to hostilities only being agreed on 31 August 1996. Arkady Babchenko was a Russian soldier drafted in to fight in the first Chechen war; he identified the Russian weaknesses as overconfidence by the senior officers, including the defence minister General Grachyov, added to which was a 'betrayal' of the Russian conscripts who were 'insufficiently trained, depressed and demoralized: they did not understand the aims of this war, and they were treated as cannon fodder'.[266]

This attitude was the same as that expressed by Putin's forces, some thirty years later.[267] But for the date, he could have been describing the Russian conscripts fighting in Putin's war against Ukraine. As with Tajikistan, there was a strong religious undercurrent to the war; the Chechen rebels, most of whom were Muslims, were aided by other Muslims from a number of countries throughout the world. and the conflict took on a religious edge. The Russians declared a ceasefire in 1996 and in 1997 they signed a peace treaty.

As might be expected all involved have political capital to make through casualty totals, so estimates of fatalities vary widely but are conservatively put at up to 100,000 civilians, in addition to some 500,000 refugees. According to Amnesty International, up to 1999, of the civilians killed in Chechnya:

> Many of these were killed during the aerial bombardments of towns and villages in the first months of the conflict. Others died during fighting, or were killed after being rounded up in mass sweep operations. Many thousands of people are believed to be buried in unmarked graves around the republic: there are reported to be 52 registered sites of mass graves in Chechnya."[268]

A report issued by the Human Rights Watch (HRW) in February 1995 highlighted the fact that Russian forces committed atrocities against the civilian population; there was widespread damage of civilian infrastructure – in particular hospitals, and residential apartment buildings. The report noted that:

> Russian forces continue to use disproportionate force to dislodge Chechen fighters from villages. In some cases villagers resent and fear Chechen fighters in their midst because of the tragedy their presence can bring. Undisciplined Russian soldiers attack civilians, systematically loot civilian property, and rob individual civilians. Russian Interior Ministry forces have brutally beaten and tortured Chechen prisoners detained at the Russian military base in Mozdok.[269]

The war dragged on until the Chechens retook Grozny in August 1996, and a cease fire was declared after which the Russian were eventually forced to leave. Politically this did nothing but store up problems for the future, as whilst the country became a de facto independent state, it also still remained officially a part of Russia, which would later give Yeltsin's successor – Vladimir Putin – the excuse he needed to re-invade Chechnya to quell 'domestic terrorism'.

The First Putin Era (1999–2008)

Putin was born in Leningrad on 7 October 1952: his early career gave no indication of his desire to run the country, but despite his apparent lack of political ambition, he displayed intense nationalism by the age of fourteen – possibly as a consequence of parental influence – and even went to the offices of the KGB in Leningrad to discuss his future career path in that organisation[270] – not something that any 'normal' fourteen-year-old would generally do. Putin was born into a working-class family that, although not wealthy, was not poor: his father was in the Soviet navy submarine branch before the outbreak of World War II, and in 1941 he had volunteered to serve in an 'extermination' battalion[271] under the command of the KGB – one of their tasks was to hunt out and eliminate all civilians who opposed rule by Moscow, and were suspected of aiding the invading German forces. Another task was the destruction of all material left behind by the retreating Russian forces, to prevent it falling into enemy hands – Stalin's 'scorched earth' policy. He was later transferred to the army, where it is claimed, he fought in the 33rd Regiment of the 86th Division, in the 5th Rifle Corps in the defence of Leningrad, and in an assault across the River Neva, he was seriously wounded. Following the end of the war, Putin's father was awarded a political position in the Leningrad government. To what extent the martial exploits of his father had an influence on the young Putin is hard to say, but it is likely that the mix of adventure, danger, nationalism and opposition to the invaders of his country must have had an impression on Putin's early life.

Following the collapse of the USSR in December 1991, there was a period of prolonged instability and widespread corruption – in both the private and public sectors. This period was overseen by two presidents, Mikhail Gorbachev and Boris Yeltsin – both of whom faced internal criticism, calls by the constituent countries of the USSR for independence, and in the case of Yeltsin, an attempted coup by the Russian military. Vladimir Putin's attitudes to the independence of various states within the USSR were largely formed during this period, and by what he regards as Russia's manifest destiny and his grievances against the West – and against the UK and USA in particular.

Putin was very introspective – Marina Manoukian (a childhood friend) claims that he liked to read a great deal[272], shunning publicity and went on to study at Leningrad University in 1970. On finishing his law degree in 1975, he joined the FSB (the successor to the KGB), and was trained at the 401st KGB School in Okhta, Leningrad, and his first job was in counter-intelligence in the USSR, before being transferred to the First Chief Directorate, where he monitored foreigners (including foreign diplomats) in the Leningrad region. He had obviously been identified as a 'high flyer', as he was sent to the Yuri Andropov Red Banner Institute in Moscow for further training in September 1984; and from 1985–1990, he served in Dresden, then in East Germany, where he was in charge of liaison with the East German 'Stasi' (secret police), ostensibly as a Russian-German translator.[273] In May 1990, the Mayor of Leningrad, Anatoly Sobchak, appointed Putin as an advisor on international affairs and on 28 June 1991 he became the head of the committee for external relations in the mayor's office – both appointments were presumably made on the strength of his experiences in the KGB and especially when he was in East Germany.

Putin (by now a lieutenant colonel), resigned from the FSB on 20 August 1991, to go into politics in Leningrad. Initially he worked for the liberal politician Anatoly Sobchak, and when Sobchak was elected mayor of Leningrad in 1991, Putin was appointed as his head of external relations and deputy mayor of the city in 1994. In June 1996 he moved to Moscow to take up the appointment of deputy chief of the presidential property management department – a role that was more important than might have been presumed as it brought into contact with a number of key people – many of whom were trying to influence the new president, Boris Yeltsin. Putin began working for Yeltsin a year later in 1997, and as deputy to Yeltsin from 26 March 1997–24 May 1998; from 25 July 1998–29 March 1999 he was also director of the FSB. His work as Yeltsin's deputy and his directorship of the FSB will have put him in good stead to take over as acting president following the unexpected resignation of Yeltsin on 31 December 1999.

Putin appeared to adopt a more 'accommodating' approach to the West than his predecessors, and his positions of responsibility seemed to confirm his growing importance. He published an open letter on the Kremlin website in which he laid out his plans for the future, and arguably sought to lull the West into a false sense of security by allaying fears they might have had of Russia under his leadership. Had they looked more closely, however, there were indications of Putin's dictatorial hardline approach already emerging: in his first televised address as acting president taking over from Yeltsin, he said: 'There will be no power vacuum…any attempt to exceed the limits of the law and the Russian constitution will be decisively crushed.'[274] The warning signs were there already, especially when viewed in conjunction with his earlier pronouncements about Russian 'humiliation.' Whilst he did not go as far as Khrushchev and threaten to 'bury' his opponents, the underlying menace was clearly visible.

Putin is no fool, and he must have realised that the great weakness of Russia lay in the country's economy, but to make Russia an economic powerhouse would require foreign investment from the West. In view of the past history of Communism, he must also have understood that it would be difficult to court the West unless he managed to convince Western financiers and business leaders that they had nothing to fear from a regime led by him. There were various strategies that he could have employed in this respect, and his previous role as a senior KGB officer must have given him unfettered access to ideas. It is likely, but not proven, that he decided to follow the long-term strategy of 'brainwashing' to deal with the West, but at the same time he needed foreign investment immediately, and the only way to achieve this was to convince Western business leaders that they were dealing with a reformed, non-Communist leader. He denounced Communism saying: 'Communism and the power of Soviets did not make Russia a prosperous country with a dynamically developing society and free people. Communism vividly demonstrated its inability to foster sound self-development, dooming our country to lagging steadily behind economically advanced countries. It was a blind alley, far away from the mainstream of civilisation.' His message was designed to reassure the West that he had learned lessons from the Soviet Union's focus on heavy industry and armaments, and to hint that the new Russia would provide an attractive market for Western goods:

> We had to pay for the Soviet economy's excessive focus on the development of the raw materials and defence industries, which negatively affected the development of consumer production and services. We are paying for the Soviet neglect of such key sectors as information science, electronics and communications. We are paying for the absence of competition between producers and industries, which hindered scientific and technological progress and prevented the Russian economy from being competitive in the world markets. This is the cost of the brakes and the bans put on Russian initiatives and enterprises and their personnel. Today we are reaping the bitter fruit, both material and mental, of the past decades...[275]

Putin outlined seven objectives that he intended to follow, designed to rescue the failing Russian economy:

1. To encourage economic growth – in particular through investment, and the attraction of foreign capital.
2. To pursue an energetic industrial policy – with a focus on advanced technology, exports (especially of fuel and energy), and the non-raw materials sector.
3. To carry out a rational structural policy – in particular to enhance financial-industrial groups, corporations, and small and medium businesses.
4. To create an effective financial system.
5. To combat the shadow economy.
6. To consistently integrate the Russian economy into world economic structures.
7. To pursue a modern farming policy.[276]

There must have been many Western leaders who were relieved to hear such talk. Putin's speeches and writing must have led many to believe that the old Cold War which died with President Gorbachev had now been well and truly buried. In his resignation speech of 31 December 1999, Yeltsin had promised the people that his successor would hold new elections on 26 March 2000. Putin honoured Yeltsin's promise, but the elections witnessed the first attempts that Putin made to give himself an undemocratic electoral advantage: as acting prime minister he had pushed through a new law in December 1999 that decreased the time between the resignation of a president and the election of a new president. This new law, entitled 'On the election of the president of the Russian Federation' allowed candidates to gather a minimum of 500,000 signatures in support of their candidacy for president, rather than the one million previously required, and within a shorter time period.[277] By now, Putin could rely on his well-oiled political machinery which made things easier for him than for an opponent. He also had another advantage as he would be in the public eye far more frequently in his capacity as acting president, and not just as a candidate. This gave him a considerable advantage over his opponents.

Few were surprised, therefore, when Putin – running as an Independent – won and was declared president in his own right on 26 March 2000, with 52.94 per cent of the vote. The conduct of the election was questioned

Vladimir Lenin (Vladimir Ilyich Ulyanov), 9th November 1917–21st January 1924.
Despite being thought of as the 'intellectual' behind the Revolution, Lenin was responsible for thousands of deaths as he founded the 'Cheka' the brutal Bolshevik secret police who terrorised the country, killing and imprisoning millions, and causing death by famine – especially in Ukraine. Photo: 1st April, 1920. (Credit: Unknown author, presumed official source. Public domain via Wikimedia Commons.)

Josef Stalin (Iosef Vissarionovich Dzugashvilli), 21st January 1924-5th March, 1953.
Official portrait of Stalin found in most schools, factories, and places of work with the objective of developing a personality cult. Stalin was the longest-serving leader, and probably the most brutal dictator of the 20th century. Stalin added vast swathes of East European territory to the Soviet Union following the defeat of Nazi Germany. (Credit: *Official frontal portrait of Stalin* (19 November 1944). Public domain, via Wikimedia Commons.)

Georgy Malenkov, 5th March 1953–7th September 1953.
A little-known leader, who was overshadowed by his predecessor (Stalin) and his successor (Khrushchev). Malenkov's period in office was unremarkable and short. (Credit: Dutch National Archives (ANEFO), Bestanddeelnummer 916-3070. CC BY-SA 3.0 NL, via Wikimedia Commons)

Nikita Khrushchev, 7th September 1953–14th October 1964.
One of the best-known Soviet leaders, principally for three reasons: he nearly brought the world to nuclear war over the Cuban Missile Crisis, he denounced Stalin as a method of 'excusing' Soviet crimes in the 1940s–1950s, and he threatened to 'bury' the West. (Credit: John Fitzgerald Kennedy Library. Public domain, via Wikimedia Commons)

Leonid Brezhnev, 14th October 1964–10th November 1982.
A hardliner, who became worried that increasing liberalisation would lead to the break-up of the Soviet Union. Under his leadership, Soviet intervention abroad increased – for example, he authorised the suppression of the 'Czech' attempt at liberalisation in 1968 and sent the tanks in to overthrow the Dubček government, and ordered the invasion of Afghanistan in 1979. (Credit: Anefo (original file), colorized by Jack Jackie Pomi (presented here in black and white). CC0, via Wikimedia Commons.)

Yuri Andropov, 10th November 1982–9th February, 1984.
Andropov was an ex-KGB man, and his Presidency was marked by his ill-health – he died suddenly whilst still President. Another unremarkable leader, who had a short time in office. (Credit: RIA Novosti archive, image #101740 (Eduard Pesov). CC BY-SA 3.0, via Wikimedia Commons)

Konstantin Chernenko, 9th February 1984-10th March, 1985.
Almost unknown outside the Soviet Union: short-lived and to be overshadowed by Gorbachev. (Credit: Mos.ru. CC BY 4.0, via Wikimedia Commons.)

Mikhail Gorbachev, 10th March 1985–25th December, 1991.
Gorbachev was the first President to introduce democracy into the USSR, and it was on his watch that the official break-up of the Soviet Union took place. His Presidency was characterised by *glasnost* (openness or transparency of government and state institutions) and *perestroika* (economic and political reform). Since he left office, his political enemies have blamed him for the economic turmoil that followed the break-up, and although remembered positively in the West, in Russia he has been blamed by Putin for Russia's socio-economic problems. Putin publicly snubbed Gorbachev when he claimed that he was 'too busy' to attend the latter's funeral in 2022. (Credit: RIA Novosti archive (image 850809). Russian International News Agency. Via Wikimedia Commons)

Boris Yeltsin, 10th July 1991–31st December 1999.
Gorbachev started the process of reform, but it was Yeltsin who really managed the change of the country's command economy to a capitalist market-led economy. To a certain extent, it was the very success of his economic reforms that led to his downfall – he allowed the market exchange rate for the Ruble, instigated widespread privatisation of industry, and lifted price controls. The result was economic chaos, as the system was not used to competing in this way. There was growing unrest, and in 1993, he ordered the dissolution of the Russian Parliament, and was nearly toppled in a military 'coup' – but loyal elements of the Army came to his rescue. (CC BY 4.0 (Creative Commons Attribution 4.0 International))

Vladimir Putin, acting President 31st December 1999–26th March 2000. President, 26th March 2000–4th March 2004, and again President, 4th March 2004–2008.
As Deputy to Yeltsin, Vladimir Putin, took over temporarily when Yeltsin resigned, on 31st December 1999. He was then elected in his own right on 26th March 2000. From the outset, he showed that he was a cunning manipulator of both people and systems, and increasingly established himself as an autocratic leader, not accepting challenges to his authority. He had to step down on 2nd March 2008, at the end of his second term, as the Constitution forbad a President from serving more than two consecutive terms. However, he still had his hand on the levers of power, and made sure that his successor (and protegé) Dimitry Medvedev would take over for one term, allowing Putin to run again at a later date.

On 7 May 2012, Putin was re-elected as President for his third term (technically his first term) with 63.6% of the vote, and again on 18th March 2018 with 77% of the vote: such a high percentage, when combined with the allegations of electoral impropriety, suggest widespread fraud. One of his first actions on assuming the Presidency in 2018 was to try to remove the Constitutional clause preventing a President from serving more than two consecutive terms. He achieved this in 2020, which meant that he could run for President twice more in succession – he could be President up until 2036. (Credit: Kremlin.ru. CC BY 4.0, via Wikimedia Commons)

Dimitry Medvedev, 2nd March 2008–6th May, 2012.
On 2nd March 2008, Dimitry Medvedev, was elected President. However, Putin (who had been 'elected' Prime Minister) continued to carry out his political agenda, using Medvedev as his 'front man'. The value of Medvedev for Putin was that it enabled Putin to claim – legitimately – that he had never been President for more than two consecutive terms. (Credit: "Dmitry Medvedev in Switzerland, September 21, 2009." CC BY-SA 3.0, via Wikimedia Commons)

Soviet Interference with Neighbours

Hungary 1956.
A T. 34/85 during the Invasion of Hungary, 1956. By 1956, the T.34 was outclassed as a Main Battle Tank (MBT), but was still useful in suppressing riots and intimidating civilians. (Credit: Jack Metzger, ETH-Bibliothek Zürich, Bildarchiv (Com_M05-0448-0002). CC BY-SA 4.0, via Wikimedia Commons)

Czechoslovakia, 1968.
Protestors burn a Russian tank sent to occupy Prague, 1968. It is difficult to tell, but it is most likely to be the victim of a 'molotov cocktail' thrown onto the engine grille where it has ignited crew belongings that are stored there. In addition, Russian tanks habitually carried a spare fuel tank on the back – in this case in the rear centre – and if this were to catch fire and reach the ammunition stored internally, the resulting explosion could totally destroy the vehicle. (Credit: The Central Intelligence Agency. Public domain, via Wikimedia Commons)

Russian Bombardment of Kyiv Radio Tower, 1 March 2022.
The destruction of civilian infrastructure is generally regarded as an act of terrorism. (Credit: Mvs.gov.ua. CC BY 4.0, via Wikimedia Commons)

"Russian Warship…Kindly go home…" (2022).
This invitation to the Russian warship to go and **** itself was issued by Roman Hrybov, on 24 February 2022. Hybov was one of thirteen Border Guards from the Izmail Border Detachment, guarding the small 'Snake Island'. His adversary was the Russian missile cruiser *Moskva*, which was sunk a year later. Hrybov's gesture of defiance was commemorated in a postage stamp. (Credit: Boris Groh. Public domain, via Wikimedia Commons.

Russian Tank near Starobesheve in East Ukraine.
Total destruction of this T-72BA; judging from the angle of the turret, it has suffered an internal explosion – probably from the ignition of stored ammunition. The dislocation of the turret appears to have blocked the driver's escape hatch, and most of the reactive explosive armour appears to be missing. (Credit: День ТВ (DenTVinform), Donetsk, Issue 13 (timestamp 13:11/13:52). CC BY 3.0, via Wikimedia Commons)

Destroyed Russian tank – one of 10,868 lost between 24th February 2022 and 27th May 2025. (Photo: Mykhailo Volkov. Licensed under the Pexels License. Uploaded 31 May 2022)

widely, especially in the Russian press, with the English-language *Moscow Times* suggesting that Putin only won through widespread voting fraud.[278] The paper was quoted as saying that: 'the worst alleged fraud took place in the republic of Dagestan'. Maura Reynolds, writing in the *Los Angeles Times*, reported that the *Moscow Times* had 'obtained copies of the vote tallies from 16 per cent of the republic's precincts and compared them to the official results reported from those precincts. The official results showed 88,000 more pro-Putin votes than the precincts' own tallies. The implications were significant: 'Given how close the vote was – Putin won with just 52.94 per cent or a slim margin of 2.2 million votes – fraud and abuse of power appear to have been decisive.'[279] For his presidential inauguration, Putin chose the Grand Kremlin Palace – a grandiose setting that had served as the official residence of the Russian Czar for much of the nineteenth century; this was entirely consistent with his view of his own importance, and it also hinted at his preoccupation with the Russian Empire.

There are a number of problems in assuming that Russia no longer presents a threat: to begin with, what Putin *says* in public and what he actually *does* are not necessarily the same, which makes him unpredictable at best, and manipulative at worst. Secondly, and perhaps more importantly, he is driven by a belief that Russia will be a great nation again, and to achieve this objective he has the power and motivation – which makes him dangerous. Finally, whilst the threat he represents may no longer be based on Communist globalism, it is every bit as dangerous as it is still focused on the establishment of a Russian empire throughout Europe with absolute control emanating from Moscow. Putin was elected for a second term on 4 March 2004: this saw him in power until 2008, when the constitution meant that he could no longer run for the presidency.

Dimitry Medvedev (2008–2012)

Putin got around the 'problem' of the constitution by hatching a plan with the then Prime Minister, Dimitry Medvedev, to alternate the presidency; Medvedev won the election on 7 May 2008, holding the position until 2012 when Putin secured the presidency once more through rigged elections. Even whilst Medvedev was president, there was widespread speculation that Putin was still in charge. Medvedev returned to being prime minister, although with effectively little or no power. Putin used Medvedev as a puppet, to allow him to avoid falling foul of the constitution.

On 7 May 2012 Putin was re-elected as president for his third term – although technically it was only his first term, as the presidency of Medvedev had ensured that there was no consecutive link between his second and third term in office – with 63.6 per cent of the vote, and again on 18 March 2018 with 77 per cent of the vote: such a high percentage, when combined with the allegations of electoral impropriety, suggest widespread fraud. One of his first actions was to set in motion a revision of the constitution, and remove the clause preventing a president from serving more than two consecutive terms – this means that he could be president up until 2036, confirming his dictatorial powers.

Putin also has another, more personal objective – the restoration of the old Russian Empire with himself as Czar. In short, his objectives remain the same as those of his Communist and Imperialist predecessors, only more dangerous as appeals to patriotism generally have a greater resonance to the domestic population than appeals based on a political philosophy. Brainwashing through constant propaganda and misinformation, coupled with overt and covert violence have been used to 'educate' the population since the formation of the Soviet Union: despite this, only a certain proportion of those under the control of Moscow genuinely believed in the political dogma of Communism. However, whilst most Russians may not believe in Communism, most do believe in the concept of 'Mother Russia' – especially the older generation. As Stalin found out during World War II, appeals to defend the nation are far stronger when they are based on patriotism; it is interesting to remember that for the Russians, there was no such thing as 'World War II', as the conflict is remembered as 'The Great Patriotic War', a label specifically designed to bring the nation together. The irony is that at the same time that Stalin was murdering the higher echelons of the Soviet officer corps, and sending millions of political prisoners to die in the Gulag concentration camps, there were still millions for whom the defence of the motherland was a real concept, and one worth dying for.

Putin has continued 'adventures' into neighbouring states almost seamlessly, either in his role as president, or initially as prime minister. These, until the latest invasion of Ukraine in 2022, appear to have been adding to his domestic popularity: this is a well-known ploy, used by dictators in trouble as it diverts attention away from domestic issues – such as inflation, unemployment, political instability – and instead gets the domestic audience focused on issues that tend to be based on things that unite them.

The Second Chechen War (1999–2000)

The First Chechen War had ended in 1996 with the signing of a peace treaty; despite this, armed resistance and instability carried on for just under another two years, with Chechen guerrillas harassing the Russian occupation forces, and attacking government installations and troop depots. This was not, however, the end of the war as in effect it was a ceasefire, rather than peace, and it allowed the Russian forces time to regroup, and reassess their strategy against the Chechens. There was increased Chechen guerrilla activity against Russians and Russian-owned property – including cross-border activity within Russia itself. This was both anathema and opportunity to Putin, who hated the attempts by the Chechens to break away, yet at the same time realised that a hard-hitting military campaign would enhance his popularity with the Russian people – we can assume that, at this time, he already had his sights on the presidency. Despite the cease-fire agreed at the end of the First Chechen War, Putin had no intention of letting the country break free of control by Moscow, and on 7 August 1999, using the excuse that Chechnya was a 'terrorist' state, Putin launched a second invasion of Chechnya. This led to more prolonged fighting, until 30 April of the following year. This second invasion boosted his ratings with the Russian voters, as it was portrayed by Russian media as an 'anti-terrorist' operation. There was prolonged fighting, until 30 April of the following year. A report written by Peter Bouckaert for the Human Rights Watch bears quoting in detail, as any analysts who had wished to predict the way in which the Russians would wage war in Ukraine, need only have looked at their record of atrocities in Chechnya:

> Russian forces have committed grave abuses, including war crimes, in their campaign in Chechnya...have indiscriminately and disproportionately bombed and shelled civilian objects, causing heavy civilian casualties... have ignored

> their Geneva Convention obligations to focus their attacks on combatants, and appear to take few safeguards to protect civilians: it is this carpet-bombing campaign which has been responsible for the vast majority of civilian deaths in the conflict in Chechnya. The Russian forces have used powerful surface-to-surface rockets on numerous occasions, causing death tolls in their hundreds... Russian commanders have threatened to use even more powerful explosives, including fuel air explosives against civilian targets.... Russian forces have often refused to create safe corridors to allow civilians to leave areas of active fighting, trapping civilians behind the front lines for months.[280]

But for the date, he could equally have been describing the Russian conscripts and the conditions faced by civilians in the occupied areas of Ukraine during the second Russian invasion in 2022, and in particular of the harrowing accounts of civilians sheltering in and around the Azovstal steel Plant, in Mariupol. The report continued, pointing out that the bombing and shelling was only the prelude to the greater horror that was to come later, when the Russian ground forces entered the cities: 'In December, Russian troops killed seventeen civilians in the village of Alkhan-Yurt while going on a looting spree, burning many of the remaining homes and raping several women. We have documented at least fifty murders, mostly of older men and women, by Russian soldiers in the Staropromyslovski district of Grozny since Russian forces took control of that district: innocent civilians shot to death in their homes and in their yards.'

There was widespread condemnation of Russian actions, including from US President Bill Clinton who said that Russia would pay a 'heavy price' for its intervention but did not elaborate further; the UK Foreign Secretary Robin Cook also condemned the invasion, without adding specifics. In the UK House of Commons, the Russian assault on Chechnya was debated seemingly in a vacuum: honourable members asked polite questions and were given equally polite and evasive answers. For example, on 6 December 1999, a Mr Harry Cohen MP asked whether Secretary of State for Foreign and Commonwealth Affairs, Robin Cook, had 'raised matters relating to the Russian military activity in Chechnya and compliance with the Geneva Conventions of 1949 and additional protocols of 1977 at the OSCE Istanbul summit'. The reply he received was from Robin Cook's deputy, Keith Vaz, who confirmed that the concerns of the UK Government with regard to Chechnya had been raised with 'Foreign Minister Ivanov, including at the Istanbul summit. We and our EU partners have reminded all parties to the conflict of the necessity to observe international humanitarian law'.[281] This answer was followed by another question, this time from a Mr Paul Marsden MP who sought clarity to the somewhat evasive answer given: he wanted to know 'what recent representations he has made to the Russian authorities over the invasion of Chechnya; and if he will make a statement'. He also received a polite 'brush-off' with little detail, simply the reply that the foreign secretary 'had regular discussions with Russian Foreign Minister Ivanov. Most recently in a telephone conversation on 3 December, urging that Russia should seek a negotiated political settlement to the conflict.'

The dangers of such ineffectual and seemingly passive communication with the Russians became apparent when, on 7 December, the citizens of Grozny were told to 'flee the city or die'. This lack of forceful opposition to the Russians was bemoaned by the Liberal Democrat Foreign Affairs spokesman, Menzies Campbell, who suggested that the West had to accept the blame for what was happening in Chechnya, as it had not reacted with sufficient force when the first invasion had taken place; he asked rhetorically whether the West had 'been supine in the face of the medieval barbarism directed against the people of Chechnya?'[282] All such inaction did was to encourage Putin in his power grab in Ukraine some years later.

It would appear that the Russian army had learned nothing from the First Chechen War, as military discipline was lax in the extreme. According to Babachenko there appeared to be more violence metered out within the Russian army, than there was to its opponents, with drunken NCOs beating recruits until 'they no longer resemble human beings' leading to very high rates of desertion, with only four soldiers left in his company[283] – the rest having 'scarpered'.[284] Putin sought to justify the actions of the Russian military when he described Chechnya as 'the place where Russia's fate is being decided'.[285] Prophetically he added: 'Unfortunately not everyone in Western nations understands this. But we will not tolerate any humiliation to the national pride of Russia or any threat to the territorial integrity of the country.' This last comment is instructive, as it is indicative of the way in which he thinks, and how, in defence of what he considers to be the Russian homeland (despite

Chechnya having proclaimed independence from Moscow), he will go to any lengths. What he apparently does not understand is that if you invade another country, and bomb, kill, rape and mutilate its citizens, they are most unlikely to ever want you as their president and to be forcibly incorporated into your country. Naturally, he could not (or would not) understand that the Chechens felt equally strongly about their territorial integrity.

Second Invasion of Georgia (2008)

As with Chechnya, the politico-military situation in Georgia had dragged on for a number of years, beginning in 1991 when the ex-Soviet republic also claimed its independence. As with other ex-Soviet republics, Vladimir Putin tried to reincorporate Georgia back into the Russian Federation, and used a tried and tested method of doing this: he claimed that there were two separatist regions of Georgia – South Ossetia and Abkhazia – that contained a high percentage of ethnic Russians who were suffering at the hands of Georgian nationalists. He claimed that these regions had been trying to rejoin Russia since the declaration of independence and for years the Russians had given covert military support, and applied economic and diplomatic pressure, to try to realise their independence, and rejoin Russia.

Low-level fighting between the separatists and the Georgian government went on for some years: in 1992–1993 Abkhazi separatists had entered into a full-scale war with Georgia, but neither side could achieve victory. Although the least-known of the three nations involved, Abkhazia was probably the most important due to its strategic location, with a coastline on the Black Sea of some 200 kilometres, which if re-allied to Russia would have given the Russian navy another warm water port. Thus, Russia had much to lose if the Abkhazi separatists eventually lost their bid for independence, and so it continued to give them both moral and matériel support. Eventually, a ceasefire was agreed, monitored by a peacekeeping force of Georgian, Russian, and Ossetian troops. Talks continued for some time, but by 2008 there still had been no agreement. In April 2008, Georgia appealed to be admitted into NATO to protect itself from Russia, citing unwarranted Russian interference in the region's affairs. The excuse for Russian intervention was provided on 1 August of that same year, when Russian-backed and -armed South Ossetian rebel forces, began to shell Georgian villages. Georgian forces were sent to engage the rebels, and this was followed by a full-scale Russian assault, which led to the Russian occupation of the towns of Gori, Poti, Senaki, and Zugdidi. The war took a nasty turn when South Ossetians began a programme of ethnic cleansing of Georgians in their region. Russia inflamed the situation further when it recognised the independence of Abkhazia and South Ossetia on 26 August, and Georgia broke off diplomatic relations with Russia. By early October, Russia had withdrawn most of its forces, but the legacy of the invasion by Russian forces remained.

Summary

The chapter clearly demonstrates the ability and willingness of the Soviet Union to interfere (covertly or overtly) in the internal politics of its neighbours, and to forcibly annex neighbouring states into the USSR. This has been going on since the days of Lenin, and was especially prevalent during the Stalin regime, and those of various premiers that followed him. Since the break-up of the Soviet Union, however, there would appear to have been little change in foreign policy: President Yeltsin interfered in the Tajikistan Civil War and launched an invasion of Chechnya in 1994. His successor, Putin has continued the 'adventures' into neighbouring states almost seamlessly, either in his role as president, or initially as prime minister.

In view of the focus of this book, it is also crucial to note that once a country had been incorporated into the Soviet Union, there was a strong reluctance to ever let it leave – as witnessed by the wars fought to prevent such nations achieving their independence and leaving – even though the Soviet Union no longer existed. The policy of repression of freedom and liberty underpinned the whole Sovietisation of post-World War II Eastern Europe; the establishment of Soviet-dominated national 'puppet' governments which obeyed the diktat of Moscow was the principal way in which control was established and maintained. The 'Iron Curtain' and the Berlin Wall showed that in their desire to control Eastern Europe and Germany, the Soviets were prepared to divide an entire continent and enslave around half of its population. If that was insufficient to subdue any thoughts of civil disobedience then Moscow was ruthless, sending in the military to crush opposition (as in Berlin in 1953, Hungary in 1956, and

Czechoslovakia in 1968), and if necessary to kill key 'agitators'. Following hard on the heels of the tanks were the various secret police organisations: such as the East German Stasi, or the Polish security office (*UB-Urząd Bezpieczeństwa*, (later security service *SB-Służba Bezpieczeństwa)* troops. 'Counter-revolutionaries' were detained and in many cases disappeared – presumed executed – or languished in prisons for years. Once again, it is obvious that, with the long-term perspective of Communism, any form of dissent would eventually be punished, regardless of how long it took; the more important the state (in economic, political, and strategic terms), the greater the Soviet efforts would be to prevent its independence – the lesson of history was that Ukraine would never be allowed to leave Moscow's orbit, the country was too important in both geostrategic and economic terms to be allowed to join the West, regardless of the desire of its citizens. As the US rock band The Eagles said in their song 'Hotel California', people can check out anytime they wish, but they can never really leave.

Chapter 4

Ukraine: The Sunflower State

'We will not give up and we will not lose.

'We will fight until the end, at sea, in the air. We will continue fighting for our land, whatever the cost. We will fight in the forests, in the fields, on the shores, in the streets…we will fight on the banks of different rivers and we're looking for your help, for the help of the civilised countries.

'We're thankful for this help and I'm very grateful to you Boris, please increase the pressure of sanctions against this country – Russia – please recognise this country as a terrorist state and please make sure our Ukrainian skies are safe. Glory to Ukraine and glory to the United Kingdom.'

Ukrainian President Volodymyr Zelensky, in a video link speech on 8 March 2022, thanking Prime Minister Boris Johnson and the UK Parliament for its support in the initial stages of the Russian attack.

The chapter begins with a brief history of modern Ukraine, after which there is an analysis of Ukrainian guerrilla resistance to Axis occupation from 1941–1944; whilst this is familiar to many, what is perhaps not quite as well-known is that some Ukrainian military units fought *with* the Axis forces *against* Communism from 1942, and in many instances, continued a guerrilla resistance to occupation by the Red Army at the end of the war. The length of time this post-war resistance lasted is open to dispute – Soviet sources try to play down the extent and longevity of anti-Communist movements, as they are indicative of a high level of dissatisfaction with Communism itself and the desire to be free of control by Moscow: a consensus suggests that most anti-Communist partisan forces were only eliminated by the mid-late 1950s, with some lasting until the 1960s. In Ukraine, armed opposition continued until 1950, in Czechoslovakia until 1953, in the Baltic republics until 1956, whilst in Romania the last resistance fighters were killed in 1962, and in Poland resistance only ceased with an amnesty introduced on 27 April 1962; even then, there were reported acts of armed resistance against the Polish Communist government, and Russian NKVD troops – the Warsaw Institute claims the last Polish partisan was killed in combat as late as 1963.[286]

The second part of the chapter analyses the importance of Ukraine to the Russians: as suggested in the preface, it is the contention of the author that the strategic objective behind Putin's invasion is the retention of Crimea, which was seized in 2014, and to do this, he needs a landbridge through eastern Ukraine. Finally, we return to the point at which the preface began the book – Putin's two invasions of Ukraine.

The Growth of Ukraine

A Short History

When examining the early history of Ukraine, it is important to bear in mind that the area that is now referred to as Eastern Europe has always been subject to shifting allegiances, changing political control, and empire-building, underpinned by the relative power of various ethnic groupings. Unlike an island country such as the United Kingdom whose borders are easy to define as they are delineated by the sea, the borders of Ukraine have been the subject of considerable dispute over the years. The area of Europe that encompasses modern-day Ukraine has been subject to constant changes in political allegiance as at various times the region (or parts of it) were controlled by Poland, Lithuania, Bulgaria, the Ottoman Turks, or Russia.

The first real state of Ukraine can probably be traced back to a loose federation of states collectively referred to Kyivan Rus, with its capital at the city of Kyiv; the story becomes more relevant from the fifteenth century when most of what we know today as Ukraine fell under the control of the Polish crown, and the southern part of the country was even controlled for a time by the Ottoman Empire. It is at this point that the tragedy of Ukraine really began when the country was annexed by three of the four major regional powers of that time: the Crimean Khanate, the Grand Duchy of Lithuania and the Kingdom of Poland. Following years of intrigue and warfare, Lithuania and Poland merged to form the Polish–Lithuanian Commonwealth, and by 1654 the 'Hetmanate' (domain) of Ukraine was allied with the Czardom of Moscow: the Pereiaslav Agreement of 1654 meant that Ukraine (led by Bohdan Khmelnytsky) became a 'protectorate' of Russia, in return the Cossacks swore allegiance to the Russian Czar. As part of the agreement, the Hetmanate was granted the status of an autonomous state within the Russian Empire; however, bearing in mind the underlying objective of Imperial Russia at the time, it is no surprise that the 'independence' of an autonomous state within Russia was not quite as 'independent' as might have been hoped. Whatever the initial expectation, Russia increasingly assumed dominance.

The war fought between the Russians and the Polish-Lithuanian Commonwealth was concluded by the Truce of Andrusovo (1667), after which Ukraine was divided between the two sides, with the largest part being awarded to Russia. Ukraine experienced many years of confusion over its national borders, and was allied at one time with the Swedes against the Russians; the various regions and groupings continued to make hostile moves towards each other, although what did unite them was their fear of the Swedes, whose empire was particularly strong, and included territories that both they and the Russians wanted – such as Finland and the Baltic states, modern-day Estonia, Latvia, and Lithuania. The Battle of Poltava (1709) saw a Russian force defeat the Swedish army, which subsequently withdrew back across the Baltic to Sweden. There was little opposition to Russian territorial ambitions and following the three partitions of Poland (1772-1795) and the Russian conquest of the Crimea, what we know today as Ukraine was subsumed within the two major powers of the day: the Habsburg Empire took over much of western Ukraine, whilst the east of the country fell into the orbit of the rapidly expanding Russian Empire. It took well over 100 years for any sense of Ukrainian nationalism to re-emerge, and then only gradually and in certain parts of the country.

Ukrainian People's Republic (March 1917–November 1921)

The establishment of a modern independent Ukraine began in March 1917, with the declaration of the Ukrainian People's Republic in Kyiv; this was administered by a Central Rada (council) led by the writer Vladimir Vinnichenko and the journalist Simon Petlyura. No sooner had this been done than the Bolsheviks sent an invasion force to put down this rebellion in January 1918 and set up their own Ukrainian Bolshevik government in an attempt to stifle any move towards independence. This Ukraine Soviet did not last long, as the Ukrainian People's Republic was officially recognised in the Treaty of Brest-Litovsk, after which, the Soviet troops left and were replaced by German troops; they appointed Pavel Skoropadsky as *hetman* (chief), but he was ousted by Ukrainian nationalist forces in December 1918 and fled to Berlin. The new Ukrainian People's Republic was not recognised by Moscow which wished to bring Ukraine once more under its control, and the period 1917–1921 was beset by violence and instability: at various times, forces loyal to the new Ukrainian government found themselves opposed by the old Russian Empire (the Whites), by the Reds (the Bolsheviks), and (until November 1918) by elements of the German and Austro-Hungarian forces. The war was fought between a number of groups including the Ukrainian nationalists, forces from the armies of Germany and Austria-Hungary, Poland and White Russian forces – each having a separate number of goals. The Bolshevik forces vastly outnumbered those of Ukraine, and the first months of 1918 saw significant Bolshevik advances – the only halt was forced on the Russians by the Ukrainian victory at the Battle of Kruty (30 January), but even this could not slow the Red forces which took Kyiv on 9 February, forcing the Ukrainian government to flee to Zhytomyr. The Bolshevik forces then continued on to occupy Bessarabia. The odds were stacked very much against Ukrainian independence as the country faced a multitude of problems: geographically, it was hemmed in on all sides by its powerful neighbours (some such as Poland, had designs on parts of Ukrainian territory) and the struggle for independence was a confused melee of forces and powerful leaders, including continued hostility by the German and Austro-Hungarian forces, but lacking an overall focus; local Bolshevik governments sprang up in Odesa, and Donetsk, and anarchists took control of the Makhnovshchina region, before allying themselves with the Bolsheviks.

The Nationalist forces, led by General Petlyura, took control once more, and managed to hold onto power until September of the following year, when they were absorbed into the Armed Forces of Southern Russia, and then defeated by the Red Army. It is claimed that this lack of political stability mitigated against military stability, and at one stage there were three Ukrainian Armies: fighting either the Bolsheviks, the White Russian forces, or even each other.[287] Needless to say that such a lack of direction and purpose ensured that they were ultimately defeated.

Once all German forces had left, the Bolsheviks reinvaded Ukraine; by now the country was effectively split into two regions: the Western Ukrainian People's Republic (WUNR) and the Ukrainian People's Republic (UNR), and these two united on 22 January 1919, with an Act of Union signed at Kyiv. The campaign lasted just over three years, from February 1918 to November 1921, until peace was declared with the signing of the Treaty of Riga; Ukraine was forcibly incorporated into the USSR and renamed the Ukrainian Soviet Socialist Republic.

Ukraine Under Communism

Following the Red Army victory, Lenin and Stalin were careful to ensure that Ukraine could never again attempt to leave Soviet control: the country was flooded with Cheka to seek out and destroy (or imprison) actual and potential leaders of Ukrainian independence movements – Ukraine became the major target of Russian activities, and the supremacy of the Soviet was cemented through various measures – in particular through the unleashing of the Cheka. Map C on page 123 shows the newly designated Soviet Ukraine incorporated into the Soviet Union in 1922.

As with the rest of the USSR, the population suffered greatly from food shortages as a consequence of agricultural collectivisation, land and property seizures, and the brutal activities of the Cheka. These murderous thugs were especially active in Ukraine, as Lenin (and later Stalin) wished to break the aspiration for independence that had been demonstrated between 1917 and 1922. The total number murdered by the Cheka is estimated by William

Chamberlain to be at least 50,000 people.[288] Even those who were to be executed could not escape humiliation before death:

> After the condemned were stripped of their clothing and other belongings, which were shared among the Cheka executioners, they were either machine-gunned in batches or dispatched individually with a revolver. Those killed in prison were usually shot in the back of the neck as they entered the execution cellar, which became littered with corpses and soaked with blood. Victims killed outside the town were moved by truck, bound and gagged, to their place of execution, where they sometimes were made to dig their own graves.[289]

Interestingly, the *Internet Encyclopaedia of Ukraine*, claims that Cheka forces not only terrorised the peasants, but that they also fought 'Ukrainian insurgents'[290], suggesting that although the country had been claimed by Moscow, there was still armed resistance to Soviet occupation. As the Civil War drew to a close, the Cheka were employed not just to search out 'saboteurs' but to hunt down 'counter-revolutionaries' – groups who were lukewarm in their support of the Bolsheviks. The Cheka increasingly assumed a proactive role, operating in intelligence-gathering and subversive activities outside the new Soviet borders, and their reputation was greatly enhanced through the discovery of plots (in many cases fabricated) against the government. Victor Suvorov suggests that during the Civil War, the Red Army fought not only the White forces, but undertook 'a series of punitive expeditions against those who did not want Communism'.[291] The commander appointed to crush internal dissent was General Mikhail Tukhachevski, described by Chris Bellamy as 'fascinating, brilliant and charismatic',[292] whilst this might have been true, Suvorov notes that once appointed commander of the 1st Army, Tukhachevski's darker side emerged: he declared that all who opposed the Communist regime were 'bandits', and as such deserved no mercy. He 'viciously exterminated not only them but also their relatives, their neighbours, and everyone who happened to come his way. The foundation of Tukhachevski's strategy was the burning of villages, whippings, and mass shootings.'[293]

The collectivisation of farms was especially significant in Ukraine, which was known as the 'breadbasket' of the USSR, and produced thousands of tons of grain each year. It is estimated that as a direct result of Communist

Map C: The Soviet Ukraine (1922).
Source: Reproduced with permission from Christian Ionita (Edmaps.com)

ideology, collectivisation led to the deaths of millions of people – mostly as a consequence of starvation.[294] It is difficult to give exact numbers as estimates vary wildly between four and twenty-five million people[295], whilst a more widely accepted figure is between seven and ten million[296]. Whatever the exact figure, it was certainly in the millions, and the disaster left a lasting collective memory of the brutality of both Communism and the Russians who imposed it – there is even a Ukrainian word for this genocide: *Holodomor*.[297] In 2017, the UK government tried to have the famine classified as 'genocide', and the process of holding the Russian government to account was debated in the House of Commons on 7 November 2017. Pauline Latham MP illustrated the extent of the man-made horror:

> Although the exact number of those who died during the holodomor is not known, it is estimated to be between 7 million and 10 million Ukrainian people. At the height of the famine, 17 people died each minute, 1,041 people died each hour and 25,000 people died each day. More than 3 million children

> born in 1932 and 1933 died of starvation. Many people died of starvation in their homes, with some trying to end the process by suicide, if they had the strength for it.[298]

However, Hiroaki Kuromiya, citing data that has been made public since the break-up of the Soviet Union, claims that evidence that the 1932–1933 famine was a deliberate assault on Ukraine was 'inconclusive'.[299] He noted that, for a combination of reasons, grain production had fallen from 76 million tons in 1930, to 61.1 million tons in 1932. At the same time, there was a rise in the percentage of harvests 'procured' by the state from 28.2 per cent of grain produced in 1930, to 32.8 per cent in 1931, and the percentage taken by the state was expected to have risen by anything up to 50 per cent by 1932, as Moscow continued to export grain as it was in need of foreign exchange.[300] Despite such doubts, the overwhelming body of evidence shows that the Ukrainian famine of 1932–1933 was caused deliberately by Stalin, who wished to ensure that Ukraine presented no danger to Soviet rule. Moscow was afraid that the Ukrainian peasantry were nationalists who wished for Ukrainian independence – what better way to prevent this happening than to engineer a famine that would kill thousands, and enfeeble many thousands more?

The persecution of the Kulaks (land owners) went on for over a decade, until 30 January 1930, when the Politburo voted for their liquidation,[301] and to achieve this 'Final Solution', they were classified into one of three groups: the first, who did not present too much of a threat were allowed to remain within their own province, but not within their own area – presumably this was designed to distance them from networks of friends and family. The second category was individuals who were to be sent far away, generally to parts of the country far from the major cities – such as Siberia or the far east or south – presumably as this group was considered more dangerous than those in the first category. Finally, there were those individuals sent to concentration camps.[302] On being asked his opinion on this, Stalin is said to have replied: 'The idea of a concentration camp is excellent.'[303]

Ukraine in World War II

Operation Barbarossa

The German attack on the Soviet Union on 22 June 1941, has gone down in history as one of the largest military operations ever: Hitler was convinced that he had to deal with Stalin before the Russian dictator launched an attack on Germany, and in the view of many authors he was correct in his assumptions, for as Victor Suvorov notes with regard to both Soviet and German troop deployments immediately prior to Barbarossa: 'The position of the divisions of the Red Army mirrored the position of the German army.' He concluded that, according to the evidence, the 'Red Army was also preparing for a sudden attack' and that there was 'no difference between the actions of Stalin and those of Hitler. Hitler just happened to strike first. If Stalin had managed to strike first, all the advantages of the deployment of German troops would have turned into disadvantages'.[304]

The Germans launched Barbarossa along three broad directions of attack, each comprising an Army Group, and aimed initially, at Leningrad, Moscow, and Kiev. Specifically, they were Army Group North, commanded by Field Marshall (FM) Wilhem Ritter von Leeb, and comprising ten divisions – seven infantry and three armoured, with Leningrad as their target. The thrust towards Moscow comprised Army Group Centre, (FM Fedor Von Bock), with fifty-one divisions – forty-two infantry and nine armoured, and finally, Army Group South (FM Gerd Von Runstedt) with fifty-two infantry divisions – of which fifteen were Romanian, two Hungarian, and two Italian, plus five armoured divisions. As Halder, German army chief of staff explained, the objectives were initially based on economic concerns; in his explanation to the Army staff and Hitler, Halder said that: 'The most important Russian armaments centre lies in the Ukraine, in Moscow and in Leningrad.'[305]

Resistance

In view of the persecution of minority groups and non-Communists within the USSR, and their brutal treatment at the hands of the successor to the Cheka – the NKVD – it is perhaps unsurprising that when Hitler launched his attack on the USSR there were many who welcomed the Germans with open arms. In many instances, German armoured units advancing through the western provinces of the Soviet Union (previously the independent states of Estonia, Latvia, and Lithuania) were met with gifts rather than bullets, as the population still held a particular loathing for the Moscow Communist regime and looked on the Germans as liberators and believed they would free them from Stalin's tyranny. Major Helmut Ritgen, of the German 6 Panzer Division confirms the adulation his units received in the first months of campaigning in the Baltic states in their drive towards Leningrad; he says that his forces: 'were often welcomed by a friendly population who regarded them as liberators from the Soviet regime, and who would exchange such things as butter and eggs for medical treatment.'[306] This welcome for the advancing Axis forces was by no means restricted to the Baltic states, for as James Lucas notes: 'In certain regions of the Soviet Union proper, notably in the Ukraine, Georgia and the Caucasus...volunteers came forward in large numbers to make common cause with the Germans against the tyranny of the Communist system.'[307] Eventually the Germans had raised volunteer anti-Communist units from all over the Soviet Union: Armenia, Belarus, Crimea, Estonia, Georgia, Latvia, Lithuania, Turkestan, and Ukraine.[308] Whilst there was, at least initially, such a positive appreciation of the Germans who were widely viewed as liberators from Communist control, there were many thousands who went one stage further and volunteered to fight with the Germans against the Russians. Initially, the majority of volunteers were recruited from those independent countries that had been occupied by the Soviets – the Baltic states, Ukraine, and the Caucasus (principally Georgia).[309] Nigel Thomas points out, that there were a variety of reasons for which people voluntarily co-operated with the Axis occupiers, with many of the non-Russian nationality groups seeking independent statehood after the war, whilst others were anti-Communist Russians who wanted to topple Stalin and Communism, and others were 'pragmatic opportunists'. By the end of the war, there were even a number of Waffen-SS divisions formed with volunteers from the various states within the USSR[310] – most, however, never reached divisional establishment:

14.Waffen-Grenadier-Division der SS (Galizische Nr.1) – Ukrainians and Poles

15.Waffen-Grenadier-Division der SS (Lettische Nr.1) – Latvians and Estonians

19.Waffen-Grenadier-Division der SS (Lettische Nr. 2) – Latvians
20.Waffen-Grenadier-Division der SS (Estnische Nr.1) – Estonians
29.Waffen-Grenadier-Division der SS (Russische Nr.1) – Russians
30.Waffen-Grenadier-Division der SS (Russische Nr.2) – Belarussians

In addition, there were other units – not forming part of the Waffen-SS – such as the 1 Kosaken Kavallerie (Cossack Cavalry) Division, which reached a strength of around 17,000 men, and the Russian National Liberation Army, officially designated 1. Russische Division, which had grown to some 13,000 men by 1943. Himmler had ordered the call-up of volunteers to form a Ukrainian division on 5 July 1943, and on 1 August, those who had volunteered were formed into the 14 Galizische SS Freiwilligen Division, from a mixture of ethnic Germans and Ukrainians. It is this historical association of some Ukrainians with the Nazis that has given Putin the excuse he needs to label all modern-day Ukrainians 'Nazis'. Whilst there might have been some who held Nazi sympathies, the overwhelming majority signed up with the Germans to fight Russian Communism and to free their land from oppression from Moscow; the motivations for recruitment are varied, and are detailed in the excellent book *The Galician Division 1943–45* by David McCormack.[311] An interesting fact is that of the six Waffen-SS divisions cited above, two (one third of the total) consisted entirely of ethnic Russian volunteers – as compared with only one that had Ukrainian volunteers. So, if Putin were to claim that Ukraine was 'Nazi' based on the country's historical associations with the Waffen-SS, it also could be argued that there were twice as many 'Nazis' in Russia than in Ukraine!

However, as a direct consequence of Hitler's inane racial policies, this warmth towards the German forces soon turned sour: in Ukraine, for example, rather than a large pro-German Ukrainian population, the activities of the *Einsatzgruppen* (extermination squads) ensured that the opportunity of raising a large anti-Communist army of Ukraine was lost. Units of the Waffen-SS Leibstandarte Division which had been greeted with flowers during its initial advance through Ukraine, were in the words of one Waffen-SS trooper, so disillusioned that they (the Ukrainians) were almost 'forced to become fanatical partisans'.[312] Initially, Ukrainian partisan units, fighting under the title of the Ukrainian Insurgent Army (UPA – Ukrainska Povostanska

Armiia), helped regular Russian forces to attack the German invader, in particular targeting the lines of supply and communication. Partisans of the UPA initially fought against the Communist partisan forces, under the illusion that their fight against the German invaders would stand them in good stead to be granted an independent Ukraine after the war.[313] They soon realised, however, that they would not be awarded a separate state by the Germans, and so began fighting them also.[314]

The leader of Ukraine's partisan forces loyal to Moscow was Timofei Strokach, who originally joined the Soviet OGPU forces in January 1924. He studied at the OGPU Border School No. 2 in Minsk, and joined the Communist Party in 1927, and between 1929-1932 he served as assistant commander (later commander) of the 56th Blagoveshchensk Border Detachment, stationed in the Far East of Russia. Various border control posts with the OGPU followed until in 1938 he was appointed commander of the 24 Mohyliv-Podilsky Border Detachment, and during that same year he also (temporarily) enlisted as a regimental commander in the 162nd Rifle Regiment, which at that time was stationed at Voroshylovhrad. At the time of Operation Barbarossa, Strokach was a deputy people's commissioner of interior for the Ukrainian Soviet Socialist Republic, and by 1942 he was in charge of all Ukrainian partisans co-ordinating their fight against the Germans, and working very closely with the Russians – in this case, General Nicolai Vatutin.[315] There were other partisan groups, but the most important was that led by Stepan Bandera – the OUN-B (Organisation of Ukrainian Nationalists-Bandera), and they also fought against the Germans.

Following the expulsion of German forces from Ukraine, the fight for Ukrainian independence continued, with an increase in guerrilla activity – now directed against Russian (as opposed to German) forces: probably as a consequence of his experience as a guerrilla organiser, Strokach was appointed to command the directorate that had been raised to combat Ukrainian 'bandits' – those forces that were not under the control of Moscow. By now the situation had become so confused and fluid that it was difficult to be sure of who was fighting whom. Put simply, Moscow-controlled partisan groups were fighting both the retreating German forces and partisan groups that were fighting for the independence of Ukraine. Despite being outgunned and outnumbered, anti-Communist Ukrainian partisans achieved one major success when they eliminated Soviet General Vatutin, who was ambushed on 28 February 1944 by partisans from the UPA as he was travelling to take up command of a unit to be involved in the forthcoming March offensive. John Erikson gives a graphic account of the ambush:

> A burst of fire suddenly ripped into Vatutin's car, setting it alight. Another burst sent a second truck with Vatutin's escort up in flames. From the snow-covered fields a force of a hundred guerrillas closed in on the burning vehicles, but machine-gun fire from the dozen men in the escort party drove them back. Vatutin categorically ordered a staff officer to withdraw, taking the operational orders and one machine-gunner with him for protection. Vatutin himself refused to leave. At sunset the general's party set about disengaging, when Vatutin was severely wounded...Vatutin never recovered from his wounds; on 15 April at the age of forty-two he died...[316]

Having been imprisoned briefly by the Germans, Bandera was released in September 1944, and tried to re-form his partisan group, but without much success. At the end of the war he fled into the US sector of Germany, where he continued to organise anti-Soviet resistance. He was considered a continued threat to the USSR through his activities aimed at Ukrainian independence, and he was assassinated by the KGB in Munich on 15 October 1959.

Why Russia Wants Ukraine

Whatever nonsense Putin and his acolytes spout, there are sound geostrategic and economic reasons why Russia wants Ukraine:

Geostrategic Reasons

In geostrategic terms, the real prize for Russia is not Ukraine *per se*, but the Crimean Peninsula,[317] which is huge – covering 10,425 square miles (27,000 square kilometres), and is shaped rather like a stylised diamond: from east to west it is approximately 175 miles at its widest point, and 125 miles north to south. The real value of Crimea lies in its position on the southern flank of Eastern Europe, and the way in which it juts out into the Black Sea. To the east is the Sea of Azov, which gives into the Black Sea via the Kerch Straight – and this is totally dominated by the Crimea; to the west lie the excellent southern Ukrainian coastal facilities at Odesa and the complex of port facilities clustered around the Sukhyi Estuary: Malodolynske, Oleksandrivka, Burlacha Balke, Pivdennyi, and Chornomorsk. In Crimea itself, the key is the magnificent deep-water harbour of Sevastopol, from where any Russian fleet could move through the Black Sea to the Mediterranean and then to the Atlantic. Control of the Crimea would also allow the Russians to bottle up the western Ukrainian port of Odesa, as the sea lane between Sevastopol and the Ukrainian south-western coastline is only around 130 miles wide: if Odesa were to remain as Ukraine's only outlet to the Black Sea, Russia could stifle Ukraine's international trade very easily. It is hard to imagine a more strategically important position than that of Crimea; the Russians desperately need the facilities provided by Sevastopol, which drove them to unilaterally invade and annex Crimea in 2014. Whilst this secured them the port, they were then faced with the question of how to supply their forces in the region – it was at the end of a long supply chain that passed through the Ukrainian provinces of Donetsk, Zaporizhzhia and Kherson, and other than by air, the only direct land connection that Russia had with Crimea was across the Kerch Bridge which could not accommodate sufficient road and rail traffic indefinitely. Logically, Russia needed a land bridge or corridor to provide a direct physical connection with Crimea, and the obvious place for this (geographically speaking) was through the three eastern Ukrainian provinces mentioned above.

Economic Reasons

Ukraine had always been of economic value to the Russians as an agricultural and economic powerhouse – producing thousands of tons of grain annually. In addition to extensive coal mining in the Donbas region, there are also significant oil and gas fields, and huge deposits of a wide variety of minerals, such as iron ore, manganese, uranium, titanium-zirconium ores, and non-metallic raw materials.[318] It was also a centre of manufacturing and heavy industry, and to make exporting easier, there was a sophisticated railway network linking the centres of production and extraction to seaports such as Odesa; there were also railways that ran through Ukrainian territory, and which brought produce from other parts of the empire. In addition, the major rivers (such as the Dnipro) that flow through the country provide valuable water resources, and there is an almost-inexhaustible supply of timber from the vast forests that cover much of the land.

Today, Ukraine still remains of high importance in economic terms – despite the war, it continues to produce thousands of tons of grain (wheat, corn, barley) – exports of which, according to the World Economic Forum, even for 2022 still amounted to US$5.1 billion, US$5.9 billion, and US$1.3 billion, respectively.[319] Added to these grain totals is the value of sunflower oil exports: US$6.4 billion, and rapeseed oil US$1.7 billion. In addition to its vast agricultural output, the value of other exports from Ukraine in 2023 amounted to:

- Iron, steel: $2.6 billion (7.3 per cent of total exports)
- Ores, slag, ash: $1.9 billion (5.2 per cent)
- Electrical machinery, equipment: $1.7 billion (4.6 per cent)
- Wood: $1.5 billion (4.1 per cent)
- Food industry waste, animal fodder: $1.4 billion (3.9 per cent)
- Machinery including computers: $957.2 million (2.6 per cent)
- Meat: $892.3 million (2.5 per cent)[320]

Control of Ukraine and especially the Crimea region were historically crucial to the Soviet Union's plans for future world-wide revolution and economic prosperity, and the same is still true today. Small wonder then, that the Ukrainians resent control from Moscow, which treated the country as a colonial possession, and bled it dry of extractive, agricultural, and manufactured products.[321] This explains why there was such a strong movement for independence, and once having achieved its independence in 1991, it also explains why the Ukrainians of today are prepared to fight in defence of their homeland, as they know the socio-economic and political history of occupation by the Russians. Despite the attempts by President Trump to initiate a ceasefire, followed by some sort of negotiated peace, Ukraine will not be bullied into accepting a forced deal, although the country is open to negotiations.[322]

First Attack on Ukraine (Donbas and Crimea, March 2014)

Background

On 24 August 1991, following discussions with the USSR, Ukraine officially became independent, but Russia still harboured thoughts of incorporating at least the eastern part of the newly independent Ukraine into the Russian Federation. The perception that Russia wished to foment was that a sizeable majority of Ukrainians wished to become part of Russia – consequently, in pursuit of the 'defence of ethnic minorities' he would be justified in 'liberating' these people and their territory (refer back to Chapter 2).

One of the conditions on which Russia granted Ukrainian independence was that there would be a national referendum on the future of the country, to be held on 1 December 1991. In the first Ukrainian presidential elections – held on 1 December 1991 – the independent candidate, Leonid Makarovych Kravchuk, won 61.6 per cent of the vote on a turnout of 84.2 per cent of the electorate. The problem from the Russian point of view, was that Ukrainian voters had chosen the 'wrong' president – i.e. someone who was pro-West, rather than a pro-Russian puppet president. Kravchuk was strongly in favour of the country joining the EU, and one of his first acts was to sign the Lisbon Protocol. This was basically an agreement that Ukraine (along with Belarus and Kazakhstan) would return to Russia any nuclear weapons that remained on their soil from the old days of the Soviet Union. This formed part of the SALT (Strategic Arms Limitation Treaty), in which the USA and Russia felt that it would be better to have all nuclear weapons under the control of as few countries as possible – reducing the possibility that such weapons could be seized by terrorist groups. There were over 3,000 nuclear warheads under the control of the three newly independent republics: Belarus (100 strategic warheads), Kazakhstan (1,400), and Ukraine (1,750).[323] As an aside, it is interesting to speculate how the current war might have developed if Ukraine had not retuned these nuclear weapons to Russia: might the fact that Ukraine would have technically been a nuclear power have made Vladimir Putin think twice before invading? Richard Paddock reported in the *Los Angeles Times* of September 1997, that the Russian politician and presidential candidate Alexander I. Lebed was claiming that Russia could still not account for around one hundred nuclear devices, each approximately the size of a suitcase. He told the press that the lax state of Russian nuclear security 'posed a danger to the whole world'.[324] In true Russian style, and in line with stage one (denial) of the 'Russian Defence' discussed earlier, the claim was categorically denied by the then Prime Minister Viktor S. Chernomyrdin, who said that this assertion was 'absolutely impossible' although he refused the offer made by the UN International Atomic Energy Agency to check that all such weapons were safely under lock and key in a secure military establishment. One cannot help but wonder why.

Russian interference in Ukrainian politics had been going on ever since Kyiv announced its independence. Professor Lucan Way, of Toronto University, writing as part of the PONARS[325] programme studying East European, Russian and Eurasian politics, has claimed that Russian interference began shortly after the collapse of the old USSR, and was initially based on thinly disguised financial and diplomatic pressures, with little sophisticated understanding of the 'dynamics of public opinion in the target countries'.[326]

Russia had been exerting as much influence as it could to ensure that the Russian-speaking peoples of the eastern Ukraine voted in favour of returning to Russia, yet the move to independence appeared unstoppable. Opinion polls in September 1992 suggested that 63 per cent of Ukrainians were in favour of independence; by October that had risen to 77 per cent, and by mid-November still further to 88 per cent.[327] The final result was a clear win for an independent Ukraine, with 28,804,071 (92.3 per cent) voting for independence, as against 2,417,554 (7.7 per cent) voting to be part of Russia, based on a turnout of 84.2 per cent of the electorate.[328] Furthermore, it is interesting to note that of the ethnic Russians living in Ukraine – mostly in the east in the Donets region – 55 per cent voted for an independent Ukraine,[329] showing that despite the months of Russian interference, anti-Kyiv propaganda, and the clandestine activities of the FSB, more than half of the citizens of these regions decided they wanted to belong to an independent Ukraine.

The current problem really began in November 2013, when Ukraine's hopes to apply for membership of the EU were dashed. The Ukrainian parliament had given approval for the government to sign an accession document, but just days before this was due to happen, the then President Victor Yanukovych reneged on his promise, and cancelled the signing ceremony, in favour of a massive political U-turn in which he announced that the country would instead be seeking closer ties with Russia, and membership of the Eurasian Economic Union (EEU) – a Moscow-controlled group set up as a direct challenge to the EU. It was obvious that he was bowing to some form of pressure from Putin, and this did not sit well with the Ukrainian population, who by a very great majority, had hoped that the future of Ukraine would be tied to that of the West in general, and the EU in particular. They also hoped to join NATO as a protection against Putin's increasingly vociferous territorial demands. There were popular demonstrations known as the 'Maiden Revolution', and the government fell; the replacement was more Western-orientated which is what the people of Ukraine wanted, but the last thing that President Putin wanted; a more Russian-orientated administration could have been persuaded to allow him to occupy Crimea and cede the land bridge to connect it with Russia.

Ukraine went through a period of political uncertainty as it faced the future. The desire of the population for a more pro-Western outlook and orientation was unmistakable, however, and the next election was won by the liberal Victor Yushchenko, who promised to steer Ukraine towards membership of the EU, and ultimately NATO: an outcome unacceptable to Putin, and Yushenko became 'inexplicably' ill with what was later diagnosed as dioxin poisoning; he nearly died, but survived with a highly disfigured face. His illness was thought to be a consequence of Russian attempts at assassination, as poisoning is a favoured FSB tool. Despite his illness, he took up office in January 2005, remaining in power until 2010. To date there has been nothing officially declared as the cause of the poisoning, although everyone suspected Russia was responsible, and this blatant attempt at regime change sparked protests in the streets. In the election held on 17 January 2010, there was no clear winner, despite the interference by Moscow and the eventually the outcome was decided by a straight run-off between the two most popular candidates: the pro-Western Yulia Tymoshenko and the pro-Russian Victor Yanukovych, who, with Russian backing attempted to win the presidency once again; Yanukovych was eventually declared the winner after another round of elections on 14 February, and began to turn the country towards Moscow. Andrei Soldatov, writing in *The Moscow Times*, reported that a note had been sent from the Ukrainian foreign ministry to Moscow on 4 April 2010, demanding to know why an FSB general (Colonel General Sergi Beseda) had visited Kyiv on 20 and 21 February, without proper accreditation with the foreign ministry.[330] The reason for concern was that the general was in command of the FSB's fifth service (operational information and international communications).

This was all part of a wide-reaching, long-term campaign by Putin to drive a wedge between Ukraine and the West, in preparation for what was to come. The street protests continued growing in size, and by November 2013 the people were now demanding Yanukovych's resignation, accusing him of corruption. Despite evidence of Russian interference in the election result, Yanukovych insisted that he had been elected democratically, and rather than reason with the demonstrators, or try to disperse them peacefully, he ordered the security services to deal with them violently. He had obviously been taking advice from his Russian advisors as to how to control street protests, and around fifty people were shot dead on 20 February 2014.[331]

In an effort to save himself, and under considerable pressure from the EU, Yanukovych promised to hold early elections, and transfer more of his presidential powers to Parliament; this did not save him however, and he was forced into exile in Russia on 22 February. This presented Putin with a problem, as Yanukovych was replaced by Petro Poroshenko who was EU-facing and wished to keep Russia at arm's length. Judging by the strength of opposition to him, Yanukovych, he would never again be able to be elected president, yet he was the only man acceptable to Moscow. Putin wanted Crimea as part of Russian territory for access to the Black Sea, and failing this, he wanted a friendly government in Kyiv that would allow Russian vessels and the Russian navy unrestricted use of the huge port of Sevastopol. He had assumed that with the election of President Yanukovych he would be able to use Sevastopol without the inconvenience of military occupation of Crimea – following the fall of Yanukovych, however, he was forced to consider other ways of achieving his goal. On the pretext of restoring law and order in Ukraine, Putin decided that the time was right to invade. Western intelligence services had got wind of what he was about to do, and various governments had warned him against it, yet nothing was really done to dissuade Putin from attacking.

The Attack

The fall of Yanukovych gave Putin the perfect excuse he needed to send his forces into Crimea on 27 February 2014, claiming that they had been invited by the deposed president (who claimed he was the victim of an illegal armed coup) and that Russian forces were there to maintain law and order which had broken down. This pretext for invasion is perfectly in line with the strategies mentioned earlier (see Chapter 2: Overt Strategies), but it does not explain, however, why Russian forces were sent to occupy Crimea, when the demonstrations had taken place in Kyiv.

The Kremlin had previously warned the West that 'any expansion of NATO military infrastructure in Ukraine would cross one of President Putin's "red lines"...'[332] This warning was based on Putin's stated opposition to a NATO member sharing a common frontier with Russia – yet this had already been the case since 18 February 1952, when Turkey joined the Alliance, on 12 March 1999 when Poland joined, and again on 29 March 2004, when Latvia and Estonia joined. Just as during the Cold War when Putin's Communist predecessors had tried to stop people receiving Western television and radio programmes such as Voice of America, he wanted to isolate the Russian public from the rest of the world. Bringing the rest of the world closer to Russia would have achieved the exact opposite. If joining NATO was indeed crossing a red line, then one is tempted to ask why Russia did nothing at all of these stages? Why did they only become significant when it was Ukraine in the spotlight? As suggested, the real reason is centred on the Crimea and Sevastopol; additionally, there is the consideration that each neighbouring state that is a member of NATO and/or the EU, represents a threat to Putin's control.

On 27 February in conjunction with some clandestine Russian irregular forces, Ukrainian dissidents in the Luhansk and Donbas regions of eastern Ukraine, began a campaign of armed rebellion against the government. The same day, Russian Special Forces – without unit identification markings and wearing face masks – were sent into Crimea to seize strategic sites. They occupied the Crimean parliament and installed the pro-Russian government led by Sergey Aksyonov, and promised to hold a referendum on whether Crimea should belong to Russia or Ukraine. The leadership of the 'free world' was in the hands of the USA, yet Putin's aggression was not countered by US President Barack Obama; his reaction to unfolding events came too late, on 28 February 2014, when he released a press statement in which he told Putin not to intervene in Ukraine, warning that: 'Any violation of Ukraine's sovereignty and territorial integrity would be deeply destabilizing, which is not in the interests of Ukraine, Russia, or Europe.'[333] Needless to say, Putin took no notice of this weedy warning – what Obama never really understood in the first place, was that destabilisation of Ukraine *was* in the interests of Russia.

Putin said that he would hold a referendum in Crimea to see the extent to which his actions had the approval of the local population. The result of the referendum, which took place on 16 March 2014, was a foregone conclusion: 97 per cent of voters expressed their desire to join the Russian Federation, and only two per cent wished to remain part of Ukraine. There were no foreign observers allowed to monitor the process, and the referendum was widely condemned as fraudulent; with a speed which suggested that the outcome had already been decided, Russia officially annexed Crimea into the Russian Federation the very next day on 17 March. As expected, and in line with the overt strategies outlined in Chapter 2, Putin defended his actions as being in line with the principle of self-determination. A Kremlin spokesman was quoted as saying that: 'Vladimir Vladimirovich Putin drew attention to the inability and unwillingness of the present authorities in Kiev to curb rampant violence by ultra-nationalist and radical groups that destabilize the situation and terrorize civilians, including the Russian-speaking population.'[334]

Reaction

There appeared to be little in the way of leadership from the then president of the USA, Barack Obama – a weak individual, who was easily outmanoeuvred by Putin. He held a telephone conversation with Putin a few days later on 1 March 2014, in which he said that the Russian invasion of Ukraine was 'a violation of Ukrainian sovereignty and territorial integrity.' Once again, Putin took no notice. This outrage seemed to be ignored by the world, and it appeared that very few outside Ukraine were interested – just as British Prime Minister Neville Chamberlain justified his lack of opposition to Hitler's invasion of Czechoslovakia in 1938, on the grounds that it was 'a faraway country of which we know nothing'. Putin attempted to justify the annexation on the grounds of self-determination of the citizens of Crimea, and had he allowed the referendum to be organised and monitored by an outside organisation, then he might have had some justification of his claim; as it was, the forced Crimean declaration of independence from Ukraine was denounced as illegal.[335]

Obama imposed financial sanctions on Russia, and personal restrictions on the bank accounts and travel permits of some of those wealthiest people close to Putin, but at the same time he refused to supply military support of any kind for Kyiv, and worse still, he seemed to give the green light to Putin when he announced: 'We are not going to be getting into a military incursion in Ukraine.'[336] Obama apparently had little understanding of how to deal with dictators, nor did he seem to appreciate the geopolitical repercussions of the Russian action and the relevance of Europe to the defence of the USA and world democracy. Until Obama, the territorial appetite of the Soviet-Union/Russia had been more or less contained by NATO: Obama was the first US president to rely totally on 'reason' and financial-economic sanctions; what he obviously failed to realise, however, was that one cannot reason with the Russians, and that even if economic sanctions are observed by all nations – highly unlikely – they may take years to have any effect. Furthermore, following Obama's feeble response, Russia placed counter-sanctions on a number of US companies and key politicians, and according to the Centre for Economic Policy Research (CEPRA), those nations on which Russia imposed their counter-sanctions, lost approximately ten times more trade by value. CEPRA estimated that over the period 2014–2016, trade lost as a consequence of Western sanctions amounted to 'to $1.3 billion, while trade lost due to the Russian counter-sanctions amounts to $10.5 billion. There appears to be no evidence that Russian importers switched between suppliers from sanctioning countries to competitors from non-sanctioning countries'.[337]

The EU froze the assets of anyone dealing with prominent Russians, in addition to a ban on named Russians from travelling to any EU country. The then UK Foreign Secretary, William Hague, condemned the annexation, and there was some reaction but it appeared half-hearted, and certainly insufficient to make Putin change his mind and withdraw his troops. For example, the leaders of the USA, UK, and Germany refused to attend the 2014 Winter Paralympics held at Sochi in Russia – although all three countries, somewhat confusingly, sent competing teams. Of perhaps greater significance was the cancellation of the planned G7 Summit also to have been held in Sochi in June, and the suspension of Russia's membership of the group. Others went further: in addition to implementing all the EU sanctions relating to trade, finance and travel, the UK also suspended all 'licenses... and applications ...

for direct export to Russia of military or dual-use items destined for units of the Russian armed forces and or other state agencies'.[338] That the UK was supplying Russia with military or dual-use items up to that point is both disturbing and scarcely believable. The Putin regime was largely unaffected by the sanctions imposed on it: they appear to have achieved so very little that not only did he continue to operate as before, but it is highly likely that this lack of retaliatory punitive measures served to encourage him to attempt the annexation of the reminder of Ukraine. As NBC's Perry Bacon put it: 'Obama will leave office with Russia having aggressively defied the United States throughout his second term, a time when Vladimir Putin reasserted his control over Russia's government and then sought to re-establish his nation as a rival power to the U.S.'[339] Whilst Obama did eventually act, he seemed more concerned to make things difficult for the incoming President Donald Trump; he left his highest-profile action until 29 December 2016, when he expelled thirty-five Russian diplomats from the USA, doubtless anticipating a Russian backlash which would no longer be his problem to deal with. Had he robustly opposed Putin earlier then Putin's later attempt to take over the rest of Ukraine might never have happened. There was the usual condemnation of Russian actions in the United Nations and more sanctions were imposed, but other than that, Putin was allowed to get away with the outrage – doubtless he saw this as a sign that he would not be prevented from taking action of a similar nature in the future, and he did just that some eight years later.

The war in eastern Ukraine had been going on sporadically since March 2014, when control by pro-Russian separatists, under the control of Russia, were encouraged and helped at the diplomatic level by Russia, and on the ground by the Russian military – including officers from the FSB – in the invasion and occupation of these areas. Since then, there have been bases from which Russian forces in conjunction with the forces of the Russian-controlled so-called Lugansk People's Republic, and the similar Donbas People's Republic, have launched attacks on eastern Ukraine. Vladislav Inozemstev made a valid point when he wrote:

> When Putin argued that he annexed Crimea to protect ethnic Russians and Russian speakers — and not to defend Russian citizens — he effectively

> rewrote the rulebook of the second half of the 20th century that drew boundaries according to political and not ethnic affiliation. If this is allowed to continue, the consequences could be very serious.[340]

He was correct in his assessment, as the relative inactivity of the West sent the wrong message to Putin, who assumed that, henceforth, he would be allowed to do whatever he wished. When Inozemstev wrote this, the attempted occupation of the remainder of Ukraine was still some eight years in the future – eight years in which the West had time to confront Putin, and at least halt further aggression and territorial annexation; but very little of import was done.

When Putin's 'land grab' began in 2014, NATO deployed additional forces in those NATO-member countries that shared a border with Russia, in particular Latvia and Estonia. At a conference of the Centre on the United States and Europe (CUSE) hosted by NATO Secretary General Anders Fogh Rasmussen, the secretary general stated that: 'Russia's military aggression in Ukraine is in blatant breach of its international commitments and it is a violation of Ukraine's sovereignty and territorial integrity.' Rasmussen added: 'We had thought that such behaviour had been confined to history. But it's back and it's dangerous. Because it violates international norms of accepted behaviour. It exports instability. It reduces the potential to cooperate and build trust. And ultimately it undermines our security.'[341] Other than these words of censure, it would appear that little of real substance was done. He concluded that:

> The only way to address such challenges is for Europe and North America to stand together. This is what we have done from the start of this crisis. NATO's clear position has been to condemn Russia's military action in Ukraine. To stand firmly in support of the government in Kiev. And to make clear that President Putin's decisions to escalate the situation have consequences.[342]

What might have helped would have been clarification: what, for example, did Rasmussen mean by the phrase 'To stand firmly in support of the government in Kiev?' How did he intend NATO to support Ukraine? Diplomatically, economically, politically, militarily, or a combination of all four? Did this 'support' include the provision of humanitarian and medical supplies, nonlethal military supplies, weapons, or even troops on the ground? What indeed are the 'consequences' for Putin of his decision to escalate the situation? To make such veiled threats is counter-productive, as it only serves to give the Russians the impression that NATO is unsure as to how best to respond. Just as when Hitler had re-occupied the Rhineland on 7 March 1936, the lack of a firm response by the major powers (Britain and France) meant that he was emboldened to make other subsequent moves.[343] The British response was a classic example of inaction, excused by the need to consult with allies and observe the letter of the law. This dithering culminated with the seizure, two years later, of the Czechoslovak Sudetenland and the annexation of Austria.

In September 2014, Putin was persuaded to negotiate with Ukrainian over the future of the territories he had seized. In a series of talks, chaired by the leaders of France and Germany, various agreements were reached – referred to as the Minsk agreements – in which both sides agreed to stop the fighting in eastern Ukraine. Despite his promises, Putin continued to arm and support the Ukrainian rebels in that region; and the world did very little other than apply more sanctions.

In June 2015, just over a year after his invasion of Crimea, Putin launched a charm offensive against the West, in an attempt to justify his invasion. In view of what he had done, the text of his interview with an Italian newspaper[344] is so outrageous that it has to be read carefully in order to appreciate the full extent of his lies, disinformation, and misdirection. He began by telling people that there was 'no need to fear Russia' suggesting that he had 'other things to think about, rather than invading other countries'. The first lie. He then tried to confuse the issue by comparing Russian military expenditure with that of NATO, which he claimed was ten times higher than that of Russia, without also comparing production costs which are considerably higher in the West. He next claimed that Russia had 'no bases abroad' – another lie, as there are Russian military bases in Armenia (a base at Gyumni, and the airbase at Erebuni airport); in Belarus (the Baranavichy Radar Station, and the Vilyeyka naval communications centre, and the joint Russo-Belarus Air Force and air defence training centre at Baranovichi); in Georgia (a large Russian military presence in the states of Abkhazia and South Ossetia); in Kazakhstan the Russians have the Sary Shagan anti-ballistic testing range, and the Kambala airbase; in Kyrgyzstan they have the 999th Air

Base, which houses numerous units relating to anti-submarine weapons, a naval communications centre, and the seismic service of the Ministry of Defence. Russia continues to maintain a military presence in Transnistria which guard a strategic ammunition dump at Cobasna. Its immense sea forces – including most of the Black Sea Fleet – are based in the port of Sevastopol in Ukraine, which, despite Putin classifying it as a part of Russia, is regarded by most of the world as Russian-occupied territory. The Russian presence in Syria has taken a blow recently with the fall of President Assad in December 2024, but when Putin was speaking it had two bases there: the Khmeimim air base, and the Tartus naval base. Much of these Russian presences were explained by Putin as necessary to counter 'terrorist' threats. The conversation then switched to Ukraine, where he said: 'In Donetsk and Lugansk people voted for independence, and the situation there is different. But the main thing, something we must always bear in mind, is that we should always respect the feelings and the choice of the people.' How the editor (Luciano Fontana) who was interviewing him kept a straight face at that point is amazing. The whole diatribe finished with what could only be described as a denial of reality, when he said that if people wanted to remain part of Ukraine, then the [Ukrainian] government should 'prove to those people that their lives would be better, more comfortable and safer within a unified state; that they would be able to provide for themselves and ensure their children's future within this state. But it is impossible to convince these people by means of weapons. These issues, issues of this kind can only be resolved by peaceful means.'

Second Attack on Ukraine (The 'Special Military Operation', February 2022)

The Build-Up

To realign Ukraine with Russia, Putin needed to oust Zelensky, and replace him with a new president who was friendly (and subservient) to Moscow. There is a sweet irony in his fear of NATO: prior to his re-invasion of Ukraine, both Finland and Sweden were staunchly neutral, as since the end of World War II, both nations had resisted invitations to join NATO, believing that neutrality would be their best protection against the Russians. Since Putin's attack on Ukraine, however, both have seen that Putin has no more respect for international borders than did his predecessors. Consequently, they voted to apply for NATO membership in May 2022: the Finnish application to join was approved on 4 April 2023, and that of Sweden on 7 March 2024. The very antithesis of what Putin wanted.

The so-called 'Special Military Operation' of 24 February 2022, was launched, according to Putin for the 'liberation' of Ukraine from Nazis; in reality however, it was 'unfinished business' left over from 2014. This time, the objective was far greater and included forced regime change within Ukraine: his first attempt in 2014 had only been partially successful, and although he now held Crimea, he had to have a Russian-friendly president in Kyiv: the current president, Volodymyr Zelensky (elected in 2019) was more pro-Western than his predecessors, and so he had to go. Putin had hoped to take the capital Kyiv within a matter of days, which would then have allowed him to replace Zelensky with a more pro-Russian and anti-EU regime, which would in turn have halted any Ukrainian moves to apply for membership of NATO. Toppling the democratically elected president and replacing him with someone who was acceptable to Moscow was a blatant return to the post-war days of the Soviet puppet regimes that Moscow installed throughout Eastern Europe. Unfortunately for Putin the Ukrainians had already suffered a foretaste of Russian occupation in 2014 and were fully aware of what being 'liberated' by the Russians actually entailed. Those areas invaded in March 2014 had suffered widespread destruction of infrastructure, continued fighting, brutal suppression, summary executions, torture, and the installation of puppet regimes. They could not allow that to happen to the rest of the country, so the invading Russian forces were met with growing resistance. Whilst Putin was compared to Hitler, Zelensky by contrast showed Churchillian steel in galvanising the national will to resist. In an address to the UK parliament, he paraphrased Churchill's most famous speech about 'never giving up': 'We will fight till the end, at sea, in the air. We will continue fighting for our land, whatever the cost. We will fight in the forests, in the fields, on the shores, in the streets.'[345] Map D opposite shows the main avenues of attack on Ukraine – of particular interest are the thrusts from Belarus and from Crimea – since 2014, this was viewed as a potential launch point for a renewed invasion by Russia.

Map D: The Russian reinvasion of Ukraine (from 2022).

Putin's speech was a curious mixture of incomprehensibly baseless slurs and accusations: 'Once again I speak to the Ukrainian soldiers…do not allow neo-Nazis and Banderites[346] to use your children, your wives and the elderly as a human shield. Take power into your own hands. It seems that it will be easier for us to come to an agreement than with this gang of drug addicts and neo-Nazis.'[347] Unfortunately, many of his entourage appeared to have been infected with the same loss of reason and detachment from reality; take for example, the rantings that emerged from the mouth of Russia's foreign intelligence service director Sergey Naryshkin, who in an outburst of pure venom, raged that 'any people, and even more so the Russian people, will be able to distinguish true patriots from scum and traitors and simply spit them out like a fly that accidentally flew into their mouths.'[348]

Even supposing these outrageous allegations were true – which they patently are not – would this give him the justification to invade Ukraine, firstly in 2014 and the again in 2022? Would it have given him the right to invade and annex the Ukrainian region of Crimea in 2014, and stir up armed rebellion in the four eastern Ukrainian *oblasts* (provinces) of Kherson, Luhansk, Donestsk, and Zaporizhzhia? Russian Foreign Minister Sergey Lavrov, writing in the state-owned *TASS* newspaper, parroted his master's accusations and claimed that the West was: 'covering up crimes of the Kiev regime in Donbass, which in the end led to Ukraine's tragedy'. In a classic implementation of the DeCaB approach discussed in Chapter 2, the Russian strategy unfolded along predictable lines – Lavrov employed stage two (counter-accuse), to claim that the Ukrainians were doing exactly what Russia had done. Bizarrely, and without presenting any supporting evidence, he went on to state: 'During this entire period, the population of DPR and LPR was subjected to abuse, perennial shelling on the part of the Kiev regime that openly adopted a course towards Russophobia and genocide.'[349] Again, a counter-accusation, which is made all the more despicable when one bears in mind the document issued to Russian invaders, and mentioned earlier in the preface.

What Lavrov failed to mention was that the so-called 'People's Republics' of Donetsk and Luhansk had been launching artillery and mortar attacks on Ukrainian forces and civilians since April 2014. Both regions had been partially occupied by armed Russian-backed 'separatists' since 7 April 2014 when they proclaimed the Luhansk People's Republic, and the Donetsk People's Republic; since then, they had launched numerous artillery, mortar and rocket attacks on the sovereign territory of Ukraine. A report published on 3 November 2020, entitled 'Armed Aggression of the Russian Federation Against Ukraine', highlighted the separatists, supported by 'regular and irregular units of the Russian Army, Don Cossack formations, and private military contractors'.[350] The 'private military contractors' refers to the Wagner group of mercenaries which have been used by Putin to carry out his dirty work when he does not want to involve the Russian army directly. Russian Special Forces and FSB agitators, have launched numerous terrorist attacks on the territory of Ukraine in an attempt to stir up resentment against the Kyiv government. The claim that these regions were subjected to 'perennial shelling' is true but it was the *Russians*, not the Ukrainians, who were responsible. Between 9 July and 5 September 2014, Ukraine reported 'more than 120 artillery attacks from Russia'.[351] Russian officials, of course denied this – stage one of the DeCaB strategy – and accused the Ukrainians of this crime (stage two, counter-accuse). Their counter-accusations have, however, been exposed for the lies that they are, by an independent Dutch-based investigative journalism group Bellingcat.[352] In a meticulously researched report, which made use of satellite imagery and measurement of mortar and artillery fire trajectories and blast impact points and shapes, the group reported that 'the Bellingcat investigation team has determined that there is compelling evidence that artillery attacks on Ukrainian territory and against Ukrainian armed forces originated from Russia'.[353]

It would appear that the Russians are guilty of state-sponsored murder through their indiscriminate use of artillery strikes on Ukrainian territory and trying to blame the Ukrainians. The Geneva Conventions Additional Protocol of 1977 prohibits:

> indiscriminate attacks and attacks or reprisals directed against the civilian population and individual civilians (articles 48 and 51) … [and attacks on] objects indispensable to the survival of the civilian population (article 54) … [it] lays down an obligation to search for missing persons (article 33) …[and] extends the protection under the Geneva Conventions to all medical personnel, units and means of transport, both civilian and military (articles 8-31)[354]

Consequently, Russian actions since 2014 in the Luhansk and Donbas regions are in flagrant breach of the International Committee of the Red Cross (ICRC) regulations and must be considered war crimes.

Response

Putin's allegations were received incredulously throughout the free world, with a piece in the UK's *The Guardian* (not normally known for its anti-Russian stance), commenting that his speech had wrecked his 'once pragmatic image'. The paper reported that Putin 'gave one of the most bizarre speeches of his twenty-two years as Russia's leader, a directive that managed to sound alarming even in a week when he has ordered tanks into Ukraine and missile strikes on Kyiv.'[355] In a conversation with Andrew Srulevitch, the Anti-Defamation League's director of European affairs, Dr David Fishman, Professor of Jewish History at The Jewish Theological Seminary – dismissed Putin's absurd allegations of Nazism in Ukraine as being part of a propaganda campaign: 'This propaganda is an attempt to delegitimize Ukraine in the eyes of the Russian public, which considers its war against Nazi Germany its greatest moment, and in the eyes of the Western publics who may not know much about Ukraine except that it's next to Russia.' He concluded by saying that: 'Putin's propaganda is so far from the truth that it doesn't survive the first contact with even a little knowledge.'[356]

As might have been expected, Putin was also at pains to silence internal opposition to his assault on Ukraine; however, one month after the invasion, US CIA Director, Bill Burns, claimed that Putin had been assured by his intelligence services that once his forces took Kyiv, the country would collapse within a matter of days.[357] A year later, this was stated via emails from the Russian FSB, and leaked to the British press[358] which confirmed that his intelligence service had underestimated the power of the Ukrainians to resist. Rather than thousands of Ukrainians rising up and overthrowing President Zelensky, the population turned to the defence of the nation: the very strength of Ukrainian resistance giving lie to Putin's excuse that he was defending the 'citizens of the Russian Federation' from 'those who perpetrated numerous bloody crimes' and the 'genocide of the Kyiv regime for eight years.' Had this been the case, then the people to whom he refers would surely have taken advantage of the invasion to have helped the invaders and attack their Ukrainian 'oppressors'?

In an interesting an informative analysis of Russian military interventions since Putin achieved power, Simon Saradzhyan has identified two conditions under which Putin sends his forces into another country, beginning with the first stage: 'Putin has to see an acute threat to Russia's vital national interests that he thinks cannot be neutralised by any means short of force…The second condition for Russia to use military force against another country is that Moscow must have a reasonable hope that such actions would yield a net reduction in threats to Russia's vital interests… both conditions need to be present for Putin's Russia to use force against other states on a large scale; neither one by itself is sufficient.'[359] This is an interesting analysis as it assumes that Russian counter-moves are motivated by a threat to the status quo and not by the advantage to be gained by any first-mover strike.

Currently, in terms of the war with Ukraine, Putin has spectacularly failed to achieve the first of these two conditions. Nor has the second condition been achieved, as Putin has made a classic error of judgement; not only has he been unable to achieve regime change in Ukraine – the very reason why he went to war in the first place – but he has also failed to prevent further Western orientation (including possible membership of NATO), by Ukraine. The Russian strategy has backfired spectacularly; Sweden and Finland (which has an extensive border with Russia) have both joined join NATO as a direct consequence of Putin's invasion of Ukraine!

Civilian Deaths

The sheer hypocrisy of Putin's allegations is breathtaking bearing in mind the 3,375 civilian deaths[360] in Ukraine that have been directly attributable to armed aggression by the Russians and their puppet regimes in the so-called People's Republics of Donetsk and Luhansk unilaterally annexed from Ukraine since 2014. This is before one takes into account the civilian deaths that are directly attributable to the second phase of the Russian attack on Ukraine, which began on 24 February 2022. In the first eighteen months of the Russian assault, the Office of the UN High Commissioner for Human Rights (OHCHR) calculated that from 24 February 2022 to 13 August 2023, the total confirmed[361] civilian casualties were 26,384: this breaks down to 9,444 killed and 16,940 injured.[362] The report also noted that of this total number of casualties, 98 per cent were caused by 'explosive weapons with wide area effects'. In other words, they were killed or injured by high explosives delivered by rockets, artillery shells, or tank shells. In a previous report, the OHCHR was even more explicit:

> Most of the civilian casualties recorded were caused by the use of explosive weapons with wide area effects, including shelling from heavy artillery, multiple launch rocket systems, missiles and air strikes. OHCHR believes that the actual figures are considerably higher, as the receipt of information from some locations where intense hostilities have been going on has been delayed and many reports are still pending corroboration.[363]

It is beyond doubt, therefore, that these civilian casualties were caused by indiscriminate shelling and/or mortar fire, which not only killed and wounded thousands, but caused widespread destruction of civilian infrastructure, including hospitals and schools, water, gas, and electricity supplies. To this we can add the number of civilians killed during the course of the two Russian invasions of Chechnya: December 1994–August 1996, and December 1999–April 2009, both of which were authorised by Boris Yeltsin and Putin; the second invasion of Chechnya resulted in an estimated 25,000 civilian deaths.

Summary

The attacks on Ukraine were predictable – it is a strategic necessity for Putin in his long-term goal of recreating the Imperial Russian Empire, and he is prepared to wait and strike at the most opportune moment. Admittedly, it was harder to predict the 2014 occupation of Crimea, but the activities of Putin's forces in Chechnya and Georgia should have shown what was likely to happen. In the short term, little was done to prevent the attack on Ukraine, even though the world was made aware of Russian troop movements along the Ukrainian border. Despite Putin's protestations to the contrary, this should have served as a warning that invasion was imminent.

The atrocities inflicted on the civilian population of Ukraine by Putin's troops are to be found in the mass graves of murdered civilians in the towns of Bucha, Mariupol, and Izyum[364], amongst many others. Added to this has been the indiscriminate bombardment of civilian infrastructure such as hospitals, schools, markets, railway stations, and power plants, in addition to the June 2023 attack in which two Russian S-300 surface-to-air missiles were fired against the Ria Pizza restaurant in Krematorsk, killing at least eight people and wounding fifty-six.[365] Thus, for Putin to cite the protection of civilians as a reason for military intervention is both hypocritical and mendacious. That these attacks are not 'justified by military necessity', means that they contravene articles of the bodies charged with punishing war crimes:

'Crimes Against Humanity'

International Military Tribunal (IMT) (1945) Article 6: 'Crimes Against Humanity'

- Murder
- Other inhumane acts committed against any civilian population, before or during the war.

International Criminal Court (ICC) (1998) Article 7: 'Crimes Against Humanity'

- Murder

'Crimes of Aggression'

ICC (1998) Article 8 bis: 'Crimes of Aggression'

- Invasion or attack by armed forces against territory
- Military occupation of territory
- Annexation of territory
- Bombardment against territory
- Use of any weapons against territory.

'War Crimes'

IMT (1945) Article 6: 'War Crimes'

- Murder
- Plunder of public or private property
- Wanton destruction of cities, towns, or villages, or devastation not justified by military necessity.

Geneva Convention (IV): the Protection of Civilian Persons in Time of War (1949)
ICC (1998) Article 8: 'War Crimes'

- Wilful killing
- Wilfully causing great suffering
- Destruction and appropriation of property.

'Genocide'

The Genocide Convention (1948) Article II

Genocide is any of the following acts committed with intent to destroy, in whole or in part, a national, ethnical, racial or religious group:

- Killing members of the group
- Causing serious bodily or mental harm to members of the group
- Deliberately inflicting on the group conditions of life calculated to bring about its physical destruction.

ICC (1998) Article 6: 'Acts of Genocide'

- Killing members of a group
- Causing serious bodily or mental harm to members of the group
- Deliberately inflicting on the group conditions of life calculated to bring about its physical destruction

Chapter 5

Russia: The Future?

'Unfortunately, there is no denying that Hitler and Stalin are alive today...under new and different guises. Their successors have adapted themselves and their style to their respective situations. They are waiting for us to forget, because this is what makes their resurrection possible. Sad to say, evil has not disappeared with the physical death of these two monsters, Hitler and Stalin.'

Simon Wiesenthal, in a speech delivered in thanks for his award of a Special Gold Medal on behalf of the US Congress. The East Room, The White House, Washington D.C., 5 August 1980

Students of history know the pernicious influence of Hitler and Stalin – two of the world's most brutal dictators of the early twentieth century. These two 'monsters' as Simon Wiesenthal calls them, are arguably the models against which the world judges Vladimir Putin. But is this a fair comparison? To what extent has Putin consciously or subconsciously modelled himself on these tyrants? For example, since his invasions of Ukraine, there have been many who have labelled Putin a Nazi and a comparative study of German Nazism and the current Putin regime does show remarkable similarities. For example, journalists such as Klaus Friedrich likened Putin's 2014 annexation of Crimea to Hitler's 1938 annexation of Austria:

> In both cases, the alleged repression of a shared ethnic group was used to foment unrest and rally support for the takeover agenda. In both cases, a carefully stage-managed popular referendum was held and, in both cases, its outcome was strongly in favor of annexation. It almost seems that Putin took a page out of Hitler's book when he described Crimea's annexation as a 'homecoming.' Hitler had welcomed Austria 'home' in the same way (*Heim ins Reich*).[366]

Vladimir Putin – the New Hitler?

As Putin himself initially introduced the concept of 'Nazism' to give what he regarded as an excuse to invade Ukraine, it is surely appropriate to make use of this benchmark to judge his own actions. Before the attack on 24 February 2022, Putin sought to justify his so-called 'Special Military Operation' on the grounds that Ukraine was a 'hotbed' of Nazis: in a televised speech[367] he announced that 'we will seek to demilitarize and denazify Ukraine, as well as bring to trial those who perpetrated numerous bloody crimes against civilians, including against citizens of the Russian Federation.' He said that he wanted to 'protect people who have been abused by the genocide of the Kyiv regime for eight years' and that his objective was the 'deNazification of Ukraine, as well as bringing to justice those who committed numerous bloody crimes against civilians'. Even taken at face value, it is difficult to understand the basis on which he made these extraordinary claims; how exactly had the people of Ukraine been 'abused by the genocide of the Kyiv regime'? As pointed out by Zak Beauchamp, such a statement is 'detached from reality…as the country's government is not even close to a Nazi regime', and 'Volodymyr Zelensky, is Jewish; he speaks proudly of how his Jewish grandfather fought against Hitler's army.' He added that the real reason for Putin's absurd claim was long-term regime change.[368] It is Putin who emerges as the 'Nazi' rather than Volodymyr Zelensky, despite Putin's allegations of 'Nazism' in Ukraine, for as Ali Soufan (a former FBI counter-terrorism agent) and Nathan Sales (former acting US Under Secretary of State) suggested, if anyone displayed Nazi leanings, it was Putin himself, pointing out that: 'Putin isn't fighting neo-Nazism. He nurtures it, making his pretext for invading Ukraine even more repellent.' They claimed that 'the Russian strongman has been supporting neo-Nazis and white supremacists for years, including mercenaries and separatists who have waged war on Ukraine since 2014'. It was also pointed out that Moscow uses the Wagner Group of mercenaries to fight wars on its behalf, and that the then leader of this group, Dmitry Utkin 'reportedly wears Nazi tattoos, including a swastika, a Nazi eagle and SS lightning bolts. Wagner mercenaries are reported to have left behind neo-Nazi propaganda in the war zones where they have fought.'[369] and most recently, Ukraine, where they were involved in the 2014 invasion of the Crimea fighting alongside Russian troops in the Donbas region. The report concluded by claiming that 'Putin has condoned and enabled a transnational white supremacist network that stretches around the globe. It's one more instrument in the toolbox Moscow uses to divide democracies and undermine democratic institutions.'[370]

Following Putin's annexation of Crimea and incursions into eastern Ukraine in March 2014, there was an outpouring of condemnation of his actions, with many commentators likening him to Adolf Hitler.[371] Some people might dismiss this comparison, based on the fatuous nonsense that is the so-called Godwin's Law – the proposition that the longer an online argument goes on, the greater the likelihood that something/someone will be compared to Hitler or the Nazis. It is an updated version of the more serious proposition by Strauss[372] in 1953, who postulated that an easy way to discredit any opponent's argument was by comparing it to Hitler or Nazism – a tactic considered by many to be a sign of desperation or intellectual laziness. Regardless of Godwin, there are sufficient grounds for actually undertaking a serious comparison between Putin and Hitler.

Before Putin had managed to stifle free speech in Russia, journalists such as Vladislav Inozemstev in *The Moscow Times* were likening Putin to Hitler in terms of his foreign policy and actions towards his neighbours. On 8 March 2022, Voice of America reported on a series of anti-war demonstrations in Skopje, North Macedonia, in which protestors held up pictures of Putin defaced to make them look like Hitler.[373] However, Charles Moore, writing in *The Spectator* magazine commented that when comparing modern events with those that led up to World War II, makes an interesting comparison between Hitler and Putin, but warns that in doing so, one runs the risk of hyperbole.[374]

In view of the outpourings in the press, and demonstrations in the streets denouncing Putin as the new Hitler, it is beholden of historians to compare key facts about the two dictators:

Invasion and Occupation

Both invaded and occupied other countries: Hitler conquered most of Europe, and then lost it. Putin appears to be more cautious, taking the long-term view: he has reasserted Russian authority in Chechnya and Georgia, and seems to be about to do the same in Ukraine.

Corruption and Electoral Fraud

Both Hitler and Putin ultimately used force and fraud to achieve power, despite the fact that initially they achieved the first stage of their ascendency through democratic means – both, however, were criticised for alleged polling irregularities. Whether these would have altered the outcome is open to debate. In the 2004 presidential election, Putin was accused of widespread ballot-rigging and in some cases, preventing his opponents from canvassing. The International Election Observation Mission that monitored the election subsequently issued a damming report, in which there were many complaints, which taken together, confirm that the election was neither free nor fair. The complaints included, amongst others:

1. Clear bias in favour of Putin by the state-controlled media
2. That the Central Election Commission 'failed to take adequate remedial action' against this bias
3. Incidents of localised election-related corruption, which 'reflected a lack of democratic culture, accountability and responsibility'
4. One candidate was 'clearly obstructed on more than one occasion in campaigning'.

The candidate Sergey Glazev was: 'clearly obstructed in getting his campaign message across to voters in some locations. This was most evident in Nizhny Novgorod, where the electricity supply was cut off at a venue where he was due to give a press conference.'[375] Timur Aliev writing in *The Moscow Times* reported that: 'While senior election officials in Chechnya reported high voter turnout in the Presidential elections, some lower ranking officials openly admitted stuffing ballot boxes.'[376] Furthermore, it was claimed that at Polling Station No. 403 in Grozny, 'local election officials at the station had stuffed 1,986 ballots on orders from higher-ranking election officials. Those officials also dictated the proportion of votes to be given presidential candidates.' The officials also added that the polling station had been issued with 2,260 ballot papers, and only 274 remained unused, yet in their experience generally no more than 200 people ever bothered to vote, implying that this was a highly unusual election.

As Hitler had done, Putin changed the constitution: this allowed him to serve as prime minister 1999–2000, and from 2008–2012, and then as president from 2012. His latest attempt to change the constitution was in January 2020, when he suggested transferring certain presidential powers to other parts of government – thereby weakening the position of any successor. On 30 June, (coincidentally the same date in 1934 as 'the Night of the Long Knives'[377]), he appealed to voters on the state-run television network and promised that the changes would only 'be valid if a majority of those casting ballots voted for them'." But as pointed out by Matthew Luxmoore: 'He neglected to mention the clause that allows him to dodge term limits and potentially remain president until 2036.'[378]

Censorship

Putin has achieved absolute power in Russia, and controls everything through censorship, and the media; this means that the Russian population have no idea what is going on in Ukraine, or why Russian forces are there, other than what Putin wants them to hear. As the BBC noted 'Since... February 2022 nearly all independent media outlets in Russia have shut down, been forced to close, or have left the country to operate from exile'.[379] Russian state-controlled media regularly broadcasts a variety of statistics and claims about the war, all of which are firstly designed to legitimise the Russian attack, and secondly to mislead the public about Russian battlefield losses.

> In Russia, the use of censorship to steer public opinion is not a new practice. The Russian government has been censoring the internet since 2012 when it first started blacklisting websites for criminal activities and terrorism. Because the scale and severity of Russian censorship have only increased, international watchdog Freedom House classifies Russia as 'not free' on their Global Freedom Index. [380]

In September 2023, the investigative journalist website *Frontline* published an analysis of censorship in Russia, in which they focused on three areas: (1) 'Journalist killings left unsolved, and journalists detained', (2) 'Laws used to repress independent journalism', and (3) 'Censorship, blocked access and shutdowns of independent media.' The situation has worsened considerably, and it is widely known that Putin is ordering closures of media outlets, and more permanent closures of 'difficult' journalists. The article also cites findings from *Reporters Without Frontiers (RSF),* which claims that more than 300 journalists fled Russia between February and October 2022.[381]

Dealing With Opponents

In addition to widespread censorship, any internal political, social, or economic opposition is eliminated through the use of a police state apparatus – Hitler used the Gestapo the state secret police and the SD (*Sicherheitsdienst* – security service), in addition to the ordinary police. Putin uses the GRU,[382] the FSB (Federal Security Service of Russia) and the SVR (the foreign intelligence service of Russia), in addition to the Armed Forces' security units and the civilian police.

Putin is the equal of Stalin, but much more subtle: not for Putin mass executions following show trials – instead, those who oppose him or those who demonstrate in public against the invasion of Ukraine are arrested by the police, and either jailed or fined or both. More dangerous for Putin are those in positions of power who voice their opposition – some of his opponents appear to suffer strange but fatal accidents, whilst others are the victims of poisoning, or shootings by unknown gunmen – most of whom have never been found:

Anna Politkovskaya: This investigative journalist was found shot dead in her Moscow apartment on 7 October 2006. She had been involved in documenting extensive human rights abuses and corruption in Chechnya. Nobody has been charged with the crime.

Stanislav Markelov: As a human rights lawyer and a journalist, Markelov would have been likely to incurred Putin's displeasure on a number of counts; he had clashed with Putin over the Russian involvement in Chechnya. On 19 January 2009, both he and the journalist and activist Anastasia Baburova were assassinated in Moscow, allegedly by Nikita Tikhonov and his girlfriend Yevgenia Khasis – both of whom received long prison sentences in 2011, although there is no objective evidence that they did in fact commit the crime.

Natalia Estemirova: A human rights activist and journalist, she was kidnapped on 15 July 2009, in Grozny, and her body was found later the same day. Nobody has ever been charged.

Sergei Magnitsky: A lawyer and auditor, who had exposed a massive tax fraud amongst Russian officials. He was arrested in 2008, on a fabricated charge, and jailed, where he suffered abuse, and was denied necessary medical treatment. He died whilst still in prison on 16 November 2009, as a consequence of severe beating and medical neglect. His death sparked an international outcry, and led to the passing of what was termed the 'Magnitsky Act' in the USA, in which any Russian official involved in corruption and human rights abuse, became the subject of personal sanctions.

Boris Berezovsky: A wealthy businessman and one-time ally of Putin, who later became highly critical of Putin and a strong supporter of the opposition. He fled to the UK but was found dead in a Berkshire hotel room on 23 March 2013: the official verdict was suicide, but it is still unclear as to why someone should kill themselves when they felt safely hidden abroad.

Boris Nemtsov: Served as deputy prime minister under Boris Yeltsin, but later became an outspoken critic of the new regime headed by Putin. Nemtsov was crossing a bridge near the Kremlin in Moscow on 27 February 2015, when he was shot dead by a person or persons unknown. Nobody was arrested, and his death remains a mystery.

Mikhail Lesin: A former Russian press minister, in addition to having his own media company. He crossed Putin and was found dead in a Washington D.C. hotel room on 5 November 2015; the official cause of death was given as an 'accidental blunt force injuries', but this was always thought to be a cover-up for his death – probably at the hand of FSB operatives, posing as diplomats at the Russian Embassy.

As Cameron Peters noted, on 14 October 2022, 'at least 15 Russian businessmen and executives have died in apparent accidents or by suicide, including a number of Putin allies. The victims range from an executive with Gazprom, a major state-owned oil company, to the managing director of a state-run development corporation'.[383]

Pavel Antov: He criticised Putin's invasion of Ukraine, and was found dead in a pool of blood at a luxury hotel in India on 27 December 2022.[384]

Yuri Shchekochikhin: Another journalist and writer, who was leading investigations of human rights abuses, and organised crime in Russia. He was also a member of the Russian Parliament (Duma) and was able to use his political position to expose corruption. On 3 July 2003 he fell ill and died from 'unknown' causes – thought to be some form of radiation poisoning.

Alexi Navalny: Navalny was a fierce opponent of Putin, and was found to have been poisoned with Novichok in 2020. After receiving treatment in Germany, he bravely returned to Russia in 2021 to prepare his campaign to challenge Putin for the presidency in the March 2024 elections. On his return he was arrested, and after a show trial, was convicted and sent to prison in Siberia, where he died under mysterious circumstances on 16 February 2024.

Vladislav Avayev: A former vice-president of Gazprombank, the third-largest bank in Russia. He and his wife and daughter were found dead, all three had suffered fatal gunshot wounds on 18 April 2022 at his Moscow flat.

Sergei Protosenya: Formerly the chief accountant of Novatek, Russia's second-largest natural gas producer, was found hanged at his villa in Barcelona, Spain, on 19 April 2022. His wife and daughter had been stabbed to death.

Anatoly Gerashchenko: The former head of the Moscow Aviation Institute, died after falling down 'several flights of stairs,' the institute reported on 21 September 2022.

According to an ex-FSB officer, in late 2024 Putin issued a new 'kill list' of individuals for whom he has ordered assassination[385] six of whom live in Britain; this might mean that the UK will be subject to more attacks such as the Novichok poisoning attempt on the life of Sergei Skripal in Salisbury. Anyone who speaks out against his war is liable for a term of imprisonment – even those who have fled the country are still subject to Putin's wrath, such as the Russian TV news producer, Marina Ovsyannikova, who denounced Putin on mainstream television saying: 'Putin is a killer. His soldiers are fascists. 352 children have been killed. How many more children need to die for you to stop?'[386] She was sentenced to eight-and-a- half years in prison, *in absentia.* Since then, she has fallen ill in Paris, reportedly the victim of poisoning.

Whilst there is no direct evidence linking these (and many other deaths) to Vladimir Putin, it is surely strange that all of them have voiced opposition to Putin and/or his war in Chechnya or Ukraine, and all have been later found dead under mysterious circumstances. Surely this cannot be simple coincidence.

What Drives Putin?

To identify the factor (or factors) that can explain Putin's action, it is necessary to look in more detail at the individual himself, and to understand what drives him. There must be some motivational factor: Hitler, for instance is on record as claiming he was driven by the injustices of the Treaty of Versailles, and to seek revenge on the Jews who he believed had caused the collapse of the German Empire. What motivates Putin to a similar degree? If US President Donald Trump's attempts to broker a ceasefire deal in Ukraine, with a view to a long-term peace agreement are to succeed, then it is necessary to understand what drives Putin in order to decide whether he can be trusted to keep to any agreement – especially in view of his long-term aims, as he broke the terms of the 2014 Minsk agreements, and he unilaterally repudiated the handing of Crimea to Ukraine.

Some have claimed that Putin is mad[387] and/or that he is terminally ill with cancer or Parkinson's disease[388]; others suggest that he has suffered a mental breakdown. This book does not concur with these theories, but instead suggests that he is driven by what he regards as his place in history – in particular the history of Russia since the break-up of the Soviet Union – and that he considers his mission is to rescue Russia from its social, moral, and economic decline. This is suggestive of at least mild fanaticism, and fanatics are difficult to negotiate with as they tend to have a fixed ideas that cannot be changed. They are generally also unpredictable. The importance of this is likely to emerge during the course of any cease-fire agreements and/or subsequent peace negotiations.

The Break-up of the Soviet Union

Putin feels that the break-up of the Soviet Union, apart from being a major disaster, was the consequence of Western interference, and that the imposition of harsh economic terms that followed were all part of a plan to destroy the USSR economically and politically. In this respect there is a clear comparison with Hitler, who described the injustices of the Treaty of Versailles as 'unreasonable, humiliating and degrading'[389] and which became the central plank of his political campaign for election. In this respect, the attitude of both men is similar, but the facts show that Hitler had a point and that the Versailles Treaty was overbearing and unworkable, and ironically provided much ammunition for moderate Germans to vote for the Nazi Party in the first place.

In addition to his resentment against the West's 'destruction of the USSR', Putin's resentment surely includes a more personal agenda – that of the loss of power and prestige that he personally suffered following his resignation from the FSB? Russians such as Putin bemoaned the Soviet Union's loss of power and world prestige, yet conveniently forget that, whilst they benefited from the Soviet empire, the states of Eastern Europe that they occupied were not so enamoured with control from Moscow – the majority sought independence as soon as they could. Eastern Europe was occupied or controlled indirectly by the Soviet Union from 1945–1991, so it was scarcely a question of other powers having imposed their economic and political will on Moscow – the reverse is true, that Moscow practiced regime change by installing puppet regimes throughout Eastern Europe, and using the Red Army to occupy and intimidate the populations of these countries. That this eventually came to an end, and was cited as an injustice by Putin is a clue as to the way his mind works.

In *Mein Kampf* Hitler gave a clear indication of his way forward, yet nobody really believed him, and the world expressed incredulity when he began to carry out the policies he had said he would. On 31 December 1999, when Putin was still prime minister but had been named by Boris Yeltsin as his successor as president, he published a long letter on the Kremlin website in which he laid out what his policies would be when he became president. This is Putin's 'road map' his *Mein Kampf* of how he intends to proceed, and it should be viewed as such. Nor should it be ignored as was *Mein Kampf* initially – we should not make the same mistake twice. Putin wrote about 'The greatness of Russia' and claimed that 'Russia was and will remain a great power'. Added to the 'tragedy' of the break-up of the USSR is the loss of patriotism. Admittedly with the benefit of hindsight, it is easy to see how Putin intended to harness the power of patriotism – just as Stalin had done fifty years earlier. For Putin, patriotism is:

> a feeling of pride in one's country, its history and accomplishments. It is the striving to make one's country better, richer, stronger and happier. When these sentiments are free from the tints of nationalist conceit and imperial ambitions, there is nothing reprehensible or bigoted about them. Patriotism is the source of our people's courage, staunchness and strength. If we lose patriotism and the national pride and dignity that are connected with it, we will no longer be a nation capable of great achievements.[390]

The importance of Russia as a 'great power' is another theme, as is the concept of 'Statism'. Worryingly, he said that: 'For Russians a strong state is not an anomaly to be gotten rid of' and suggested that the public 'looks forward to a certain restoration of the guiding and regulating role of the state, proceeding from Russia's traditions as well as the current state of the country.' Taken in context with the previous statements, his promise that Russia will not adopt the liberal values of the USA or UK, shows an authoritarian streak that does not accept challenge: 'Russia will not become a second edition of, say, the US or Britain, where liberal values have deep historic traditions.' All of which, if people had taken him at his word, would have been indicative of the future focus of President Vladimir Putin.

Regaining an Empire

Putin is obsessively focused on regaining what he considers to be the territory 'taken' from Moscow when countries (including Ukraine) gained their independence following the break-up of the Soviet Union. Andrew Roth, made a highly perceptive observation that Putin's invasion speech 'seemed to be ripped from an alternate reality – or from World War II, where Putin appears to be spending more of his time as he launches the kind of broad military offensive not seen in Europe for nearly 70 years.'[391] Dmitry Muratov, the editor of *Novaya Gazeta*[392] was quoted as saying that Putin's emotions are deeply rooted in what he perceives as the injustices inflicted on Russia since the fall of the Soviet Union, and that the Russian president was a man with 'a historical map in his mind and a plan to use his military to achieve it'.

This belief, coupled with a determination to achieve power at any cost, should have served as a warning to the West that Putin must be taken seriously, as he is very serious about what he intends to do, and he continues to blame the West (and the USA in particular) for all the problems and dangers that have beset Russia. Very cleverly, through a mixture of state propaganda and elimination of any media criticism (foreign or domestic) he has managed to persuade millions of Russians of the voracity of this lie. In March 2013, one year before the Russian invasion of the Crimea and the eastern *oblasts* of Luhansk and Donbas, a survey found that only one Russian in one hundred viewed Russian-EU relations negatively; by January 2015, this anti-EU perception had risen to one in four.[393]

Mental State

Despots such as Mao, Stalin, Hitler, and Putin did not suddenly emerge onto the political stage as fully-formed monsters – as with all human beings, they were the product of their childhood and adolescence: their experiences of early life helped shape their attitudes, thoughts, and prejudices that typified them in later life. Having said this, according to psychologists, each of these leaders also had some personality flaw, or something in their history that made them different from other people. According to James Fallon, there are traits that are shared by all such psychopaths, whom he describes as people who are generally 'charming, charismatic and intelligent'. They exude self-confidence, are highly independent and 'exude sexual energy'. However, he points out that they also tend to be 'self-absorbed, masterful liars, compassionless, often sadistic, and possess a boundless appetite for power'. He concluded that for an individual to develop into a dictator, they needed to have 'aggressive gene variants and a dysfunctional frontal lobe and amygdale' and he claims that in addition, such people have frequently been seriously abused during childhood, and might also have lost 'important caretakers, such as biological parents'.[394]

Despite his condemnation of 'Nazis' in Ukraine, it would appear that Putin admires Hitler and Stalin as nationalist 'strong men' who led their countries out of difficult times and received the admiration of their citizens. On 10 May

2015, in an interview in which German Chancellor Angela Merkel also participated, Putin justified the much vilified Molotov-Ribbentrop Pact of 1939 (which allied Soviet Russia with Nazi Germany) as 'a statesmanlike act defending Russia's national interests.' In a highly perceptive piece, which presented an interesting analysis of Putin's character and his way of thinking, Stephen Blank of *Newsweek* commented at length on Putin, suggesting that one of his objectives is a partnership with a major power – in particular he views Germany as important in this respect. He also believes that within the Russian zone of influence, he will not recognise any outside interference. It is also interesting to note that Putin 'refuses to acknowledge that the pact [Molotov-Ribbentrop] resulted in the death of millions of Poles, Jews and other East Europeans.... While Germany has visibly repented for its crimes, Russia cannot bring itself to talk honestly about Stalinism'. Blank comments that Putin's behaviour is a 'classic manifestation of overcompensation; Russia is deeply insecure and sensitive to what the West thinks.'[395]

The problem is that the West seems incapable (or unwilling) to understand the Russian menace, and those who do voice their fears are derided as 'reactionaries', 'anti-Russian', or 'right wing' with a hidden agenda of regime change in Russia. Possibly so, but under the current aggressive dictatorship of Vladimir Putin, regime change in Russia might well usher in a safer world than that which we currently inhabit. In April 2022, IPSOS published the findings from a twenty-seven-country survey: one of the questions asked was: 'What level of risk do you think the war in Ukraine poses to your country?' The highest level of risk was felt in Japan (87 per cent of respondents), Poland (77 per cent), South Korea (77 per cent), and Sweden (75 per cent).[396] The Polish and Swedish responses are easiest to explain, as both nations were feeling vulnerable to Russian attacks on their territory: Poland because it is an immediate neighbour to Russia, and Sweden as it was not then a member of NATO. Whilst Japan and South Korea are nowhere near Ukraine, it is likely that concerns expressed in those countries reflect that fear that if Putin were successful, then that might be seen as a green light for Chinese or North Korean military operations against Taiwan and South Korea respectively.

Despite the international recognition of an independent Ukraine – including recognition by the then Russian President Boris Yeltsin, Vladimir

Putin resents Ukraine leaving the Moscow sphere of control.[397] In an infamous rambling diatribe he claimed that Ukraine was not an independent country, that modern Ukraine had been 'made' by the Soviet Union, criticised the decision to hand over the Crimea to Ukraine, and accused the West of developing Ukraine as a barrier against Russia. This rant of historical inaccuracies and unsubstantiated accusations was published on 12 July 2021, on the official Kremlin website, and included the following statement which might well be taken as a route map for his relations with Ukraine:

> Russians and Ukrainians were one people – a single whole…The right for the republics to freely secede from the Union was included in the text of the Declaration on the Creation of the Union of Soviet Socialist Republics and, subsequently, in the 1924 USSR Constitution. By doing so, the authors planted in the foundation of our statehood the most dangerous time bomb… In 1954, the Crimean Region of the RSFSR was given to the Ukrainian SSR, in gross violation of legal norms that were in force at the time… We respect the Ukrainian language and traditions… We respect Ukrainians' desire to see their country free, safe and prosperous…[398]

His comment relating to the 'time bomb' of cessation from the Soviet Union, is particularly instructive as it shows two things: firstly, that he considered that cessation was dangerous and should never have been allowed, and secondly, he did not examine the reasons *why* any of the former Soviet republics should wish to leave the Union. After claiming that he desired to see Ukraine 'free and safe', he then launched an all-out military assault on the country some seven months later!

Strong Man: Strong State

Since his assumption of the presidency in May 2000, Putin has cultivated a 'strongman' image, inundating the press with pictures of him bare-chested, helping with harvests, riding horses, fishing, firing sniper rifles, or dressed in military camouflage fatigues riding on a tank or in modern fighter jets. All of which are highly reminiscent of pictures of Mussolini in the 1930s, when the Italian dictator was trying to cultivate his 'strongman' image, and to relate more directly to the average Italian peasant (rural) voter. Before World War II, Mussolini wanted to be loved by the Italian people, and to this end he devoted much of his energies to grandiose projects that would improve the life of the average Italian citizen – such as draining the malaria-ridden Pontine marshes to the south of Rome, significantly curtailing the power of the Mafia, keeping the north and south of the country united, and he was even reputed to have made Italian trains run on time!

Putin has tried to cultivate a 'man of the people' image, openly giving material goods with one hand, whilst clandestinely taking away democratic freedoms with the other. He has tried to evoke the spirit of Russian unity by referring to the Russian experience in World War II: in 2020, the BBC reported that 'he has made the Soviet victory in World War II a key element of Russia's national idea.'[399] For historians this is instructive, as it shows the extent to which Putin understands the Russian mentality based on history – or at least a Russian interpretation of history. When Stalin's hold on power was at its weakest, just after the German invasion of June 1941, what saved him was a number of factors, but arguably the most important of which was his ability to unite the country through his appeals to the population to 'Defend the Motherland'. By this clever use of a 'propaganda umbrella' he managed to unite a diverse country, in which the peoples of the various Soviet republics put aside their differences with Moscow, and united against what was perceived as the common enemy.

Rehabilitation of Stalin

To understand the significance of Stalin to Putin and Russia, one has to look at Stalin through Russian, rather than Western eyes. To the West, Stalin represents the worst excesses of Communist evils, yet to many Russians (especially the older generation) he was the 'Man of Steel' who saved the USSR from Hitler. In an attempt to get the population on his side, Putin is trying to link the current war with the 'heroic' struggle of the Soviet peoples during World War II – to this end, as long ago as 2019, Putin began to rehabilitate Stalin. Irina Sherbakova, a founding member of the human rights group Memorial wrote:

> Vladimir Putin's rise to power came accompanied by a new version of patriotism relying on "heroic" and "bright" aspects of the Soviet past. An image of Stalin as a strong leader who had ensured victory in World War II and led a Soviet

> superpower re-emerged. Television propaganda again worked hard to create that image. The millions who perished in waves of political repression were pushed to the margins of collective consciousness.[400]

Whilst accepting that Stalin made many mistakes, Putin reveres Stalin's patriotic strongman image: unfortunately, he also appears to have started to rehabilitate the dictator, telling the film director Oliver Stone that Stalin could be compared to Oliver Cromwell[401] or Napoleon Bonaparte. As part of this rehabilitation drive, in the same interview he excused Stalin as a 'product of his time', and complained that the excessive 'demonisation of Stalin' was 'a means to attack [the] Soviet Union and Russia'.[402]

Containing Putin

Containing Putin's aggressive activities has become a major source of worry for most European nations: if he is allowed to get away with his illegal seizure of vast tracts of Ukrainian territory, where will he go next? The most likely targets are immediate neighbours which are not members of NATO: another reason why he has focused on Ukraine. After Ukraine, the most likely targets would be the complete take-over of Transnistria and Moldova – whilst to many Europeans and Americans, these may represent 'a quarrel in a faraway country, between people of whom we know nothing,'[403] they form part of the geostrategic jigsaw currently being assembled by Vladimir Putin, in whose reality they still remain part of the old Russian Empire, and are therefore subject to 're-incorporation'. This could be achieved quicker and much easier if Ukraine were to be annexed by Russia. There are three possible strategies to contain his activities: (1) appeasement, (2) sanctions, and (3) military confrontation.

Appeasement

One strategy when dealing with despots is that of appeasement: partially giving in to their demands in the hope that they will not demand more. As Winston Churchill famously observed: 'Each one hopes that if he feeds the crocodile enough, the crocodile will eat him last. All… hope that the storm will pass before their turn comes to be devoured.'[404] Unfortunately this policy plays into the hands of the despot, who generally perceives it as a sign of weakness, not as a desire to reach an accommodation. The natural inclination of someone who is accountable to nobody is to demand more – there is a psychological tendency to associate the reward received by appeasement as confirmation that the initial demand was a correct strategy – after all, it achieved the desired result, did it not?

Historically there are many examples of the failure of appeasement: possibly the most famous is when Hitler was making territorial demands and incursions in Europe. Basically, the problem when dealing with Hitler in the 1930s was that the West said and did too little too late. At that time, Britain amongst others was heavily involved in preventing future wars through the negotiations taking place through the Conference for the Reduction and Limitation of Armaments (the Geneva Conference) 1932–1934, and the focus of the nation was on maintaining peace as agreed at that conference. The policy of appeasement, though viewed as a mistake with the benefit of hindsight, was widely supported at the time; understandably so, given the legacy of the horrendous war of 1914–1918: nobody wished to see another industrial war that might kill even more than the first.[405] Richard Evans points out that, for Britain and France there was a genuine fear that the potential death count would be very high, as a consequence of battlefield casualties, in addition to civilian deaths from the much-feared aerial bombardment of large cities and 'possibly even social revolution as well'.[406] Winston Churchill was one of the few who opposed appeasement, and remained unconvinced by the Allied inaction, pointing out to the British parliament the dangers of not dealing forcefully with the Nazis before they developed their domestic power and defences further. On 6 April 1936 he made an impassioned speech warning against the folly of trying to placate Hitler:

> Herr Hitler has torn up treaties and has garrisoned the Rhineland. His troops are there, and there they are going to stay. All this means that the Nazi régime has gained a new prestige in Germany, and a most powerful and sustained impression of their strength has been spread abroad through all the neighbouring countries.[407]

Simply by replacing certain words, the similarities with the situation in relation to Vladimir Putin are revealing:

> *Vladimir Putin* has torn up treaties and has garrisoned *eastern Ukraine.* His troops are there, and there they are going to stay. All this means that *Putin's* régime has gained a new prestige in *Russia*, and a most powerful and sustained impression of their strength has been spread abroad through all the neighbouring countries.

Sanctions

The underlying theme of this book is that history repeats itself – and the West appears to have made the same mistakes again with Putin that they made with Communist Russia, and before that with Bolshevik Russia; they have seemingly preferred to excuse atrocities and violence with a variety of excuses and apologies – amongst which, commerce appears to have been predominant. This has been evident from as long ago as 1927, from a discussion in the UK Houses of Parliament, between Sir Archibald Sinclair (Secretary of State for Scotland) and Sir Robert Horne (formerly leader of the UK-Russia Trade Delegation), both MPs, and is worth quoting at length; Sinclair, despite accepting that the new Russian government could not be trusted to keep their word:

> When Russia indicated her willingness to give a written pledge that she would cease her hostile activities against us, he frankly believed that she would try and keep her word. I see the right hon. Gentleman nods his head, but, if he ever dreamed that this Bolshevist Government, as at present constituted, would ever cease to strive for world revolution, then he was living in a world of solitary illusion.

He then went on to state:

> The reasons for entering into this arrangement with Russia were quite different. The reasons given were not hatred, or love of Russia, or, still less, of the Bolshevist Government. The reasons were to try and do something to restore our British trade and to help our unemployed people here. That was the first and big reason. We have got the trade.[408]

Fast forward some ninety years, and one could be forgiven for thinking that little had changed: when President Donald Trump introduced his wide-ranging package of tariffs on goods coming into the USA from 185 countries, neither Russia (nor its ally Belarus) appeared on the list[409] – but bizarrely, Ukraine had a 10 per cent tariff imposed on exports to the USA.[410] A spokesperson for the White House suggested that there was little point in imposing tariffs on Russian goods entering the USA, as there were so few at present due to a combination of sanctions and the Russia-Ukraine war.[411] This is not strictly true, however, as according to the same source – German international broadcaster Deutsche Welle – whilst trade between Russia and the USA has indeed suffered a dramatic fall from US$36 billion in 2021 to US$3.5 billion in 2024, trade between the two nations still remains important, especially as the USA imports strategic goods such as inorganic chemicals and fertilisers. Why Trump should avoid placing tariffs on Russia and Belarus is inexplicable at first sight. There is, however, another explanation: he has no wish to annoy Putin any more than necessary as his long-term objective is the resumption of 'normal' trade with Russia after the cessation of hostilities in Ukraine. Short-term economic sanctions are 'trumped' by long-term economic pragmatism!

All of which explains why sanctions do not generally work – too many people continue to make too much money through trade. After the Russian seizure of Crimea and their incursions into eastern Ukraine in 2014, the US oil and gas giant ExxonMobil made a US$500 million deal for exploration in the Arctic, with Rosneft – Russia's largest oil company. In deference to sanctions imposed following the 2014 Russian invasion, the deal was put on hold in 2015 but reactivated in 2017 – presumably because both parties felt that everyone would have forgotten about the invasion and the sanctions.[412] There are many multinationals that continue to trade with Russia. More recently, the news agency Reuters carries out an investigation of those EU companies that have continued to trade with Russia, despite sanctions. The report found, for example:

> Much trade still flows between the bloc's 27 countries and Russia – a result of successful lobbying, the EU's unwillingness to take a harder economic hit, and concerns about ripple effects on global supply chains... In 2021, Russia was

> the EU's fifth-largest trading partner with goods exchange worth 258 billion euros, according to the EU executive European Commission. The main EU imports were fuel, wood, iron and steel and fertilizers...[413]

Sanctions against Russia are of little value for many reasons: in the first place, there are countries that are politically-aligned with Russia, and do not even entertain the idea of sanctions against Moscow – such as North Korea[414], Belarus, and Cuba. There are other countries willing to act as sanction-busting conduits for goods in and out of Russia – in this respect, the UAE is a major culprit.[415] In addition, even from within those countries that officially maintain sanctions, there are companies that will break them for profit: in November 2023, a report in the *Financial Times* claimed that 127 British companies admitted to having broken sanctions against Russia.[416] More recently, and in response to Russia's re-invasion of Ukraine, there are still companies trying to evade sanctions. In a recent study it was found that sanctioning countries had reduced their exports to Russia of those products that attracted sanctions by 80 per cent, and those that did not attract sanctions by 40 per cent.[417] So, even within those countries that are supposedly obeying sanctions regulations, there are companies that are still exporting to Russia around 20 per cent of products that are supposedly prohibited! In view of this, it is scarcely surprising that the same study found that sanctioning countries continue to export around 60 per cent of non-sanctioned products to Russia. As might be imagined, those countries that do not officially recognise the sanctions appear to have taken advantage of the situation, and *increased* their exports to Russia of sanctioned products by some 40 per cent. The figures were roughly the same for imports *from* Russia.

There is no wonder that sanctions have relatively little effect: one is tempted to conclude that they are imposed on an errant country such as Russia simply to demonstrate that the target has done wrong, rather than part of an effective economic strategy that hits the target economy hard and makes the leaders of that country regret their errant ways. The author has come to the conclusion that sanctions are perhaps best compared to being told to 'sit on the naughty step' – everyone can see that you have done wrong and are being punished, even though the punishment will end once those administering it grow tired of the economic consequences to their own economies. If countries are serious in the implementation of sanctions – which is doubtful – then why bother identifying certain sectors? Simply do not trade at all with the errant country. Do *no* trade: neither import nor export. Nothing at all. If not, the whole exercise is simply 'window-dressing' to keep critics at bay, until normal trade can be resumed.

Confrontation

As neither appeasement nor sanctions appear to have worked in containing Putin, the moral dilemma for the West is whether it feels sufficiently confident to employ the only remaining option – that of confrontation? Critics might argue that to adopt a confrontational attitude towards Putin's regime might lead to another war – possibly nuclear – and that this should be avoided at all cost: they argue that Putin should be included in international discussions, and made to see the error of his ways through a mixture of persuasion, appeasement, or sanctions. Whilst there is a certain logic in this, history has shown such arguments to be fallacious: indeed, in many instances, such an approach has been counter-productive: as any accommodation is perceived as a sign of weakness. Churchill's observation on the Soviet lack of respect for what they perceive as military weakness was proven correct: witness the stand-off between US and Soviet tanks at Checkpoint Charlie on 27 October 1961, when the US refused to give in to Soviet attempts to restrict movement by the Western Allies in and out of Berlin.

In terms of the current Ukraine-Russia conflict, and the possibility of military confrontation, for Putin to attack a NATO state would be, at least in theory, to invite retaliation. However, since January 2025, there has been a 'wild card' in this calculation – Donald Trump, who has threatened that if NATO member states do not make their appropriate financial contribution to the Alliance, he would not defend them.[418] It remains to be seen exactly whether the new Trump administration in Washington will honour the promise made on behalf of all NATO members.[419] Despite these uncertainties, as suggested earlier, it is very unlikely that Putin would undertake such a move, although in October 2022, he did threaten to use nuclear weapons.[420] In early 2023, the stockpile of Russian nuclear weapons was estimated by the Federation of American Scientists' Nuclear Information Project as comprising 'approximately 4,489 nuclear warheads assigned for use by long-range strategic launchers and shorter-range tactical nuclear forces'. The same report gave figures for strategic warheads (1,674 deployed) and those in storage were estimated at around 1,000 strategic, and 1,816 'non-strategic' (ie. tactical) warheads.[421] There is, however, one key consideration that negates the importance of any nuclear arsenal: logically, if Putin were to launch a nuclear attack on Ukraine in order win the conflict and annex the strategically important territory that he wanted to claim for Russia, why would he risk turning this same territory into a nuclear wasteland, and losing it forever – or until the radioactive pollution has subsided sufficiently to allow human re-occupation of the polluted territory? It does not make sense. Furthermore, history has shown us that what Putin says and what he does generally bear little resemblance to each other. Moreover, despite their public proclamations, it equally likely that Putin's key political allies (including Foreign Minister Lavrov), and the top Russian military figures, would prevent him triggering a nuclear war. This leaves, however, the question of conventional warfare – such as is currently destroying Ukrainian infrastructure and killing its population.

The Russian Steamroller?

What people tend to overlook in the nuclear age, however, is the importance of conventional weaponry – whilst the *nuclear* threat can be largely discounted as predictable Pyrrhic sabre-rattling, that still leaves the vast Russian arsenal of conventional weaponry. As the war in Ukraine has demonstrated, conventional weapons are effective especially when supplemented by the widespread use of drones, and this largely negates the advantage that a large economy (Russia), has over a smaller economy (such as that of Ukraine). In view of the territorial objectives of Putin, conventional weaponry may prove even more useful than nuclear weapons.

It is undoubtedly true that many Western leaders are afraid of the military might of Russia, and this is perhaps what has dissuaded them from acting as they should have done in defence of world democracy. The irony is that, since their invasion of the Ukrainian Crimea, Luhansk and Donbas regions in March 2014, the Russians have shown that they are not as strong as their propaganda would have us believe, but they are a 'paper tiger'. This has become particularly obvious since February 2022, when Putin thought that he could take Kyiv within a matter of days (weeks at most), as the Ukrainian forces would collapse under the weight of the Russian 'steamroller'. In March 2022, an Irish analyst predicted that Ukraine would disintegrate within two weeks.[422] However, as has been seen, it was the Russians who have all but collapsed, losing some 77,000 military personnel killed between 24 February and 11 September 2022; in one day alone, they apparently lost around 700.[423] By January 2025, nearly three years into the war, the Russians had lost an estimated 800,000 dead, according to British military intelligence. By the start of the winter of that year, updates from Ukrainian intelligence gave Russian losses up to 1 November 2025 as 1,143,670 killed. By the same date, the Ukrainians also claimed to have destroyed 11, 316 tanks, 34,162 artillery systems, 428 aircraft and 346 helicopters.[424]

Added to this is the number of seriously wounded personnel up to September 2022 (estimated at 45,000)[425]. As an aside, any student of military history would find these figures strange, as in every conflict it is usual to find that the number of wounded generally far exceeds the number of dead (by this date, some 77,000 had been killed): to have 77,000 wounded and 45,000 dead would be more like the ratio that might have been expected, but even this would be considered extraordinarily high. Horrifyingly, there may be an explanation for this unusual ratio, as captured Russian soldiers have confirmed that if their wounded were unable to walk, they were 'finished off' by their officers – there are a number of reports of Russian officers 'despatching' their wounded on the battlefield.[426] One source claimed:

> In a harrowing account to Ukrainian journalist Volodymyr Zolkin, the young intelligence soldiers described how one lieutenant colonel asked a wounded comrade if he could walk. When the badly injured soldier replied that he could not, the high-ranking officer reportedly shot him – as well as several others – dead. Another soldier told Zolkin, who has reported about Russian prisoners for Open Media Ukraine, that officers have finished off their wounded.[427]

Added to the 'butcher's bill' of human misery, is, as of January 2025, the destruction of 4, 353 Russian MBTs (Main Battle Tanks) of various vintage;[428] in addition, Russia had lost 21,157 AFVs[429], 23,626 artillery systems, 1,299 multiple launch rocket systems, 1081 air defence systems, 26,645 UAVs[430],

38,444 vehicles and bowsers (unarmoured vehicles, such as trucks, jeeps etc) and fuel tankers, and 370 aircraft.[431] In addition, the Russians have lost numerous boats captured or destroyed – so much so that the Russian navy had been moved out of the range of Ukrainian air-surface and naval surface 'kamikaze' drones, which have proven highly effective – even taking out a submarine. This does not include the 117 tanks captured in working order by the Ukrainians in the first months of the Russian assault and turned against their former owners.[432]

However, since Putin launched his attack on Ukraine, a number of considerations have emerged that might make the balance of power seem considerably less weighted in Russian favour: briefly, they are a combination of material and psychological factors:

1. Extensive and deep-seated corruption within the Russian military, which means that supplies cannot always be given to new recruits. For example, Danielle Ong, writing in the *International Business Times*, claimed: 'that Russian soldiers were reportedly told to buy their own equipment, including a helmet, boots and combat vest: a serviceman would need to spend about a month's worth of pay on equipment'.[433] A Ukrainian media channel reported that some Russian soldiers stole footwear from Ukrainians
2. A second factor is the poor state of armaments with which they have been issued: one recent report by Reuters claimed that several draftees from the Donbas region of occupied Ukraine were issued with a Mosin rifle[434] 'which went out of production decades ago…Images shared on social media, that Reuters has not been able to verify independently, also showed Donbas fighters with Mosin rifles.'[435]
3. Despite the above, however, the single most important factor in explaining the poor Russian performance thus far, is the level of morale and lack of determination. The Russians by and large do not want to fight, as many consider the attack on Ukraine is wrong, and dangerous for the new recruits who they feel are being used simply as 'cannon fodder'. As reported recently: 'Russian conscripts have been filmed boarding buses to Ukraine 'drunk' as recruits go on vodka fuelled drinking sessions ahead of deployment to the frontline. A video reportedly recorded in

> the Russian enclave of Kaliningrad appears to show soldiers boarding Russian army buses boozed up and in the full knowledge that 'they are cannon fodder.'[436] Consequently, many desert at the first opportunity – either preferring captivity by the Ukrainian forces, or simply run away and hide somewhere; others try to cross the frontier to Kazakhstan or Georgia. There was a mass exodus of Russian males when Putin announced conscription 21 September 2022, and by the end of October, an estimated 370,000 people had fled abroad – around 200,000 to Kazakhstan, 66,000 to Georgia, Finland and Estonia, and around 12,000 to Mongolia.[437]

As the deputy director of the Transatlantic Defence and Security Programme at the Centre for European Policy Analysis (CEPA) observed: 'The Russian military is exhausted and low on morale; they've suffered enormous costs in terms of battlefield casualties and desertions with some estimates suggesting these could be as high as 80,000.' The situation has become so desperate for the Russian commanders that 'Russian forces have likely started deploying "barrier troops" or "blocking units" to deal with their own retreating soldiers who are unwilling to fight "due to low morale." These units threaten to shoot their own retreating soldiers in order to compel offensives.'[438]

Then there is the arrival of troops from the Democratic People's Republic of Korea (North Korea, NK), thought to number tens of thousands. Despite its size, the NK military was considered largely ineffective – a report in the *National Interest* suggested that the bulk of their equipment is 'outdated', such as their tank force which consists of the Soviet T-54 and T-62 variants (from 1954 and 1962 respectively). The same report claimed that the NK infantry are 'plagued by basic equipment shortages and...crippling malnutrition'.[439] Furthermore, the NK forces were generally considered too unreliable to ever be used outside North Korea, as the army in particular would be likely to suffer a very high rate of desertion should the force ever be launched in invasion of South Korea; it was felt that many North Korean military would take advantage of being outside the 'prison' to desert. Such estimates of their reliability were to prove accurate, as from the first batch of troops assigned to the Kursk front, a reported eighteen deserted to the Ukrainians. The deployment of North Korean forces in Russia came as a surprise to most military observers and was interpreted as a desperate move on the part of Putin.

All this is in stark contrast with the Ukrainian forces, who have the motivation to defend their homeland – including their villages and families, who may have an intimate knowledge of the terrain over which they are fighting, and since their counter-offensive in the north in September 2022 and their incursions into the Kursk region in August 2024, have seen a significant boost to their morale. In a report from early September 2022, Ukraine claimed that it had photographic evidence of 'high morale' amongst Ukrainian forces that were attacking the Kherson region. This was compared with the Russian forces that appear to be 'suffering from extremely low morale amid failures of military leadership'.[440]

Now is the time for the West to take active measures to topple Putin – not to invade Russia, but to foment revolution within the country. To date, the Ukrainians have suffered the Russian onslaught by themselves; it is time for the West to confront Putin's corrupt regime, and in doing so greatly increase the chances of a coup against him, led probably by some of the senior military figures who are seeing their authority and prestige drain away with each casualty, or possibly by a group of oligarchs who have paid a high financial price for their association with Putin. A third possibility is that there could be a 'palace coup' engineered by discontented politicians and members of Russia's secret service and intelligence forces – they have been publicly blamed by Putin for providing faulty intelligence that directly contributed to the heavy losses thus far.

Summary

This chapter brings us back to the central question of this book – could history have predicted the Russian war on Ukraine? In short, as suggested in the preface, the answer is undoubtedly 'yes'. The history of Russia (Imperial, Communist, or Nationalist) has demonstrated that there is only one direction of travel: the annexation (or control) of neighbouring states. It shows how, rather than presenting the opportunity of a new hope for relations with Russia, Vladimir Putin has simply followed the agenda set hundreds of years ago – to annex and absorb adjacent states and harness their assets to the benefit of Moscow. Where the annexation and absorption of territories is deemed not possible (e.g. Cuba), or undesirable (Afghanistan), then governments are established that are subservient to Moscow. These puppet regimes will do what they are told to do, and should their populations (or even the governments) object the subservient position in which they find themselves, then Moscow – geography allowing – does not hesitate to send in its armed forces as a reminder – as in Ukraine in 1917, Poland in 1919 (and again in 1939), Georgia in 1921, Berlin in 1953, Hungary in 1956, Czechoslovakia in 1968, Afghanistan in 1979, Tajikistan in 1992, Chechnya in 1994, and finally Ukraine again in 2014 and 2022.

NATO and the EU would do well to remember that from Putin's point of view, the re-absorption of Ukraine into the Russian Empire is essential: he began in 2014 with the seizure of Crimea, and the fomentation of instability in eastern Ukraine; he was then forced to pause for some seven years (regrouping, developing new tactics and weapons, and Covid), before he resumed the attacks in 2022. The West makes the mistake of assuming that it can trust Putin to keep his word – yet his breaking of the Minsk agreement (2015) shows that he cannot be trusted. All a ceasefire would do, would be to give him another period of grace to re-arm and reposition his forces, before renewing the onslaught. Putin can afford to wait: he has the training and experience of an FSB officer, and we saw how the KGB (the forerunner to the FSB) has always adopted the long-term view, even if things take a generation to come to fruition. Furthermore, Putin's opponents are democracies that re-elect every five years – all he has to do is wait, and a new president or prime minister will come along who may be more sympathetic to his cause, or open to 'persuasion'.

The lack of strong response from the West emboldened Putin to think that any further action would be only weakly opposed – if at all – and that he could continue his land grab with impunity. After sending his troops into Crimea, Putin justified this flagrant breach of international law on the grounds that he was protecting ethnic Russians from 'far-right' extremists. Once again, this is the sort of hyperbole that has been used by his predecessors as part of a 'smear' campaign (see Chapter 2: Covert Strategies – Discreditation) is a tactic employed by other administrations. Perhaps Putin will manufacture reasons for the seizure of the Baltic republics, citing the numbers of ethnic

Russians living in these states who have been 'persecuted': there are around 300,000 Russians living in Estonia, and in Latvia they comprise around 30 per cent of the population, and around 25 per cent in Lithuania. Within the old 'client states' of Eastern Europe, there are significant numbers of Russians: 31,000 in Bulgaria, 30,000 in Romania, and 20,000 in Hungary. All of whom could be used by Putin as an excuse for invasion and annexation of territory.

What the world in general, and Russia's neighbours in particular, have to remember is that the bear never sleeps – he may appear inactive, but is using this time to regroup and prepare for the next onslaught. This should be borne in mind in relation to the 'ceasefire' that US President Trump was trying to organise between Russian and Ukrainian forces in May 2025. Later that same year, Trump proposed a 28-point 'peace plan',[441] which appeared to give Putin everything he asked for, and which was obviously unacceptable to Ukraine. It included the provision that Putin could keep all Ukrainian territory that his troops held at the time of a ceasefire; an incredibly stupid clause, as if implemented, not only would it effectively reward Russian aggression, but it would also encourage Putin to escalate his attacks on Ukraine with a view to gaining as much ground as possible before the deadline. In addition, Kyiv would be obliged to cap the size of its military, and pledge never to join NATO. The talks to date show the dangers of involving Trump, who appears incredibly naive, probably believing that he is dealing with another 'businessman' who will honour any agreement (or 'deal' as Trump likes to call it) that has been made.

In return, Putin would promise not to invade again, and Ukrainian independence would be guaranteed by NATO under Article 5 of NATO's North Atlantic Treaty. Bearing in mind Putin's track record to date in terms of keeping his word, and what this book suggests is his ultimate objective, this first draft of Trump's 28-point plan must be 'dead in the water' even before it is discussed. As to NATO guaranteeing Ukraine's security through Article 5, this has been examined earlier, but it is worth re-examining to see exactly what it promises:

> The Parties agree that an armed attack against one or more of them in Europe or North America shall be considered an attack against them all and

> consequently they agree that, if such an armed attack occurs, each of them, in exercise of the right of individual or collective self-defence recognized by Article 51 of the Charter of the United Nations, will assist the Party or Parties so attacked by taking forthwith, individually and in concert with the other Parties, such action as it deems necessary, including the use of armed force, to restore and maintain the security of the North Atlantic area.[442]

It is hard to see why Putin is prepared to accept the defence of Ukraine underpinned by NATO, yet not that Ukraine join NATO. As both would (at least in theory) provide for NATO military backing, one is forced to ask why Putin appears to regard them as different concepts? The key to this apparent dichotomy lies in the specific wording of the Treaty obligations; the NATO website explains the semantics behind the language used:

> Article 5 applies only in case of an 'armed attack'. An obvious example would involve an invasion by one state of the territory of another state. This type of threat continues to be a serious concern, and constitutes a major focus of NATO's efforts to maintain and develop its capacity to defend all Allies... Events that lack an *international* element, such as purely domestic acts of terrorism, do not trigger Article 5 (though NATO Allies can and often do offer assistance in such cases).[443]

There are two key phrases, which undoubtedly explain Putin's stance, they are firstly, 'armed attack' being the 'invasion by one state of the territory of another'. Secondly, there is the caveat that article 5 is *not* triggered by an event that lacks an *international* element. As we have seen previously, Putin twists words to his advantage, and has done so with regards to Ukraine which he regards as part of Russia, and therefore precludes international involvement. If peace were based on the promises made under Article 5, then Putin would be still able to continue his destabilisation and subversion within Ukraine leading to internal revolution and/or the overthrow of the Kyiv government. As history has shown, Putin could use the anarchy he had created to provide the excuse for armed intervention It would *not* be an 'armed attack' on another state, but would be a cry for help (probably at the 'request' of a rebel group), designed to stabilise the situation, restore order, and protect civilian lives – especially of any ethnic Russians. Thus, he would have achieved his objective without the danger of NATO intervention: he would then be free to turn his attention to other former Russian-empire states. In essence, as has been explained earlier in the book, the Russians prefer the long-term approach, and would prefer that Ukraine were to fall into Moscow's hands as a result of internal chaos or civil war, rather than through the use overt force. This is not to say that force would not be used, as was apparent in 2022; but it is something that is probably the last page in his playbook.

Conversely, if Ukraine to become a fully-fledged member of NATO, then two major considerations would come into play: (1) such a state of anarchy would be unlikely to develop in a democracy in the first place, and (2) even if it were to happen, it would be neighbouring NATO states, rather than the Russians, that would be called on to supply peacekeeping forces. In other words, Putin would have no excuse for intervention.

At the time of going to press, the outcome of Trump's various attempts at peace are unclear. Whatever is ultimately agreed, Putin could simply wait and then try again later – probably after the inauguration of a different US president, who may choose not to drag NATO into a war in defence of Ukraine. It should also be remembered that, since the start of his presidency, Trump has consistently stated that he wishes to reduce the military and financial contribution to NATO, and he feels that European defence should be increasingly a matter for European nations to fund, organise and implement.[444] Bearing this in mind, there is a danger that any promised military defence of non-NATO Ukraine would be left to the European members of NATO, and given the political in-fighting and lack of unity, this would not bode well for Kyiv.

At best, it would keep Ukraine dependent on the USA for the foreseeable future.

What is certain, however, is that if Putin cannot get what he wants now, he will simply bide his time and acquire it at a later date. As the Russian author Leo Tolstoy once said: 'The two most powerful warriors are patience and time'.

Appendices

Appendix A: The Ten Objectives of The Communist Manifesto

1. Abolition of property in land and application of all rents of land to public purposes.
2. A heavy progressive or graduated income tax.
3. Abolition of all rights of inheritance.
4. Confiscation of the property of all emigrants and rebels.
5. Centralisation of credit in hands of the state by means of a national bank with state capital and exclusive monopoly.
6. Centralisation of the means of communication and transport in the hands of the state.
7. Extension of factories and instruments of production owned by the state; bringing into cultivation wastelands, and improvement of the soil in accordance with a common plan.
8. Equal liability of all to work. Establishment of industrial armies, especially for agriculture.
9. Combination of agriculture with manufacturing industries; abolition of distinction between town and country by more equable distribution of the Proletarians and Communists populace.
10. Free education for all children in public schools.

Appendix B: Countries Invaded/Occupied by the USSR (1917–1999)

- Ukrainian War of Independence (1917–1921)
- Polish War of Independence (1919–1921)
- Georgian War of Independence (1921–1924)
- Occupation of Xinjiang (1937)
- Border Incidents with Japan (1938–1939)
- The Attack on Finland (1939–1940)
- Occupation of Eastern Poland (1939–1941)
- Occupation of Bessarabia and Northern Bukovina (1940)
- Occupation of Iran (1941–1946)

- Occupation of Northern Norway (1944–1946)
- Occupation of Bulgaria (1944–1991)
- Occupation of Ukraine (1944–1991)
- Occupation of Hungary (1944–1991)
- Occupation of Germany (1944–1991)
- Occupation of Moldova (1944–1991)
- Third Invasion of Poland (1944–1991)
- Occupation of Transnistria (1944–1991)
- Occupation of Czechoslovakia (1944–1991)
- Occupation of Romania (1944–1991)
- Occupation of The Kuril Islands (1945)
- Occupation of Bornholm (Denmark) (1945–1946)
- Occupation of Austria (1945–1955)
- Occupation of Manchuria (China) (1945–1946)
- Involvement in The Korean War (1950–1953)
- Suppression of the Berlin Uprising (1953)
- Suppression of the Hungarian Uprising (1956)
- The Erection of the Iron Curtain and the Berlin Wall (1961)
- Suppression of the 'Czech Spring' Uprising (1968)
- Invasion of Afghanistan (1979–1921)
- Intervention in the Tajikistan Civil War (1992–1997)
- The First Chechen War (1994–1996)
- The Second Chechen War (1999–2000)
- The Second Invasion of Georgia (2008)
- The First Attack on Ukraine (Donbas and Crimea, 2014)
- The Second Attack on Ukraine ('Special Military Operation' 2022)

Appendix C: The 14 Galizische SS Freiwilligen Division

The division was organised as a type 44 Division: it had three infantry regiments, each comprising two infantry *abteilungen* (battalions). There was a third *abteilung* from each regiment: these were reorganised as the *14. SS Fusilier Battalion* (comprising four companies), and the *14 Feldersatz (Replacement) Battalion* (five companies). In line with the overall policy relating to volunteer units, the division received a change of name on 22 October 1943, to become the *14. Galizische SS Freiwilligen Infanterie Division*, and the infantry regiments (each with only two battalions) became the 29th, 30th, and 31st Freiwilligen Grenadier Regiments. The artillery regiment and all other units were numbered 14.

Appendix D

Sources for Maps

Map A: The Growth of Imperial Russia, 1547–1725
This map is reproduced from a file available on Wikimedia Commons. The original image (Growth_of_Russia_1547-1725.png, 636 × 365 px, 92 KB, PNG format) was created on 26 October 2012 and uploaded on 19 November 2014. The map can be accessed at: https://commons.wikimedia.org/wiki/File:Growth_of_Russia_1547-1725.png

Map B: Area Lost by Russia Following the Treaty of Brest-Litovsk (1918)
This map illustrates the territorial concessions imposed on Russia by the Treaty of Brest-Litovsk in March 1918. The file (Map_Treaty_of_Brest-Litovsk-en.jpg) is hosted on Wikimedia Commons and is available at: https://commons.wikimedia.org/wiki/File:Map_Treaty_of_Brest-Litovsk-en.jpg

Map C: The Soviet Ukraine (1922)
This map was created by Cristian Ionita of Edmaps.com. Permission and attribution inquiries may be directed to the author at: informations@edmaps.com.

Map D: The Russian Re-Invasion of Ukraine (2022)
This map and its associated animation were created by Viewsridge and are available through Wikimedia Commons. Attribution information is provided at: https://commons.wikimedia.org/w/index.php?title=File:2022_Russian_invasion_of_Ukraine.svg

Additional related files include 2022 Russian Invasion of Ukraine Animation F15 & F16.svg and the animated GIF version, both uploaded on 27 May 2022.

Permissions

Extracts from the following are reproduced with permission from the author/publisher:

Atzil, Boaz and Min Jung Kim, 'Buffer Zones and International Rivalry: Internal and External Geographic Separation and Mechanisms.' *International Affairs* Vol 99 (2) 2023.

Engel, David, *Facing a Holocaust: The Polish Government-in-Exile and the Jews, 1943–1945.* (Chapel Hill & London: The University of North Carolina Press, 1993).

Kramer, John M., 'Political Corruption in the USSR (Union of Soviet Socialist Republics)' *Western Political Quarterly,* Vol. 30 (2), June 1977, pp. 213–224.

Lucas, James, *War on the Eastern Front 1941-1945: The German Soldier in Russia* (Greenhill Books, London).

Matthews, Owen, 'Vladimir Putin's new plan for world domination.' *The Spectator* (22 February 2014).

Peter Rutland and Neil Shimmield, 'Putin's dangerous campaign to rehabilitate Stalin.' *The Washington Post* (13 June 2019).

Plokhy, Serhii, *Forgotten Bastards of the Eastern Front.* (London: Penguin Random House UK, 2020).

Service, Robert, *Lenin: A Biography* (London: Pan Books Ltd., 2010).

Service, Robert, *Blood on the Snow: The Russian Revolution 1914–1924* (Picador: London, 2023).

Simon Saradzhyan, 'When Does Vladimir Putin's Russia Send in Troops?' *Russia Matters* (7 August 2018).

Walker, Shaun and Andrew Roth, 'They took our clothes': Ukrainians returning to looted homes. *The Guardian* (11 April 2022).

The following maps are reproduced with permission from the author/publisher:

Ionita, Cristian (Edmaps.com) Map: The Soviet Ukraine (1922).

Endnotes and Sources

Preface

1. HRW, 'Ukraine: Executions, Torture During Russian Occupation.' *Human Rights Watch* (18 May 2022).
2. James S. Lucas, *War on the Eastern Front 1941–1945: The German Soldier in Russia* (London: BCA, 1979), p.55.
3. Erika Kinetz, 'Kill everyone!' Russian violence in Ukraine was strategic.' *Associated Press* (27 October 2022).
4. Laura Wamsley, 'Rape has reportedly become a weapon in Ukraine. Finding justice may be difficult.' (Washington: NPR); 30 April 2022.
5. Quoted in: Robert Service, *Lenin: A Biography*. (London: Pan Books, 2010), p.403.
6. Jeffrey Veidlinger, 'The Killing Fields of Ukraine.' *Tablet* (23 February 2022).
7. Veidlinger, 'The Killing Fields of Ukraine'.
8. Martin Latsis, *Red Terror* [Krasnyi Terror] 1918 no. 1, (Prague: Kazan, 1 November 1918, p.2.) Quoted in George Leggett (1981). *The Cheka: Lenin's Political Police. The All-Russian Extraordinary Commission for Combatting Counter-Revolution and Sabotage, December 1917 to February 1922.* (Oxford: Clarendon Press, 1981), p.114.
9. Veidlinger, 'The Killing Fields of Ukraine'.
10. Tim Snyder, 'Russia's Genocide Handbook: The Evidence of Atrocity and Intent Mounts', (translated from Russian propaganda article: 'What Should Russia Do with Ukraine?'), *Mgrublian Centre for Human Rights* (Claremont McKenna College), 14 April 2022.
11. Shaun Walker and Andrew Roth, "They took our clothes': Ukrainians returning to looted homes' *The Guardian* (11 April 2022).
12. Walker and Roth, *The Guardian* (11 April 2022).
13. Jorge Santayana, *The Life of Reason: Reason in Common Sense (New York: C. Scribner's & Sons,* 1905), p.284.
14. Sean McMeekin, *Stalin's War* (London & New York: Penguin Random House, 2021).
15. US Embassy, 'World War II Allies: US Lend-Lease to the Soviet Union, 1941–1945' *US Embassy & Consulates in Russia.*
16. Denis Havlat, 'Western Aid for the Soviet Union During World War II: Part 1' *The Journal of Slavic Military Studies,* Vol. 30 (2), 2017, pp. 290–320.
17. Begun in 2014 after the annexation of Crimea and completed in 2018.
18. (a) Anthony Blair, 'Russian Revolution: Adolf Putin' graffiti sprayed across Russian buildings as thousands protest President 'acting like Hitler' *The Sun* (25 February 2022)
    (b) Jesse Clark, "Hitler Vs Putin-Their Biggest Similarities and Differences" *Grunge,* (2 March 2022)

(c) Ryan Thomas, 'Is Putin Comparable to Hitler? Who's the Closest Historical Match for Vladimir Putin?' *Hubpages* (12 March, 2022)
(d) John Blake, 'Putin is making the same mistakes that doomed Hitler when he invaded the Soviet Union' *CNN* (2 April 2022).

19. Such as aluminium, asbestos, lime, lead, gypsum, iron ore, bauxite, gallium, boron, mica, potash, platinum, rare earths, pig iron, cadmium, arsenic, magnesium, phosphate, silicon, uranium, tellurium, vanadium, tungsten, cobalt, graphite, and copper.
20. Prior to 2022 Russia accounted for 31 per cent of the world's diamond production; 'Alrosa' the state-owned diamond company extracted around 90 per cent of Russian diamonds, worth US$4 billion in 2021 (Fátima Rodriguez, 'Russia: Importance of Diamond Industry', *Lupicino,* (19 December 2023).
21. For example, in 2021 Russia earned $110.2 billion from exports of crude oil, $468 billion from oil products, and $454.2 billion from natural gas – mostly supplied through the 'Nordstream 1' pipeline. See: Reuters, 'Russia's oil and gas revenue windfall' (21 January 2022).
22. BBC News, 'Nordstream 1: How Russia is cutting gas supplies to Europe.' *BBC* (29 September 2022).
23. Donald Trump was instated as president of the USA in January 2025. It remains to be seen what he will do in respect of the war, but as we move into 2026 things are not looking better for Ukraine.
24. Elena Salvoni, 'Why is Putin massing troops on the border of Finland? Military build-up similar to the prelude to Ukraine war sparks alarm in NATO' *Mailonline* (12 May 2025)
25. For Putin's 'Special Military Operation', President Alexander Lukashenko of Belarus allowed Russian forces to train on Belarusian territory, and from there to launch a major advance towards the Ukrainian capital Kyiv.
26. Piece-by-piece destruction: 'one small slice at a time'.
27. AP, 'Putin warns again that Russia is ready to use nuclear weapons if its sovereignty is threatened.' *Associated Press* (13 March 2024).
28. Yevgeny Yevtushenko, 'Foreword' in Brian Moynahan, *The Russian Century: A History of the last Hundred Years* (London: Pimlico, 1994), p.vii.

Chapter 1: Imperial Russia – The Schizophrenic State

29. Ivan L. Rudnytsky, 'The Soviet Ukraine in Historical Perspective.' *Canadian Slavonic papers/Revue Canadienne des Slavists,* Vol. 14 (2), 1972, pp. 235–236.
30. Boaz Atzil and Min Jung Kim, 'Buffer Zones and International Rivalry: Internal and External Geographic Separation and Mechanisms.' *International Affairs* Vol 99 (2) 2023. pp. 645–665.
31. Prior to 2022, Sweden and Finland were staunchly neutral, however, when they saw what had happened to Ukraine, they were scared into joining NATO themselves. The outcome is exactly what Putin did *not* want, as Finland has a 830-mile-long common land border with Russia, and the Swedish Navy and Air Force dominate the Baltic – effectively 'bottling-up' Russian naval forces based in St Petersburg and Kaliningrad.
32. The Finns declared war on Russia on 25 June 1941, in what they called the 'Continuation War' – they regarded it as 'unfinished business' – revenge for the unprovoked Russian assault on Finland during the winter of 1939–1940.

33. Quoted in: Richard Pipes (ed.), *The Unknown Lenin: From the Secret Archives* (New Haven: Yale University Press, 1996), p.90.
34. Petrograd was declared the capital of Russia in 1712, and remained so until the new Bolshevik government under Lenin moved it back to Moscow in March 1918, in fear of the city being taken by advancing German troops.
35. Tim Blanning, *Frederick the Great: King of Prussia* (London: Random House, 2016), p.688.
36. Jerzy Zukowski and Hubert Zawadzki, *A Concise History of Poland* (Cambridge: CUP, 2001), p.84.
37. Alexander Hill, 'Deep-rooted Russian fear of the West has fuelled Putin's invasion of Ukraine.' *The Conversation* (3 March 2022).
38. Stalin sent thousands of Soviet military personnel captured during the war to the Gulags on their release from German captivity, simply because they had come into contact with 'Western' ideas. The best account of the horrors inflicted on returned Soviet POWs, is to be found in Nikolai Tolstoy, *Victims of Yalta* (London: Corgi Books, 1979).
39. Hill (3 March 2022).
40. Richard M. Connaughton, *Rising Sun and Tumbling Bear: Russia's War with Japan* (London: Orion Publishing Company, 2004), pp. 28-30.
41. Barbara W. Tuchman, *The Guns of August* (New York: Bantam Books., Inc, 1976), p.75.
42. Luís Pásara, "El Guano y la Penetración Inglesa", in Jorge Basadre (ed.), *Reflexiones en Torno a la Guerra de 1879* (Lima: Centro de Investigación y Capacitación, 1979), p.36. [Original Spanish: *'Un país no gana una guerra solo cuando está mejor armado; primero es indispensible que sea un país.'*]. This, according to Pásara, was the reason for the defeat of the Bolivian-Peruvian alliance during the War of the Pacific (1879-1884). Peru was thought by most contemporary military observers to have the most powerful military in South America, yet was socio-politically fractured and disunited – leading to an overall lack of national purpose and effort – and subsequently the alliance was decisively defeated by Chile.
43. Daron Acemoglu and James A. Robinson, *Why Nations Fail: The Origins of Power, Prosperity, and Poverty* (London: Profile Books, 2012), p.86.
44. Robert B. Asprey, *The German High Command at War: Hindenburg and Ludendorff and the First World War* (London: Warner Books, 1994), p.80.
45. Asprey, p.80.
46. Max Hastings, *Catastrophe: Europe Goes to War 1914* (London: William Collins, 2014), pp. 275–285.
47. Quoted in: Geoffrey Jukes, *Carpathian Disaster: Death of an Army.* (London: Pan/Ballantine, 1973), p.87.
48. Andrew Knighton, 'The Great Retreat: Germany Captured 1 million Russians in 1915.' *War History Online* (30 May 2018); https://www.warhistoryonline.com/world-war-i/the-great-retreat-germanys-gorlice-tarnow.html
49. Robert Service, *Blood on the Snow: The Russian Revolution 1914–1924* (Picador: London), p.150.
50. Norman Stone, *The Eastern Front 1914–1917* (Penguin Books: London,1975), p.20.
51. Stone, p.21.
52. Another example of the Russian paranoia identified earlier.
53. Such as Prince Georgy Yevgenyevich, who had been born in Dresden, Germany.

54. David Lloyd George, *War Memoirs of David Lloyd George, Volume 1.* (London: Odhams Press, 1938), p.261.
55. Dominic Lieven, *Nicholas II: Emperor of All the Russias* (London: BCA, 1994), p.236.
56. Paul Kennedy, *The Rise and Fall of The Great Powers: Economic Change and Military Conflict from 1500 to 2000.* (London: Fontana Paperbacks, 1990), p.307.
57. Lloyd George, p.842.
58. Michael T. Florinsky, 'The Russian Mobilization of 1914', *Political Science Quarterly,* Vol. 42 (2), 1927, pp. 203–227.
59. Nicholas Golovin, 'The Russian War Plan of 1914', *The Slavonic and East European Review,* Vol. 14 (42), 1936, pp. 564-584; some sources give higher estimates, such as Strachan, who claims that in 1914, Russia mobilised 6.5 million men, and another 5 million the year after (Hew Strachan, *The First World War* (London: Simon & Schuster UK Ltd., 2003), p.140.
60. John Bushnell, 'Russian Peasants and Soldiers during World War I: Home and Front Interacting,' (Guest Editor's Introduction), *Russian Studies in History,* Vol. 56 (2), 2017, p.65.
61. Kennedy, p.302.
62. Service, *Blood on the Snow,* p.107.
63. Stone, p.295.
64. David Lloyd George, 'PROVISIONAL GOVERNMENT'. House of Commons Debate (HC Deb), *Hansard* (19 March 1917), Vol. 91 (c.1536).
65. William Philpott, *Bloody Victory: The Sacrifice of the Somme.* (London: Abacus, 2009), p.495.
66. Hart, Peter, *The Great War 1914-1918* (London: Profile Books Ltd., 2014), p.300.
67. Robert Outhwaite, 'KERENSKY GOVERNMENT'. House of Commons Debate (HC Deb), *Hansard* (12 November 1917), Vol. 99, cc 9-11 (c.9).
68. Outhwaite, 'KERENSKY GOVERNMENT'. (HC Deb), *Hansard* (12 November 1917), c.10.
69. Hart, p.30.
70. Nikolay Pashin, 'Did Allied Assistance make a difference for Russia in World War I?' *Russia Beyond* (10 November 2018).
71. Hew Strachan, p.141.
72. Lyn Macdonald, *1915 The Death of Innocence* (London: Headline Book Publishing, 1993), p.60.
73. Strachan, p.142.
74. Ambassador David R. Francis to Secretary of State Robert Lansing, (No. 1056), File no. 861.00/272. Papers Relating to the Foreign Relations of the United States, 1918, Russia, Volume 1 (25 February 1917). Just under one month later he was writing that 'Revolutionists have absolute control in Petrograd' and that the Duma [Russian parliament] had 'refused to obey the Emperor's order of adjournment.' This should have served as a warning but did not.
75. Ambassador David R. Francis to Secretary of State Robert Lansing, (No. 1753), File no. 861.00/520. Papers Relating to the Foreign Relations of the United States, 1918, Russia, Volume 1 (15 September 1917).
76. Joseph King, "BRITISH AMBASSADOR (PETROGRAD)." House of Commons Debate (HC Deb), *Hansard,* (12 November 1917), vol.99 (c. 99).

77. Arthur Balfour, "RUSSIA", House of Commons Debate (HC Deb), *Hansard* (26 November 1917), Vol. 99, c. 1614 (c.1614).
78. Quoted in: John Reed, *Ten Days that Shook the World* (London: Penguin Classics, 2007), p.60.
79. Quoted in: John Terraine, *Mons: The Retreat to Victory* (London: B.T. Batsford, 1960), p.182.
80. Service, Robert, *Lenin*, p.177.
81. Acemoglu and Robinson, p.389.
82. Service, *Lenin*, p.352.
83. Charles P. Vincent, *The Politics of Hunger: the Allied Blockade of Germany, 1915–1919.* (Athens, Ohio: Ohio University Press, 1986), p.141.
84. Quoted in: Service, *Lenin*, p.403.
85. Antony Beevor, *Russia: Revolution and Civil War 1917-1921* (London: Weidenfeld & Nicholson, 2022)
86. Robert Cecil, 'BRITISH SUBJECTS IMPRISONED', House of Commons Debate (HC Deb) *Hansard*, Vol. 110 (31 October 1918), c.1753.
87. A derogatory term, used to mean someone who is mean or 'tight-fisted': it was applied to most landowner farmers, especially those considered sufficiently 'wealthy' to employ others to work the land.
88. Nicolas Werth, 'Dekulakisation as Mass Violence', *Mass Violence and Resistance* (23 September 2011).
89. Yuri Shapoval and Marta D. Olynyk, 'The Holodomor: A Prologue to Repressions and Terror in Soviet Ukraine.' *Harvard Ukrainian Studies*, Vol. 30 (1), 2008, p.101.
90. Gill Bennett, 'What's the Context? 20 December 1919: Formation of the Cheka, the first Soviet Security and Intelligence agency.' *History of Government* (20 December 2017).
91. The 'All Russian Extraordinary Committee to Combat Counter Revolution and Sabotage'.
92. Beevor, *Russia: Revolution and Civil War*, p. 136
93. Jennifer Llewellyn, Michael McConnell, and Steve Thompson, 'The Red Terror' *Alpha History* (5 March, 2022).
94. 'Novaia zhizn', "Executions Continue" *Novaia zhizn*, No. 71 (19 April 1918), p. 3. Taken from the translation into English and published in James Bunyan and Harold H. Fisher (eds.), *Bolshevik Revolution, 1917-1918; Documents and Materials* (Stanford: Stanford University Press, 1934), p.577.
95. Sergey P. Melgunov, *'Red Terror' in Russia* (London and Toronto: J.M. Dent & Sons, 1925), p.4.
96. Quoted in: Victor Sebestyen, *Lenin the Dictator: An Intimate Portrait* (London: Weidenfeld & Nicholson, 2017), p.348.
97. Melgunov, p.178.
98. Leggett George, *The Cheka: Lenin's Political Police. The All–Russian Extraordinary Commission for Combating Counter–Revolution and Sabotage, December 1917 to February 1922.* (Oxford: Clarendon Press, 1981), pp.197-198.
99. Members of the Socialist Revolutionary Party (SR) were probably considered more dangerous by the Bolsheviks than were the representatives of the Duma or even the Czar's military. Prior to the revolution, the SR had acrimoniously split with the Bolsheviks over ideology; the SR drew most of its support from rural areas, and their

leadership presented an ideological challenge to Lenin – who in his role as self-appointed dictator, brooked no opposition.

100. Anna Reid, *A Nasty Little War: The West's Fight to Reverse the Russian Revolution.* (London: John Murray Press, 2023), p.55.
101. Quoted in: Victor Sebestyen, *Lenin the Dictator: An Intimate Portrait.* (London: Weidenfeld & Nicholson, 2017), pp. 417-418.
102. Mikhail Khvostov, *The Russian Civil War (1): The Red Army,* (Oxford: Osprey Publishing, 1996), p.3.
103. Phoebus Athanassiou, *Armies in Southern Russia, 1918-19,* p. 22 (Oxford: Osprey Publishing Ltd., 2021).
104. Athanassiou, p.4.
105. Reid, p.31.
106. Reid (2004).
107. Cecil Malone, 'UKRAINE', House of Commons Debate (HC Deb), *Hansard,* Vol. 113 (5 March 1919) c.382.
108. Cecil Harmsworth, 'UKRAINE', (HC Deb), *Hansard,* Vol. 113 (5 March 1919) c.382.
109. Andrew Bonar Law, 'ALLIED EXPEDITIONS', House of Commons Debate (HC Deb) *Hansard,* Vol. 110 (29 October 1918), c.1254.
110. Peter Kenez, *Red Advance, White Defeat: Civil War in South Russia 1919-1920.* (Washington, DC: New Academia Publishing, 2004), pp. 20–23.
111. Frederick E. Guest, 'GENERAL DENIKIN (AIR SERVICE)', House of Commons Written Answers to Questions, *Hansard,* Vol.122 (2 March 1921), c.57w.
112. This had formed part of the old Austro-Hungarian Empire, which had been dissolved on 16t October 1918. Geographically it was broadly located in Southern Poland, and Western Ukraine, and was claimed by both countries.
113. Winston S. Churchill, 'GALICIAN TROOPS', House of Commons Debate (HC Deb) *Hansard,* Vol. 122 (2 December 1919), cc.186-187.
114. Mikhail Khvostov, *The Russian Civil War (2): White Armies* (Oxford: Osprey Publishing Ltd., 1997), pp.13–17.
115. Robert Gellately, *Lenin, Stalin, and Hitler: The Age of Social Catastrophe.* (New York: Knopf Doubleday Publishing Group, 2008), p.7.
116. Khvostov, *The Russian Civil War (2),* pp.11–12.
117. Geoffrey Best, *Churchill and War. Bloomsbury Academic* (London: Bloomsbury Academic, 2005).
118. Charlotte Alston, 'British Journalism and the Campaign for Intervention in the Russian Civil War, 1918–20'. *Revolutionary Russia.* Vol. 20 (1), 2007, pp.35–49.
119. Damien Wright, *Churchill's Secret War with Lenin: British and Commonwealth Military Intervention in the Russian Civil War, 1918–1920.* (Warwick: Helion & Company, 2017), p.302.
120. Ian C.D. Moffat, 'Forgotten Battlefields – Canadians in Siberia 1918-1919.' *Canadian Military Journal.*
121. The best translation of this title is 'fellowship'.
122. David Bullock, *The Czech Legion 1914–1920* (Oxford: Osprey Publishing Ltd., 2009), p.3.
123. Eric Toussaint, 'Russia: Origin and Consequences of the debt repudiation of February 10, 1918', *Committee for the Abolition of Illegitimate Debt (CADTM),* (8 February 2024).

124. Winston S. Churchill, 'MIDDLE EAST', House of Commons Debate (HC Deb) *Hansard*, Vol 460 (26 January 1949) c.948.

Chapter 2: Communist Russia -The Subversive State

125. A graphic account of the murders is provided by Lieven, p.244.
126. Joseph A. Weydemeyer, 'The Dictatorship of the Proletariat' *Turn-Zeitung*, New York (1 January 1852).
127. Hal Draper, *The Dictatorship of the Proletariat from Marx to Lenin* (New York: Monthly Review Press, 1987).
128. Foreign military intelligence agency of the Armed Forces of the Russian Federation.
129. Viktor Suvorov, *The Chief Culprit: Stalin's Grand Design to Start World War II* (Annapolis, Maryland: Naval Institute Press, 2013), p.2.
130. Suvorov, p.6.
131. Harold Fisher, *The Communist Revolution: An Outline of Strategy and Tactics*, (California: Stanford University Press, 1955), p.13.
132. 'COMINTERN Communist International' /Third International. GlobalSecurity.org; http://www.globalsecurity.org./ military/world/int/comintern.html
133. Suvorov, p.6.
134. 'Peaceful coexistence' was a term coined by Soviet Premier Nikita Khrushchev in 1955 in an attempt to allay Western fears over Soviet intentions towards the rest of the world.
135. For example: Albania, Bosnia and Herzegovina, Bulgaria, Croatia, Czechoslovakia, Estonia, Hungary, Latvia, Lithuania, Macedonia, Montenegro, Poland, Romania, Serbia, Slovenia, and Ukraine.
136. Ronald Reagan. Address to the UK Parliament, 8 June 1982.
137. Winston S. Churchill 'The Sinews of Peace'. Speech given at Westminster College, Fulton, Missouri, 5 March 1946.
138. Paul Ratner, '39 Years Ago, a KGB Defector Chillingly Predicted Modern America", *The International Chronicles* (24 April 2024).
139. Winston S. Churchill, 'The Sinews of Peace'.
140. Ronald Reagan: address to the National Association of Evangelicals, Orlando, Florida, (8 March 1983).
141. Stephen E. Ambrose, *Rise to Globalism: American Foreign Policy Since 1938 (3rd Edition).* (Harmondsworth, Middlesex: Penguin Books Ltd., 1984), p.123.
142. The tactic of eroding an opponent's economic-political-military power incrementally: one small piece at a time, so as not to be too obvious and attract countermeasures.
143. Marcus Samuel, 'RUSSIA (BROADCASTS)'. House of Commons Debate (HC Deb), *Hansard*, vol 321 cc. 3–5 (1 March 1937) col 4.
144. Anthony Eden, 'RUSSIA (BROADCASTS)'. House of Commons Debate (HC Deb), *Hansard*, vol 321 cc. 3–5 (1st March 1937) col 4.
145. Zhores A. Medvedev, 'Two decades of dissidence', *The New Scientist*, Vol. 72 (1025), (2 November 1976) pp.264–266.
146. HRW, 'Russia: with War, Censorship Reaches New Heights.' *Human Rights Watch* (28 February 2022).
147. The Constitution of the Russian Federation, Chapter 2 (Article 29); www.constitution.ru/en/1000300-03

148. It is interesting to note that the current UK Labour government (elected July 2024) uses a similar tactic when trying to discredit its opponents, by labelling them 'far right'.
149. Winston Churchill, 'Europe Unite: Speeches 1947 and 1948' (London, Cassell, 1950).
150. Surorov, p.xi.
151. This is a lesson that the current UK Labour government of Keir Starmer would do well to learn.
152. Paul Kirby, 'Giorgia Meloni: Italy's far-right wins election and vows to govern for all' BBC News (26 September 2022).
153. Mark Lowen, 'Georgia Meloni: Far-right leader poised to run Italy' *BBC News* (26 September 2022).
154. Roberto Saviano, 'Georgia Meloni is a danger to Italy and the rest of Europe.' *The Guardian* (24 September, 2022)
155. Katy Watson, 'Brazil election: a moment in history as Lula returns' *BBC News* (31 October 2022).
156. Committee on un-American Activities (1951) 'Communist Tactics Among Veterans' Groups (testimony of John T. Pace).' *Hearing before the Committee on Un-American Activities, House of Representatives Eighty-second Congress* (first session. July 13), p.1948 (US Government Documents, Boston Public Library, Additional Collections).
157. Christopher Andrew, 'The Threat of Subversion' *MI5 Security Service.*
158. Owen Matthews, 'Vladimir Putin's new plan for world domination' *The Spectator* (22 February 2014).
159. Russia carried out its first nuclear test on 29 August 1949 – despite the fact that it had been secretly developing nuclear weapons since 1943.
160. The History of CND; https://cnduk.org/who/the-history-of-cnd
161. Toby Helm,' Labour left breaks with Jeremy Corbyn over sending weapons to Ukraine.' *The Guardian* (26 February 2023).
162. Dan Falvey, 'Putin apologist' Corbyn desperately defends Russia record after attacking NATO for war.' *Express* (10 March 2022).
163. John Pilger, *Hidden Agendas* (Vintage/Random House: London, 1999), p.3.
164. Pilger, *Hidden Agendas*, p.23.
165. For example, the Soviet invasions and/or occupation of: Poland (1939), Finland (1939–1940), The Baltic States (1940–1991), Bessarabia (1941–1991), East Germany (1945–1991), Hungary (1945–1991), Czechoslovakia (1945–1991), Afghanistan (1979–1989), Transnistria (1992–present day), and Abkhazia and South Ossetia (August–October 2008)
166. Pilger, *Hidden Agendas*, p.29.
167. John Pilger, 'In Ukraine, the US is dragging us towards war with Russia.' *The Guardian* (13 May 2014).
168. Freddy Mayhew, 'Journalist John Pilger says ex-Russian spy poisoning case is a "carefully constructed drama in which the media plays a role".' *Press Gazette* (20 March 2018).
169. John Fisher, *Burgess and Maclean: A New Look at the Foreign Office Spies* (London: Robert Hale Ltd., 1977).
170. Larry Holzworth, 'This Spy Ring Betrayed the US and British to the Soviet Intelligence.' *History Collection: Cold War* (15 April 2021).
171. Steve Vogel, *Betrayal in Berlin: George Blake, the Berlin Tunnel, and the Greatest Conspiracy of the Cold War.* (London: John Murray, 2019).

172. Barry Strauss, 'Pre-emptive Strikes and Preventive Wars: A Historian's Perspective." *Strategika,* Hoover Institution, Stanford University (29 August 2017)
173. Suvorov, *The Chief Culprit: Stalin's Grand Design to Start World War II.* This book is fascinating reading for anyone who has an interest in the start of the Second World War, Nazi-Soviet relationships, and the rearmament programmes of the mid-to-late 1930s.
174. Alexander Velez-Green, 'Russian Strategists Debate Pre-emption as Defense Against NATO Surprise Attack.' *Russia Matters,* (Cambridge, Massachusetts: Harvard Kennedy School, Belfer Center for Science and International Affairs (14 March 2018).
175. Charter of the United Nations; Chapter VII – Action with respect to Threats to the Peace, Breaches of Peace, and Acts of Aggression (Article 51); https://legal.un.org/repertory/art.51.shtml
176. The North Atlantic Treaty, Washington D.C. – 4 April 1949; https://www.nato.int/cps/en/natolive/official_texts_17120
177. Robert Edwards, *White Death: Russia's War on Finland 1939-1940* (London: Weidenfeld & Nicholson, 2006), p.105.
178. Edwards, p.106.
179. Edwards, p.107.
180. Snejana Farberov, 'Russia plans "false flag" attack on Kherson dam ahead of battle for region: report.' *New York Post,* (20 October 2022).
181. Paul Adams, 'Ukraine Dam: Floods devastate tracts of rich farmland', *BBC News* (8 June 2023).
182. Max Hastings, *Chastise: The Dam Buster's Story 1943* (London: William Collins, 2019), p.38. In view of the current assertion that the Russians blew up the dam by explosives placed underground in the centre of the dam, it is interesting to note that the British team led by Barnes Wallis, had studied the 'physics of explosions, and especially by the scope for harnessing the power of water, and indeed of earth, dramatically to increase the impact of underwater or underground explosions.' (p.38).
183. Lidia Kelly, 'Evidence suggests Russia blew Kakhovka dam in Ukraine: NYT.' *Reuters* (18 June 2023).
184. Julian Borger and Peter Beaumont, 'Russia steps up Ukraine "dirty bomb" claim in letter to the United Nations', *The Guardian* (25 October 2022).
185. Hamish de Bretton-Gordon, 'Putin's Wild Claims of a Dirty Bomb Show Just How Badly his Army is Faring.' *The Guardian* (25 October 2022).
186. *Guardian staff,* 'UN nuclear inspectors shut down Russian "dirty bomb" claim against Ukraine' *The Guardian* (4 November 2022).
187. *Guardian staff,* 'UN nuclear inspectors shut down Russian "dirty bomb" claim against Ukraine'.
188. Adolf Hitler, closing speech at the NSDAP Conference in Nuremberg , 12 September 1938.
189. Klaus Friedrich, 'Uncomfortable Parallels: Hitler and Putin: Artfully Mixing the toxic spirit of national and personal humiliation.' *The Globalist* (21 March 2015).
190. Jane Clinton, 'Why did Russia annex Crimea? What happened when Putin invaded in 2014 and how Nato reacted to annexation.' *Inews* (29 January 2022).
191. UN Office of Legal Affairs. Article 2 (4), p.22; https://legal.un.org/repertory/art2/english/rep_supp7/vol.1/art2/4.pdf

192. Charter of the United Nations, Article 51, p. 22; https://legal.un.org/repertory/art2/english/rep_supp7_vol1_art2_4.pdf
193. SBS News, 'Putin Announces "Special Military Operation in Ukraine"' *Special Broadcasting Service* (24 February 2022).
194. Zach Cheung, 'Protecting' Ethnic Russians by Expanding the Definition of 'Self-Defence' *McGill Journal of Political Studies* (19 May 2022).
195. BBC News: 'Kazakhstan: Why are there riots and why are Russian troops there?' *BBC* (10 January 2022).
196. The use of the word 'terrorists' is interesting, as it suggests an excuse for armed intervention that is both understandable and acceptable to most nations. The Russians always use the word 'terrorist' to describe any anti-Soviet/Russian resistance.
197. Ali Shoaib, 'Blinken issues warning to Kazakhstan. "Once Russians are in your house, it's sometimes very difficult to get them to leave."' *Business Insider* (8 January 2022).
198. Alix Culbertson, 'Ukraine crisis: Putin says military drills "purely defensive" and "not a threat" as Western leaders warn invasion imminent.' *Sky News* (18 February 2022).
199. Sergey Lavrov, 'West was covering up crimes of Kiev regime that led to Ukraine's tragedy' *Military Operation in Ukraine, TASS* (25 February 2022).
200. Gerald Reitlinger, *The SS: Alibi of a Nation 1922–1945* (New York: The Viking Press Inc., 1957).
201. An excellent example of this strategy is the speech made by Soviet Premier Nikita Donetsk to the 20th Party Congress of the Communist Party of the USSR, on 25 February 1956, (three years after the death of Stalin). In this speech he denounced Stalin as a 'despot', and accused him of murder, genocide, and betraying both the USSR and the Communist Party. The speech was designed to acknowledge the Stalin-era wrongs whilst showing that the *current* government was not responsible.
202. 54[2] 46'20" N/31[3]47'24" E
203. David Engel, *Facing a Holocaust: The Polish Government-in-Exile and the Jews, 1943–1945.* (Chapel Hill & London: The University of North Carolina Press, 1993), p.71.
204. Engel, p.71.
205. Benjamin B. Fischer, 'The Katyn Controversy: Stalin's Killing Field'. *Studies in Intelligence* (Winter, 1999–2000). Center for the Study of Intelligence.
206. Service, *Stalin*, p.471.
207. Service, *Stalin*, p.471.
208. Timenote, 'Katyn Massacre: Russian Communists Authorize Order No. 394/5 Allowing NKVD to kill 22,000 Polish Army Officers.' *Timenote* (17 October 2022).
209. Quoted in Engel, p.71.
210. Joseph Goebbels, *The Goebbels Diaries (1942–1943).* (New York: Doubleday & Company, 1948).
211. George Sandford, *Katyn and the Soviet Massacre of 1940: Truth, Justice And Memory* (London and New York: Routledge, 2005).
212. Steven J. Zaloga, *The Polish Army, 1939-1945* (London: Osprey Publishing Ltd., 1982), p.17.
213. Rob Hopmans, 'Russian Brutality: Massacres by Russian Soldiers During WW2.' *WW2Gravestone* (30 April 2018).
214. Eugenjusz A. Komorowski, *Night Never Ending* (Washington D.C.: H. Regnery Publishing, 1974).

215. Quoted in: Serhi Plokhy, *Forgotten Bastards of the Eastern Front.* (London: Penguin Random House UK, 2020), p.209.
216. Susan Butler (ed.), *Dear Mr Stalin: The Complete Correspondence of Franklin D. Roosevelt and Josef V. Stalin* (Yale University Press: New Haven & London, 2005), p.184.

Chapter 3: Relations with Neighbours

217. Service, *Lenin*, p.4.
218. Service, *Lenin*, p.4.
219. Jukes, p.57.
220. Rudolph J. Rummel, *Lethal Politics: Soviet Genocide and Mass Murder Since 1917.* (Piscataway, NJ: Transaction Publishers, 1990), p.55.
221. Service, *Stalin*, p.4.
222. Service, *Stalin*, p.9.
223. Joseph Stalin: 'Speech at Celebration Meeting of the Moscow Soviet of Working People's Deputies and Moscow Party and Public Organisation.' *Twenty-Fifth Anniversary of the October Revolution* (6 November 1942).
224. Edwards, p.29.
225. Anthony Eden, 'RUSSIA (EXECUTIONS)'. House of Commons Debate (HC Deb), *Hansard,* Vol. 296 c. 1340 (20 December 1934), col. 1340.
226. Palash R. Ghosh, "How Many People Did Joseph Stalin Kill?" *International Business Times* (13 May 2013).
227. Iosef G. Dyadkin, *Unnatural Deaths in the USSR* (London: Routledge, 1983).
228. Norman Davies, *Europe at War 1939-1945: No Simple Victory* (London: Pan Books Ltd., 2006).
229. Augustinas Zemaitis, 'The Occupation of Latvia (1940-1990)' *World War 2 and Later in Latvia* (2004).
230. Josef Stalin, 'On the Death of Lenin" (30 January 1924). Speech delivered at Second All-Union Congress of Soviets, Moscow (26 January–2 February 1924). Printed in Pravda 30 January 1924.
231. Roger Manvell and Heinrich Fraenkel, *Hitler: The Man and The Myth.* (London: Granada Publishing Ltd., 1978), p.13. Also: Michael Burleigh, *The Third Reich: A New History* (London: Pan Macmillan Ltd., 2000).
232. Robert Edwards, *White Death: Russia's War on Finland 1939–1940.* (London: Weidenfeld & Nicholson, 2006).
233. Valters Nollendorfs and Uldis Neiburgs, 'Soviet Mass Deportations from Latvia', *The Gulag Expedition* (2006).
234. Anne Applebaum, *Iron Curtain: The Crushing of Eastern Europe* (London: Penguin Books Ltd., 2013), p.136.
235. Ineta Ziemele, *State Continuity and Nationality: The Baltic States and Russia: Past, Present and Future as Defined by International Law.* (Leiden: Martinus Nijhoff Publishers, 2005), p.25.
236. Lester H. Brune (ed.), *The Korean War: Handbook of the Literature and Research* (Westport, Connecticut: Greenwood Press, 1996), p.25.
237. Timothy Jones, 'Berlin Marks East German Uprising of 1953.' *Deutsche Welle* (17 June 2017).
238. Vogel, pp. 85–95.

239. Harold Macmillan, *The Macmillan Diaries (Vol II- Prime Minister and After 1957–1966)* (ed. Peter Catterall) (London: Pam Macmillan, 2011), pp. 199-200.
240. Thomas Powers, *The Man Who Kept the Secrets: Richard Helms and the CIA.* (New York: Alfred A. Knopf, 1981), p.130.
241. Khrushchev, Nikita S., *Khrushchev Remembers (Vol. 1)* (Harmondsworth: Penguin Books Ltd., 1971), p.523.
242. Winston Churchill, Speech given at Westminster College, Fulton, Missouri (5 March 1946).
243. Khrushchev, p.523.
244. Max Hastings, *Abyss: the Cuban Missile Crisis 1962.* (London: William Collins, 2022), p.141
245. Khrushchev, p.525.
246. Khrushchev, p.528.
247. NATO designation SS-17 Sadler.
248. The brutal Soviet repression led to 10-15 deaths and over 100 wounded in East Berlin; repression in Hungary was even worse, leading to around 2,500 deaths and over 2,000 fled across the border into Austria.
249. Sergey Radchenko, 'Why Were the Russians in Vietnam?' *New York Times* (27 March 2018).
250. Rakesh Krishna Simha, 'Vietnam War: The critical role of Russian weapons' *Russia Beyond (Rossiyskaya Gazeta)* (30 April 2015).
251. Ben Fowkes, *Eastern Europe 1945–1969: from Stalinism to Stagnation* (London: Longman, 2000), pp. 64–85.
252. Rob Cameron, 'Soviet 1968 invasion: Czechs still feel Cold War shivers.' *BBC News* (21 August 2018).
253. Ruth Fraňková, "Historians Pin Down Number of 1968 Invasion Victims." *Radio Praha: English* (18 August 2017).
254. The U.S Helsinki Watch Committee was founded in 1979 to promote domestic and international compliance with the human rights provisions of the 1975 Helsinki Accord.
255. Jeri Laker and Barnett Rubin, 'Tears, Blood and Cries – Human Rights in Afghanistan Since the Invasion, 1979–1984.' *A Helsinki Watch Report* (New York and Washington: Helsinki Watch Committee, December 1984), p.1.
256. Laker and Rubin, p.4.
257. Amongst the first to declare their independence from Russia were Estonia (16 November 1988), Latvia (4 May 1990), and Lithuania (18 May 1991).
258. Katie Sanders, 'Did Vladimir Putin call the breakup of the USSR "the greatest geopolitical tragedy of the 20th century?"' *Politifact* (6 March 2014).
259. However, it is worthwhile speculating as to whether he was upset about the loss of the USSR (and all its 'client states'), or whether he was more concerned as to a direct correlation between the demise of the Soviet Union and the demise of Russia – and it was the demise of Russia that concerned him most of all.
260. John M. Kramer, "Political Corruption in the USSR (Union of Soviet Socialist Republics)" *Western Political Quarterly,* Vol. 30 (2), June 1977, pp. 213–224.
261. Khrushchev, p.252.
262. Equivalent to some £60,870,000 in 1952 (Harold Marcuse, 'Historical US Dollars to German Marks Currency Converter'; https://marcuse.faculty.history. Ucsb.edu/projects/currency.htm#egerm).

263. Frederick Taylor, *The Berlin Wall: 13 August 1961–9 November 1989.* (London: Bloomsbury Publishing, Plc, 2007), p.119.
264. Madsen Pirie, 'When Hungary Began Dismantling the Iron Curtain' *Adam Smith Institute* (2 May 2019).
265. Carlotta Gall and Thomas de Waal suggest up to 5,000 Russian fatalities in *Chechnya: Calamity in the Caucasus.* (New York: NYUP, 1998), p.96.
266. Arkady Babchenko, *One Soldier's War in Chechnya* (London: Portobello Books Ltd., 2008), p.viii.
267. Leon Aron, 'Putin's cannon fodder: an anthem for Russia's doomed youth", *The Spectator* (6 October 2024).
268. AI, "Amnesty International Issues Reports on Disappearances", *North Caucasus Weekly*, 8:21, (24 May 2007), p.1.
269. HRW, 'Russia: Three Months of War in Chechnya' *Human Rights Watch*, Vol. 7 (6), 28 February 1995.
270. He was apparently told to join the military or take a law degree and not to approach the KGB again – presumably as they feared he would be put on file by Western intelligence agencies, and this might later harm any KGB career he might subsequently have. (Marina Manoukian, 'The Truth About Vladimir Putin's KGB career' *Grunge*, 20 May 2022).
271. Also known as destruction battalions.
272. Manoukian, "The Truth About Vladimir Putin's KGB career" *Grunge*, 20 May 2022);
273. There are also reports that he served as an undercover operative in New Zealand – as an undercover 'Bata' shoe salesman in Wellington and Auckland.
274. George McKevitt, '"He is an Introvert – A Man of Deeds not Words": How Vladimir Putin Rose to Power in Russia.' *BBC* (30 December 2024).
275. Vladimir Putin, "Russia at the Turn of the Millennium", *Signs of the Times* (31 December 1999);
276. Putin, "Russia at the Turn of the Millennium", *Signs of the Times* (31 December 1999).
277. Federal Law 31.12.99 N 228-FZ
278. Website, https://www.themoscowtimes.com
279. Maura Reynolds, 'Russia Election Chief Rejects Fraud Claims in Presidential Vote" *Los Angeles Times* (13 September 2000).
280. Peter Bouckaert, 'War Crimes in Chechnya and the Response of the West' (Testimony before the Senate Committee on Foreign Relations), *Human Rights Watch* (29 February 2000).
281. Keith Vaz, 'CHECHNYA.' House of Commons Debates, (HcDeb) *Hansard* vol. 340, cc 400-401 (6 December 1999), cc 400–401.
282. BBC News, 'UK Condemns Chechnya Ultimatum', *BBC* (7 December 1999). (news.bbc.co.uk/1/hi/uk-politics/554075)
283. At this time, a company of Russian infantry should have comprised around 100 men.
284. Babchenko, p.113.
285. Henry E. Hale, 'Putin's Policy Positions" *Strengthening Democratic Institutions Project, Russian Election Watch* (Cambridge, Massachusetts: John F. Kennedy School of Government, Harvard University, 2000), p.3.

Chapter 4: Ukraine: The Sunflower State

286. Karol Wołek, 'A post-war War. The Years of 1944-1963 in Poland." *The Warsaw Institute* (1 October 2018).
287. Khvostov, *The Russian Civil War (2)*, p.34.
288. William H. Chamberlain, *The Russian Revolution 1917-1921.* (2 vols., reprint) (Princeton, N.J: Princeton University Press, 1987).
289. Leggett, p.199.
290. International Encyclopaedia of Ukraine (2001) 'Cheka' *Canadian Institute of Ukrainian Studies, Toronto.*
291. Suvorov, p.8.
292. Chris Bellamy, *Absolute War: Soviet Russia in World War II.* (London: Pan MacMillan Ltd, 2007), p.33.
293. Suvorov, p.82.
294. Stéphane Courtois *et.al. The Black Book of Communism: Crimes, Terror, Repression.* (Cambridge MA: Harvard University Press, 1997), p.159.
295. Courtois *et.al*, p.159.
296. Some suggest up to 25 million died as a direct consequence of famine-induced starvation (Courtois *et.al.*, p.159).
297. Anne Applebaum, "Holodomor: Ukrainian History", *Britannia* (16 May 2003).
298. Pauline Latham, 'UKRAINIAN HOLODOMOR '. House of Commons Debate (HC Deb), *Hansard*, vol 630 cc.544-560 (7 November 2017), column 545.
299. Hiroaki Kuromiya, 'Ukraine and Russia in the 1930s', *Harvard Ukrainian Studies*, Vol. 18 (3/4), pp. 327–341, (p.329).
300. Kuromiya, p.328.
301. This would be considered 'genocide' today.
302. Service, *Stalin*, p.267.
303. Service, *Stalin*, p.158.
304. Suvorov, p.xx
305. Quoted in: John Keegan, *Barbarossa: Invasion of Russia 1941.* (London: Macdonald & Co., Ltd, 1971), p.38.
306. Helmut Ritgen, *The* 6th *Panzer Division 1937-45.* (London: Osprey Publishing Ltd., 1982), p.19.
307. Lucas, p.2.8
308. For a good guide as to the numerous 'Foreign Legions' of volunteers, consult the excellent book by Nigel Thomas, *Hitler's Eastern Legions 1942–45.* (Oxford: Osprey Publishing Ltd., 2020).
309. Carlos Caballero Jurado, *Foreign Volunteers of the Wehrmacht 1941–45* (London: Osprey Publishing, 1983), p.12.
310. Nigel Thomas, *Hitler's Russian & Cossack Allies 1941–45* (Oxford: Osprey Publishing, 2015), p.4.
311. David McCormack, *The Galician Division 1943–45: Ukrainian Volunteers and Conscripts in the Waffen SS.* (Stroud: Fonthill Media, 2022).
312. Herbert Maeger, *Lost Honour, Betrayed Loyalty: The Memoir of a Waffen-SS Soldier on the Eastern Front.* (London: Frontline Books, 2019), p.57.
313. A comprehensive analysis of partisan and anti-partisan warfare in Eastern Europe during World War II can be found in the text edited by Ben Shepherd and Juliette

Pattinson, *War in a Twilight World: Partisan and Anti-Partisan Warfare in Easter Europe, 1939–45.* (Basingstoke: Palgrave Macmillan, 2010).
314. John Erikson, *The Road to Berlin* (London: Weidenfeld & Nicholson, 1983), p.182
315. Erikson, p.123.
316. Erikson, p.182.
317. The Crimea had been 'given' by Khrushchev to the then autonomous Socialist Republic of Ukraine on 19 February 1954, as a gesture of goodwill to mark the 300th anniversary of the Treaty of Pereiaslav signed in 1654.
318. The US administration of President Donald Trump has expressed interest in securing mining rights for US companies in Ukraine. See: Gracelin Baskaran and Meredith Schwartz, 'Breaking Down the US-Ukraine Minerals Deal.' *Centre for Strategic and International Studies* (27 February 2025).
319. Spencer Feingold, "Food Security: Ukraine's food exports by the numbers." *World Economic Forum* (12 December 2022).
320. Daniel Workman, 'Ukraine's Top Ten Exports.' *World's Top Exports* (2023).
321. Nazim Gorin, 'Soviet Economic Integration or Industrial Colonialism?" *Heinrich-Böll-Siftung-Ukraine* (1 September 2022).
322. Janina Dill, Marnie Howlett, and Carl Müller-Crepon, 'Ukraine Will Not Surrender to Russia.' *Foreign Affairs* (26 February 2025).
323. Robert S. Norris, 'The Soviet Nuclear Archipelago' *Arms Control Today*, January/February 1992, p.25.
324. Richard C. Paddock, 'Lebed Says Russia Has Lost Track of 100 nuclear bombs' *Los Angeles Times* (9 September 1997).
325. Program on New Approaches to Research and Security (PONARS) in Eurasia, Institute for European, Russian and Eurasian Studies, Elliott School of International Affairs, George Washington University, Washington D.C.
326. Lucan A. Way, 'Russian Foreign Election Interventions Since 1991', PONARS (Washington D.C: Institute for European, Russian and Eurasian Studies, Elliott School of International Affairs, George Washington University), March 2018, p.2.
327. Andrew Wilson, *Ukrainian Nationalism in the 1990s: A Minority Faith* (Cambridge: CUP, 1996), p.128.
328. Dieter Nohlen and Philip Stöver, *Elections in Europe: A Data Handbook*, (Oxford: OUP, 2010), p.1976.
329. Daniel Treisman, *The Return: Russia's Journey from Gorbachev to Medvedev* (New York: The Free Press, 2011), p.178.
330. Andrei Soldatov, 'The True Role of the FSB in the Ukraine Crisis.' *The Moscow Times* (15 April 2014), p.2.
331. Daniel Sandford, 'Ukraine Crisis: what we know about the Kiev snipers.' *BBC News* (3 April 2014).
332. Reuters, 'Kremlin says NATO expansion in Ukraine is a "red line" for Putin', *Reuters* (27 September 2021).
333. Staff reporter, 'Stern words, economic sanctions and a diplomatic boycott: The action Obama took to deter Putin from invading Crimea' *MailOnline* (7 December 2021).
334. Mike Collett-White and Ronald Popeski, *Reuters.* (16 March 2014).
335. Christian Marxsen, "The Crimea Crisis: An International Law Perspective." *Heidelberg Journal of International Law,* Vol. 7 (2), 2014, pp. 367–391.

336. Dan Roberts, Ian Traynor, and Alec Luhn (2014) 'Obama extends sanctions against Russia to include wealthy Putin allies.' *The Guardian* (21 March 2014).
337. Jan Hanousek and Matěj Bělín (2019) 'Making Sanctions Bite: The EU-Russian Sanctions of 2014' *CEPRA/VoxEU* (29 April).
338. Jessica Gladstone, 'Russia, Ukraine: the Impact of US and EU Sanctions on International Business', *The Law Society of England & Wales,* (22 April 2014).
339. Perry Bacon, 'Obama Administration Sanctions a Challenge to Putin and Trump.' NBC News (29 December 2016).
340. Vladislav Inozemstev, 'A Subtle Similarity Between Hitler and Putin." *The Moscow Times* (16 April 2014).
341. Fred Dews, 'NATO Secretary-General: Russia's Annexation of Crimea Is Illegal and Illegitimate." (19 March 2014).
342. Dews (19 March 2014).
343. Britain was one of the signatories and guarantors of the Locarno Pact (1925), along with France, Germany and Italy. The Locarno Pact guaranteed the post-World War I borders of European countries, and included a provision for the demilitarisation of the Rhineland.
344. Vladimir Putin: interview with Luciano Fontana, Editor of *Il Corriere della Sera.*
345. Emma Cotton, 'Zelensky Channels Churchill's famous words in defiant speech to UK Parliament: 'We will not give up."' *Fox News* (18 March 2022).
346. The term *Banderite* is not, as English-speaking readers might suppose, a term for a 'bandit', but is derived from the group of Ukrainian nationalists led by Stepan Bandera in World War II (explained earlier). They fought with the Germans against the Soviets, and against both the Germans and the Soviets, which explains why there is some ambiguity as to their historical allegiances. However, from the Russian point of view their real crime was to have resisted the Soviet occupation of Eastern Galicia. In an attempt to delegitimise the activities of the group, Soviet propaganda has associated it with radical Ukrainian nationalism, carrying on a tradition established by Stalin. Putin uses the term 'Banderite' as a slur designed to discredit Ukrainians in general, and specifically anyone who opposes Russian efforts to reincorporate Ukraine into Russia. For an assessment of Ukrainian resistance to occupation by both the Nazi and Soviet regimes, see: Clarence D. Manning, *Ukrainian Resistance* (Bayonne, New Jersey: Jersey Printing Co., 1949).
347. Andrew Roth, 'It's not rational: Putin's bizarre speech wrecks his once pragmatic image.' *The Guardian* (25 February 2022).
348. Jamie Seidel, 'Russia-Ukraine war: Vladimir Putin's bizarre claim Russia "saving" Ukraine from West's Nazi dictatorship.' *New Zealand Herald* (10 April 2022).
349. Sergey Lavrov, 'West was covering up crimes of Kiev regime that led to Ukraine's tragedy, Lavrov says' *Military Operation in Ukraine, TASS*, (25 February 2022).
350. Euromaidan Press Staff, 'Largest-yet report on Ukraine invasion documents Russian army in Donbas' *Euromaidan Press,* Kyiv (14 January 2021).
351. Bellingcat Team, 'Origin of Artillery Attacks on Ukrainian Military positions in Eastern Ukraine Between 14 July 2014 and 8 August 2014.' (17 February 2015) p.1.
352. Bellingcat is a Netherlands-based group of investigative journalists that specialise in fact-checking and open-source intelligence (OSINT); it investigates war zones, human rights abuses, and criminality, and was founded by British journalist Eliot Higgins in July 2014.

353. Bellingcat, 'Origin of Artillery Attacks on Ukrainian Military positions in Eastern Ukraine…'
354. ICRC, 'Additional Protocol 1 Relating to the Protection of Victims of International Armed Conflicts,' *Additional Protocols to the Geneva Conventions of 1949.* (Geneva: International Committee of the Red Cross, 1977), p.2.
355. Andrew Roth, 'It's not rational: Putin's bizarre speech wrecks his once pragmatic image'
356. Andrew Srulevitch, 'Why is Putin Calling the Ukrainian Government a Bunch of Nazis?' *Anti-Defamation League* (4 March 2022).
357. Jake Epstein and Charles R. Davis, 'Putin thought Russia's military could capture Kyiv in 2 days, but it still hasn't in 20.' *Business Insider* (15 March 2022).
358. Tariq Tahir, "Putin thought he could take Ukraine in three days, leaked emails reveal', *The Sun* (23 February 2023).
359. Simon Saradzhyan, 'When Does Vladimir Putin's Russia Send in Troops?' *Russia Matters* (7 August 2018).
360. From 14 April 2014 to 31 January 2021, there were 3,077 'conflict-related' civilian deaths, and this total rises to 3,375 if we include the 285 people killed when Malaysian Airlines MH17 was shot down by Donetsk separatists, on 17 July 2014. Source: United Nations Office of the High Commissioner for Human Rights, 'Report on the Human Rights Situation in Ukraine: 1 August 2020– 31 January 2021.' (OHCHR, March 2021), p.7.
361. Individual cases verified by OHCHR, actual numbers are considerably higher.
362. OHCHR, 'Ukraine: Civilian Casualty Update 14 August 2023.' United Nations Office of the High Commissioner for Human Rights (14 August 2023).
363. OHCHR, 'Ukraine: Civilian Casualty Update 23 January 2023.' United Nations Office of the High Commissioner for Human Rights (OHCHR, January 2023).
364. Ewelina U. Ochab, 'New Mass Graves Found in Ukraine as Putin's Atrocities Continue' *Forbes* (22 September 2022).
365. AFP, '8 Dead, 56 Injured in Russian Strike on Ukraine Restaurant', *The Moscow Times* (28 June, 2023) [NB: this report has since been removed from *The Moscow Times* website]

Chapter 5: Russia: The Future?

366. Klaus Friedrich, 'Uncomfortable Parallels: Hitler and Putin: Artfully Mixing the toxic spirit of national and personal humiliation.'
367. SBS, 'Putin Announces "Special Military Operation in Ukraine"' (24 February 2022).
368. Zak Beauchamp, 'Putin's "Nazi" rhetoric reveals his terrifying war aims in Ukraine' *Vox* (24 February 2022).
369. Ali Soufan and Nathan A. Sales, 'One of the Worst Ways Putin is gaslighting the world on Ukraine' *Think: Opinion, Analysis, Essays* (5 April 2022).
370. Soufan and Sales, 'One of the Worst Ways Putin is gaslighting the world on Ukraine.'
371. (a) Paul Johnson, 'Is Vladimir Putin Another Adolf Hitler?' *Forbes* (16 April 2014);
(b) Rebecca English, 'Exclusive: "Putin is behaving just like Hitler", says Charles. Prince's controversial verdict on Russian leader's invasion of Ukraine.' *Daily Mail* (20 May 2014);
(c) Klaus Friedrich, 'Uncomfortable Parallels: Hitler and Putin: Artfully Mixing the toxic spirit of national and personal humiliation.' *The Globalist* (21 March 2025).

372. Leo Strauss, *Natural Right and History*, Chicago: University of Chicago Press, 1953, p.42.
373. Steve Herman, 'Is Putin the New Hitler?' *Voice of America* (8 March 2022).
374. Charles Moore, 'What Putin has in Common with Hitler' *The Spectator* (26 February 2022).
375. International Election Observation Mission (Russian Federation Presidential Election, 14 March 2004), pp. 2-5.
376. Timur Aliyev, 'Chechen Officials Fill Out Ballots Themselves', *The Moscow Times* (15 March 2004), p.3. [This report has subsequently been removed from *The Moscow Times* website].
377. This was the night Hitler liquidated all internal politico-military opposition to his rule, including the murder of Ernst Röhm, the leader of the para-military group known as the 'Brownshirts' – *Sturmabteilung* (SA). The parallels with Putin and the Wagner Group are uncanny.
378. Matthew Luxmoore, 'The Putin Constitution: How Will It Change Russia?' *Radio Free Europe/Radio Liberty,* (1 July 2021).
379. BBC, 'Russia Media Guide', *BBC News* (6 March 2023).
380. Theodor Porutio, 'Censorship in Russia: How to get around online Restrictions.' *Vpn Overview* (8 November 2022).
381. Kaela Malig, 'How Russia's Press Freedom has Deteriorated Over the Decades Since Putin came to Power.' *Frontline* (26 September 2023).
382. Replaced the KGB.
383. Cameron Peters, 'Russian businessmen keep dying. No one knows why.' *Vox* (14 October 2022).
384. Staff Reporter, 'Indian police investigate Russian politician's hotel death.' *The Guardian* (27 December 2022).
385. Tayrn Pedler, 'Secret declassified document reveals list of Vladimir Putin's assassination targets for the first time as memo accuses the Russian president of "authorising killings abroad."' *Mail Online* (24 November 2024).
386. Mark Alfred, 'Russian Journalist Turned Putin Critic Sentenced to 8.5 Years in Prison' (4 October 2023).
387. Dov Alfon, 'Vladimir Poutine, le fou de Moscou.' *Liberation* (22 February 2022); Judson Berger, 'Has Putin Actually Lost His Mind?' *National Review* (26 February 2022); Mark Bennets, 'Bitter, isolated – Putin may have lost the plot!' *The Sunday Times* (27 February 2022); Aliss Higham, 'Has Putin gone mad? The 'Putin Paradox' that will lead to his downfall.' *Express* (UK – 1 March 2022); Carlos Alberto Montaner, '¿Está loco Vladimir Putin?' *El Independiente* (Colombia – 3 March 2022).
388. Jack Newman, 'Vladimir Putin "DOES have Parkinson's and pancreatic cancer", leaked Kremlin spy documents claim.' *Mailonline* (2 November 2022).
389. Richard J. Evans, *The Third Reich in Power: How the Nazis Won Over the Hearts and Minds of a Nation* (London: Penguin Books Ltd., 2005), p.618.
390. Vladimir Putin, 'Russia at the Turn of the Millennium – a Strategy for Russia's Revival.' *SOTT* (*Signs of the Times*, 31 December 1999).
391. Roth, 'It's not rational: Putin's bizarre speech wrecks his once pragmatic image'.
392. An independent Russian newspaper that, as a consequence of its criticism of Vladimir Putin, has been shut down.

393. Maria Lipman, 'How Russia has come to loathe the West.' *European Council on Foreign Relations* (13 March 2015).
394. James Fallon, 'The Mind of a Dictator: Exploring the Minds of Psychopaths and Dictators.' *Psychology Today* (11 November 2011).
395. Stephen Blank, 'What Putin's Praise of the Hitler-Stalin Pact Means' *Newsweek* (29 May 2015).
396. Nicolas Byrom, 'The World's Response to the war in Ukraine', *IPSOS: A 27 – Country Global Advisory Survey*. (19 April 2022).
397. Putin's resentment at the break-up of the Soviet Union is the root cause of much of his belligerent attitude and actions.
398. Vladimir Putin, 'On the Historical Unity of Russians and Ukrainians' (12 July 2021).
399. Steve Rosenberg, 'Strongman Putin stokes patriotism in small-town Russia', BBC News (15 January 2020).
400. Irina Sherbakova, 'Vladimir Putin's Russia is rehabilitating Stalin. We must not let it happen.' *The Guardian* (10 July 2019).
401. He obviously does not understand what a divisive figure Oliver Cromwell is to the British: for some he was the man who brought down the king; for others, he was a dangerous revolutionary responsible for regicide; for others, he was a dictator; for others he brought democracy.
402. Peter Rutland and Neil Shimmield, 'Putin's dangerous campaign to rehabilitate Stalin.' *The Washington Post* (13 June 2019).
403. British Prime Minister, Nevil Chamberlain, on his return from Czechoslovakia after having given in to Hitler's demands to annex the Sudetenland region of that country, as it contained ethnic Germans (27 September 1938).
404. Winston Churchill, 'Invitation to War', *Time*, Vol. 35 (5), (29 January 1940), p.27.
405. Deaths of UK military Service personnel in World War I amounted to 886,000 with many thousands more crippled for life. (Source: TNA, 'Deaths in the First and Second World Wars' *The National Archives*, 2023).
406. Richard J. Evans, *The Third Reich in Power* p.6.
407. Winston Churchill, 'INTERNATIONAL SITUATION'. *Hansard* (HC Deb) vol 310, (6 April 1936), cc2479-2511 col.2484.
408. Archibald Sinclair, 'ANGLO-RUSSIAN RELATIONS'. House of Commons Debate (HC Deb), *Hansard*, Vol. 203, cc. 599-675 (3 March 1927), cc 602-603.
409. Vitaliy Shevchenko, 'Russia not on Trump's tariff list.' *BBC* (3 April 2025);
410. Dominic Culverwell, 'How Trump's tariffs will impact Ukraine.' *The Kyiv Independent* (3 April 2025).
411. Alexey Strelinkov and Alex Izmaylov, 'Trump's tariffs: why are Russia and Belarus not targeted?' *Deutsche Welle* (4 May 2025).
412. Emma Nolan 'Which Companies are still trading with Russia?' *Naritatrading.com* (17 September 2022).
413. Gabriela Baczynska, 'Factbox: EU keeps on doing business with Russia despite sanctions' *Reuters*, (29 March 2023).
414. North Korea has even sent troops to help the Russians fight the Ukrainians; estimates of numbers vary, but are generally thought to be around 10,000 (Kelly Ng, 'What we know about North Korean troops fighting Russia's war.' *BBC News* (24 December 2024). Korean losses are, by early 2025, thought to be their thousands (*Reuters* 'What we

know about North Korean troops joining Russia's war in Ukraine.' *Reuters* (18 February 2025);
415. Fank Millard, *et. al.* 'Why the UAE is Becoming a Liability: The Case of Russian Sanctions Evasion' *The Bruges Group and Tactics Institute* (London: The Bruges Group and Tactics Institute, 2024).
416. Suzi Ring, 'Over 100 British companies admit breaching sanctions on Russia', *Financial Times* (5 November 2023).
417. Haishi Li, Yulin Wang, Zhi Li, and Jing Wu, 'To Comply or Not to Comply: Understanding Neutral Country Supply Chain Responses to Russian Sanctions,' *CESifo* Working Paper no. 11110 (5 May 2024).
418. Trevor Hunnicutt and David Brunnstrom, 'Trump: If NATO members don't pay, US won't defend them.' *Reuters* (7 March 2025);
419. Ellie Cook, 'Trump Has More Than One Way Out of Nato' *Newsweek*, (22 March 2025).
420. Reuters, 'Will Russia use nuclear weapons? Putin's warnings explained' *Reuters* (4 October 2022).
421. Hans M. Kristensen, Matt Korda, and Eliana Johns, 'Nuclear Notebook: Russian nuclear weapons, 2023' *Bulletin of the Atomic Scientists* (9 May 2023).
422. Declan Power, 'State of Ukraine will "collapse within a fortnight" – security expert.' *Raidió Teilifís Éireann*, (3 March 2022).
423. Aisla Slisco, 'Putin's Military Suffers Over 700 Deaths in One Day of War: Ukraine' *Newsweek* (11 September 2022).
424. Stavros Atlamazoglou, 'The Jaw-Dropping Loss of Human Life in the Russia-Ukrainian War' *The National Interest* (12 January 2025).
425. UKinform; https://www.net/rubric-ato/4056510-russian-army-losses-1190-soldiers-and-helicopters-in-war-against-ukraine
426. Maria Tsvetkova, 'Some wounded Russian soldiers find compensation elusive, despite Putin's pledge' *Reuters* (29 July 2022).
427. Yaron Steinbuch, 'Captive Russian troops claim commanders kill their own wounded soldiers' *New York Post* (16 May 2022).
428. Steinbuch, *New York Post* (16 May 2022).
429. T-72 (2,130 losses), T-80 (1,475), T- 62 (335), T-90 (257), T-64 (146), T-55 (10). Source: Yuri Clavilier and Michael Gjerstad, 'Combat losses and manpower challenges underscore the importance of 'mass' in Ukraine.' *International Institute of Strategic Studies* (10 February 2025); https://web-opti-prod.iiss.org/online-analysis/military-balance/2025/02/combat-losses-and-manpower-challenges-underscore-importance-of-mass-in-ukraine.
430. AFV = Armoured Fighting Vehicle. This nomenclature covers a range of vehicles, from armoured troop carriers (without defensive weaponry) to vehicles that are armoured by also have weapons – these are generally light guns, and the vehicles are designed to support the MBTs.
431. UAV = Unmanned Aerial Vehicle i.e, drone.
432. David Axe, 'The Ukrainian Army Has More Tanks Now Than When the War Began – Because it Keeps Capturing Them from Russia.' *Forbes* (24 March 2022).
433. Danielle Ong, 'Russian Soldiers Have to Buy Their Own Equipment For Ukraine War: Report' *International Business Times* (22 May 2022).

434. Generally referred to as a 'Mosin-Nagant' rifle: this was first manufactured in 1891 and went through a number of variants. See: Joseph E. Smith, *Small Arms of the World (10th edition)* Revised. (Harrisburg, Pennsylvania: A& W Visual Library, 1973), pp.578-582.
435. Reuters, 'Conscripts sent to fight by pro-Russia Donbas, get little training, old rifles, poor supplies.' *Reuters* (4 April 2022).
436. Tim McNulty, 'Russian conscripts boarding buses to Ukraine drunk as soldiers "know they're cannon fodder"', *Express* (3 November 2022).
437. Isabel Van Brugen, 'Putin's Mobilization Backfires as 370,000 flee Russia in two weeks.' *Newsweek,* (4 October 2022).
438. Isabel Van Brugen, 'Russian Army Threatening to Shoot Deserters amid Low Morale' *Newsweek* (4 November 2022).
439. Matthew Dooley, 'North Korean troops desert frontline days after arriving to support Russia against Ukraine." *Daily Express US* (17 October 2024).
440. Leia Paxton, 'Ukrainian soldiers boast of high morale as troops cheered onto frontline in Kherson' *Express* (7 September 2022).
441. Mariam Khan, 'Trump administration's 28-point Ukraine-Russia peace plan presented to Zelenskyy' *Abc News* (21 November 2025); https://abcnews.go.com/international/trump-administration-29-point-ukraine-russia-peace-plan/story
442. NATO, 'Collective defence and Article 5' (https://www.nato.int/en/what-we-do/introduction-to-nato/collective-defence-and-article-5)
443. NATO, 'What counts as an 'armed conflict' under Article 5' (https://www.nato.int/en/what-we-do/introduction-to-nato/collective-defence-and-article-5)
444. Eli Stokols, 'Trump wants one thing from the NATO summit. Europe is going to give it to him. *Politico* (21 June 2025); https://www.politico.com/news/2025/06/21/trump-nato-defence-spending

Bibliography

Acemoglu, Daron and James A. Robinson, *Why Nations Fail: The Origins of Power, Prosperity, and Poverty* (London: Profile Books, 2012), ISBN 9-781-846-686-108

Adams, Paul, 'Ukraine Dam: Floods devastate tracts of rich farmland', *BBC News* (8 June 2023); https://www.bbc.co.uk/news/ world-europe-65838771

AFP, '8 Dead, 56 Injured in Russian Strike on Ukraine Restaurant', *The Moscow Times* (28 June 2023); https://www.themoscowtimes.com/23/06/27/8-dead-56-injured-in-russian-strike-on-restaurant-a81669 [This report has now been deleted from *The Moscow Times* website]

AI, 'Amnesty International Issues Reports on Disappearances', *North Caucasus Weekly*, Vol. 8:21, (24 May 2007); https://jamestown.org/program/amnesty-international-issues-report-on-disappearance

Alfon, Dov, 'Vladimir Poutine, le fou de Moscou' *Liberation* (22 February 2022); https://www.liberation.fr/international/europe/le-fou-de-moscou

Alfred, Mark, 'Russian Journalist Turned Putin Critic Sentenced to 8.5 Years in Prison' (4 October 2023); https://uk.news.yahoo.com/russian-journalist-turned-putin-critic-163011466.html

Alston, Charlotte, 'British Journalism and the Campaign for Intervention in the Russian Civil War, 1918–20' *Revolutionary Russia*. Vol. 20 (1), 1 June 2007, pp.35–49

Aliyev, Timur, 'Chechen Officials Fill Out Ballots Themselves', *The Moscow Times* (15 March 2004) [This report has now been deleted from *The Moscow Times* website]

Ambrose, Stephen E., *Rise to Globalism: American Foreign Policy Since 1938 (*3rd *Revised Edition).* (Harmondsworth, Middlesex: Penguin Books Ltd., 1974)

Andrew, Christopher, 'The Threat of Subversion' *MI5 Security Service,* https://www.mI5.gov.uk/the-threat-of-subversion (undated)

AP, 'Putin warns again that Russia is ready to use nuclear weapons if its sovereignty is threatened.' *Associated Press* (13 March 2024); https://apnews.com/article/russia-ukraine-war-putin-nuclear-weapons

Applebaum, Anne, 'Holodomor: Ukrainian History', *Britannia* (16 May 2003); https://www.britannia.com/event/holdomor

Applebaum, Anne, *Iron Curtain: The Crushing of Eastern Europe* (London: Penguin Books Ltd., 2013), ISBN: 9-780-141-021-874

Aron, Leon, 'Putin's cannon fodder: an anthem for Russia's doomed youth', *The Spectator* (6 October 2024); https://www.spectator.co.uk/article/putins-cannon-fodder-an-anthem-for-russias-doomed-youth.

Asprey, Robert B., *The German High Command at War: Hindenburg and Ludendorff and the First World War* (London: Warner Books, 1994), ISBN-13-978-075-151-038-6

Athanassiou, Phoebus, *Armies in Southern Russia, 1918-19* (Oxford: Osprey Publishing Ltd., 2021). ISBN: 978-1-4728-4476-7

Atlamazoglou, Stavros, 'The Jaw-Dropping Loss of Human Life in the Russia-Ukrainian War' *The National Interest* (12 January 2025); https://nationalinterest.org/blog/jaw-dropping-loss-of-human-life-russia-ukraine-war-214355

Atzil, Boaz and Min Jung Kim, 'Buffer Zones and International Rivalry: Internal and External Geographic Separation and Mechanisms.' *International Affairs* Vol 99 (2) 2023. pp.645-665

Axe, David, 'The Ukrainian Army Has More Tanks Now Than When the War Began—Because It Keeps Capturing Them from Russia.' *Forbes* (24 March 2022); https://www.forbes.com/sites/davidaxe/2022/0324/

Babchenko, Arkady, *One Soldier's War in Chechnya* (London: Portobello Books Ltd., 2008). ISBN -13: 9-781-846-270-406

Bacon, Perry, 'Obama Administration Sanctions a Challenge to Putin and Trump.' NBC News (29 December 2016); https://www.nbcnews.com/politics/white-house/Obama--administration-sanctions-challenge-putin-trump-n701286

Baczynska, Gabriela, 'Factbox: EU keeps on doing business with Russia despite sanctions' *Reuters*, (29 March 2023); https://www.reuters.com/world/europe/eu-keeps-doing-business-with-Russia-despite-sanctions-2023-03-29

Balfour, Arthur, 'RUSSIA', House of Commons Debate (HC Deb), *Hansard* (26 November 1917), Vol. 99, c. 1614

Baskaran, Gracelin, and Meredith Schwartz, 'Breaking Down the US-Ukraine Minerals Deal.' *Centre for Strategic and International Studies* (27 February 2025); https://www.csis.org/analysis/breaking-down-us-ukraine-minerals-deal

BBC News, 'UK Condemns Chechnya Ultimatum', *BBC* (7 December 1999) news.bbc.co.uk/1/hi/uk-politics/554075)

BBC News: 'Kazakhstan: Why are there riots and why are Russian troops there?" *BBC* (10 January 2022); https://www,bbc.co.uk/news/explainers-59894266

BBC News, 'Nordstream 1: How Russia is cutting gas supplies to Europe.' *BBC* (29 September 2022); https://www.bbbc.co.uk/news/world-europe-60131520

BBC News, 'Russia Media Guide', *BBC* (6 March 2023); https://www.bbc.co.uk/news/world-europe-17840134

Beauchamp, Zak, 'Putin's 'Nazi' rhetoric reveals his terrifying war aims in Ukraine' (24 February 2022); https://www.vox.com/2022/2/24/22948944/putin-ukraine-nazi-russia-speech-declare-war

Beevor, Antony, *Russia: Revolution and Civil War 1917-1921* (London: Weidenfeld & Nicholson, 2023). ISBN: 9-780-333-780-220

Bellamy, Chris, *Absolute War: Soviet Russia in World War II.* (London: Pan MacMillan Ltd, 2007), ISBN 9-780-333-780-220

Bellingcat Team, 'Origin of Artillery Attacks on Ukrainian Military positions in Eastern Ukraine Between 14 July 2014 and 8 August 2014.' (17 February 2015); https://www.bellingcat.com/news/uk-and-europe/2015/02/17/origin-of-artillery-attacks

Bennets, Mark, 'Bitter, isolated – Putin may have lost the plot!' *The Sunday Times* (27 February 2022); https://www.thetimes.co.uk/article/bitter-isolated-putin-may-have-lost-the-plot

Bennett, Gill, 'What's the Context? 20 December 1919: Formation of the Cheka, the first Soviet security and intelligence agency.' *History of Government* (20 December 2017); https://history.blog.gov.uk/2017/12/20/whats-the-context-20-december-1917-formation-of-the-first-soviet-security-and-intelligence-agency.

Berger, Judson, 'Has Putin Actually Lost His Mind?' *National Review* (26 February 2022); https://www.nationalreview.com/corner/has-putin-actually-lost-his-mind.

Best, Geoffrey, *Churchill and War. Bloomsbury Academic* (London: Bloomsbury Academic, 2005), ISBN 10-185-285-464-2

Blair, Anthony, 'Russian Revolution: ' "Adolf Putin" graffiti sprayed across Russian buildings as thousands protest President "acting like Hitler"', *The Sun* (25 February 2022): https://www.thesun.co.uk/news/177776125/Russia-Ukraine-news-protests-vladimir-putin- hitler.

Blake, John, 'Putin is making the same mistakes that doomed Hitler when he invaded the Soviet Union.' *CNN* (2 April 2022); https://edition.cnn.com/2022/04/02/world/putin-invasion-mistakes-hitler-blake-cec/index.html

Blank, Stephen, 'What Putin's Praise of the Hitler-Stalin Pact Means' *Newsweek* (29 May 2015); https://www.newsweek.com/what-putins-praise-hitler-stalin-pact-means-337185

Blanning, Tim, *Frederick the Great: King of Prussia* (London: Random House, 2016). ISBN 0-812-988-736

Bonar Law, Andrew, 'ALLIED EXPEDITIONS', House of Commons Debate (HC Deb) *Hansard,* (29 October 1918), Vol. 110 c.1254

Borger, Julian and Peter Beaumont, 'Russia steps up Ukraine "dirty bomb" claim in letter to the United Nations', *The Guardian* (25 October 2022); https://www.theguardian.com/world/22/oct/25/russia-to-raise-ukraine-dirty-bomb-accusation-at-un-security-council

Bouckaert, Peter, 'War Crimes in Chechnya and the Response of the West' (Testimony before the Senate Committee on Foreign Relations), *Human Rights Watch* (29 February 2000); http://hrw.org/news/2000/02/29/war-crimes-chechnya-and-response-west

Brune, Lester H., (ed.), The Korean War: Handbook of the Literature and Research (Westport, Connecticut: Greenwood Press, 1996), ISBN: 0-313-289-697

Bullock, David, *The Czech Legion 1914-1920* (Oxford: Osprey Publishing Ltd., 2009), ISBN 9 781-846-032-363

Bunyan, James and Harold H. Fisher (Eds.) *Bolshevik Revolution, 1917-1918: Documents and Materials* (Standford: SUP, 1934)

Burleigh, Michael, *The Third Reich: A New History* (London: Pan Macmillan Ltd., 2000). ISBN 0-330-487-574

Bushnell, John, 'Russian Peasants and Soldiers during World War I: Home and Front Interacting,' (Guest Editor's Introduction), *Russian Studies in History,* Vol. 56 (2), 2017, pp.65-72

Butler, Susan, (ed.), *Dear Mr Stalin: The Complete Correspondence of Franklin D. Roosevelt and Josef V. Stalin* (Yale University Press: New Haven & London, 2005), ISBN 13-9-780-274-745-562

Byrom, Nicolas, 'The World's Response to the war in Ukraine', *IPSOS: A 27 – Country Global Advisory Survey.* (19 April 2022); https://www.iposos.com/en-us/news-polls-war-in-ukraine-april-2022

Caballero Jurado, Carlos, *Foreign Volunteers of the Wehrmacht 1941-45* (London: Osprey Publishing Ltd., 1983). ISBN: 9-780-850-455-243

Cameron, Rob, 'Soviet 1968 invasion: Czechs still feel Cold War shivers' *BBC News* (21 August 2018); https://www.bbc.co.uk/news/world-europe-451-680-62

Cecil, Robert, 'BRITISH SUBJECTS IMPRISONED', House of Commons Debate (HC Deb) *Hansard,* (31 October 1918), Vol. 110, c.1753

Chamberlain, William H., *The Russian Revolution 1917-1921.* (2 vols., reprint ed.) (Princeton, N.J: Princeton University Press, 1987). ISBN: 0-691-008-140

Cheung, Zach, 'Protecting' Ethnic Russians by Expanding the Definition of 'Self-Defence' *McGill Journal of Political Studies* (19 May 2022); https://www.mjps.ssmu.ca/2022/05/19/protecting-ethnic-russians-by-expanding-the-definition-of-self-defence

Churchill, Winston S., 'GALICIAN TROOPS', House of Commons Debate (HC Deb) *Hansard*, (2 December 1919), Vol. 122, cc. 186-187

Churchill, Winston S, 'INTERNATIONAL SITUATION", House of Commons Debate (HC Deb) *Hansard*, (6 April 1936), Vol 310, cc. 2479-2511

Churchill, Winston S., 'Invitation to War', *Time*, Vol. 35 (5), 29 January 1940, p.27

Churchill, Winston S., 'The Sinews of Peace' Speech given at Westminster College, Fulton, Missouri (5 March 1946); https://www.nationalchurchillmuseum.org/sinews-of-peace-iron-curtain-speech.html

Churchill, Winston S., 'MIDDLE EAST', House of Commons Debate (HC Deb) *Hansard*, (26 January 1949), Vol 460, c. 948

Churchill, Winston S., 'Europe Unite: Speeches 1947 and 1948' (London: Cassell, 1950)

Clark, Jesse, 'Hitler Vs Putin-Their Biggest Similarities and Differences', *Grunge* (2 March 2022):https://www.grunge.com/784872/hitler-vs-putin-their-biggest-similarities-and-differences

Clavilier, Yuri and Michael Gjerstad, 'Combat losses and manpower challenges underscore the importance of 'mass' in Ukraine.' *International Institute of Strategic Studies* (10 February 2025); https://www.iss.org/online-analysis/military-balance/2025/02/combat-losses-and-manpower-challenges-underscore-the-importance-of-mass-in-ukraine

Clinton, Jane, 'Why did Russia annex Crimea? What happened when Putin invaded in 2014 and how Nato reacted to annexation.' *Inews* (29 January 2022); https://inews.co.uk/news/world/russia-annex-crimea-why-putin-invaded-2014-what-happened-nato-annexation-explained-1424682

Collett-White, Mike, and Ronald Popeski, "Crimeans vote over 90 percent to quit Ukraine for Russia.' *Reuters.* (16 March 2014); https://www.yahoo.com/news/crimea-vote-joining-russia-moscow-wields-u-n-024050097-finance.html

'COMINTERN Communist International' /Third International. GlobalSecurity.org; http://www.globalsecurity.org./military/world/int/comintern.html

Committee on Un-American Activities, 'Communist Tactics Among Veterans' Groups (testimony of John T. Pace).' *Hearing before the Committee on Un-American Activities, House of Representatives Eighty-second Congress* (first session. July 13 1951), US Government Documents, Boston Public Library, Additional Collections. (File: urn: oclc: record: 654790876)

Connaughton, Richard M., *Rising Sun and Tumbling Bear: Russia's War with Japan* (London: Orion Publishing Co., 2004). ISBN-10:0-304-366-576

Cook, Ellie, 'Trump Has More Than One Way Out of Nato.' *Newsweek*, (22 March 2025); https://www.newsweek.com/donald-trump-nato-exit-us-army-europe-2044325

Cotton, Emma, 'Zelenskyy Channels Churchill's famous words in defiant speech to UK Parliament: "We will not give up."' *Fox News* (18 March 2022); https://www.foxnews.com/world/zelenskyy-channels-churchill-defiant-speech-we-will-not-give-up

Courtois, Stéphane, Nicolas Werth, Jean-Louis Panné, Andrzej Paczkowski, Karel Bartošek, and Jean-Louis Margolin, *The Black Book of Communism: Crimes, Terror, Repression.* (Cambridge MA: Harvard University Press, 1997)

Culbertson, Alix, 'Ukraine crisis: Putin says military drills "purely defensive" and "not a threat" as Western leaders warn invasion imminent.' *Sky News* (18 February 2022); https://news.sky.com/story/ukraine-crisis-putin-says-military-drills-purely-defensive-and-not-a-threat-as-western-leaders-warn-invasion-iminent-1254284

Culverwell, Dominic, 'How Trump's tariffs will impact Ukraine.' *The Kyiv Independent* (3 April 2025); https://kyivindependent.com/how-trumps-tariffs-will-impact-ukraine/

Davies, Norman, *Europe at War 1939-1945: No Simple Victory* (London: Pan Books Ltd., 2006) ISBN 9-780-330-521-23

de Bretton-Gordon, Hamish, 'Putin's Wild Claims of a Dirty Bomb Show Just How Badly his Army is Faring.' *The Guardian* (25 October 2022); https://www.theguardian.com/world/22/oct/25/russia-to-raise-ukraine-dirty-bomb-accusation-at-un-security-council

Dews, Fred, 'NATO Secretary-General: Russia's Annexation of Crimea Is Illegal and Illegitimate.' (19 March 2014); www.brookingsedu/blog/brookings-now/2014/03/19/nato-secretary-general-russias-annexation-of-crimea-is-illegal-and-illegitimate

Dill, Janina, Marnie Howlett, and Carl Müller-Crepon, 'Ukraine Will Not Surrender to Russia.' *Foreign Affairs* (26 February 2025); https://www.foreignaffairs.com/russia/ukraine-will-not-surrender-russia.

Dooley, Matthew, 'North Korean troops desert frontline days after arriving to support Russia against Ukraine.' *Daily Express US* (17 October 2024); https://www.the-express.com/news/world-news/151837/north-korean-troops-desert-frontline-ukraine-russia

Draper, Hal, *The 'Dictatorship of the Proletariat' From Marx to Lenin* (New York: Monthly Review Press, 1987). ISBN: 9-780-853-457-268

Dyadkin, Iosef G., *Unnatural Deaths in the USSR* (London: Routledge, 1983); ISBN 0-878-559-191

Eden, Anthony, 'RUSSIA (EXECUTIONS)'. House of Commons Debate (HC Deb) *Hansard,* (20 December 1934), Vol. 296, col. 1340

Eden, Anthony, 'RUSSIA (BROADCASTS)'. House of Commons Debate (HC Deb), *Hansard,* (1st March 1937) Vol 321, cc. 3-5

Edwards, Robert, *White Death: Russia's War on Finland 1939-1940* (London: Weidenfeld & Nicholson, 2006), IBSN-13: 9-780-297-846-302

Engel, David, *Facing a Holocaust: The Polish Government-in-Exile and the Jews, 1943-1945.* (Chapel Hill & London: The University of North Carolina Press, 1993), ISBN 0-807-920-695

English, Rebecca, 'Exclusive: "Putin is behaving just like Hitler", says Charles. Prince's controversial verdict on Russian leader's invasion of Ukraine.' *Daily Mail* (20 May 2014); https://www.dailymail.co.uk/news/article-2634400/Putin-behaving-just-like-Hitler-says-Charles-Princes-controversial-verdict-Russian-leaders-invasion-Ukraine

Epstein, Jake, and Charles R. Davis, 'Putin thought Russia's military could capture Kyiv in 2 days, but it still hasn't in 20.' *Business Insider* (15 March 2022); https://www.businessinsider.com/vladimir-putin-russian-forces-could-take-kyiv-two-days-2022-3

Erikson, John, *The Road to Berlin* (London: Weidenfeld & Nicholson, 1983), ISBN 0-297-772-384

Euromaidan Press Staff, 'Largest-yet report on Ukraine invasion documents Russian army in Donbas', *Euromaidan Press,* Kyiv (14 January 2021); https://www.euromaidanpress.com/ 2021/01/14/russian-army-in-donbas-2014-2015/

Evans, Richard J., *The Third Reich in Power: How the Nazis Won Over the Hearts and Minds of a Nation* (London: Penguin Books Ltd., 2005), ISBN 1-397-801-410-097-66

Fallon, James, 'The Mind of a Dictator: Exploring the Minds of Psychopaths and Dictators.' *Psychology Today* (11 November 2011); https://www.psychologytoday.com/us/blog/the-psychology-inside-201111/the-mind-dictator

Falvey, Dan, 'Putin apologist' Corbyn desperately defends Russia record after attacking NATO for war.' *Express* (10 March 2022); https://www.express.co.uk/news/politics/1578570/jeremy-corbyn-news-russia-ukraine-war-nato-criticism

Farberov, Snejana, 'Russia plans "false flag" attack on Kherson dam ahead of battle for region: report.' *New York Post,* (20 October 2022); https://www.nypost.com/22/10/20/russia-planning-false-flag-attack-to-blow-up-kherson-dam

Feingold, Spencer, 'Food Security: Ukraine's food exports by the numbers.' *World Economic Forum* (12 December 2022); https://www.weforum.org/agenda/2022/07/ukraine-s-food-exports-by-the-numbers/

Fischer, Benjamin B., 'The Katyn Controversy: Stalin's Killing Field.' *Studies in Intelligence,* Winter, 1999-2000. Center for the Study of Intelligence; https://www.cia.gov/resources/csi/ static/Stalins-killing-field.pdf

Fisher, Harold, *The Communist Revolution: An Outline of Strategy and Tactics*, (California: Stanford University Press, 1955)

Fisher, John, *Burgess and Maclean: A New Look at the Foreign Office Spies* (London: Robert Hale Ltd., 1977) ISBN 0-091-647-93

Florinsky, Michael T., 'The Russian Mobilization of 1914', *Political Science Quarterly,* Vol. 42 (2), 1927, pp.203-227

Fowkes, Ben, *Eastern Europe 1945-1969: from Stalinism to Stagnation* (London: Longman, 2000), ISBN: 7-980-582-326-934

Francis, David R. (US Ambassador), to (US Secretary of State) Robert Lansing, (No. 1056), File no. 861.00/272. Papers Relating to the Foreign Relations of the United States, 1918, Russia, Volume 1 (25 February 1917)

Francis, David R. (US Ambassador), to (US Secretary of State) Robert Lansing (No. 1753), File no. 861.00/520. Papers Relating to the Foreign Relations of the United States, 1918, Russia, Volume 1 (15 September 1917).

Fraňková, Ruth, 'Historians Pin Down Number of 1968 Invasion Victims.' *Radio Praha: English* (18t August 2017); https://www.radio.cz/en/section/curraffrs/historia

Friedrich, Klaus, 'Uncomfortable Parallels: Hitler and Putin: Artfully Mixing the toxic spirit of national and personal humiliation.' *The Globalist* (21 March 2015); https://www.theglobalist.com/uncomfortable-parallels-hitler-and-putin

Gall, Carlotta and Thomas de Waal, *Chechnya: Calamity in the Caucasus* (New York: NYUP, 1998). ISBN-13: 9-780-814-729-632

Gellately, Robert, *Lenin, Stalin, and Hitler: The Age of Social Catastrophe.* (New York: Knopf Doubleday Publishing Group, 2008), ISBN 9-781-400-032-136

Ghosh, Palash R., 'How Many People Did Joseph Stalin Kill?' *International Business Times* (13 May 2013); https://www.ibtimes.com/how-many-people-did-joseph-stalin-kill-1111789

Gladstone, Jessica, 'Russia, Ukraine: the Impact of US and EU Sanctions on International Business', *The Law Society of England & Wales,* (22 April 2014);

https:www.debevoise.com/insights/publications/2014/04/Russia-ukraine-the-impact-of-us-and-eu-sanctions

Goebbels, Joseph, *The Goebbels Diaries (1942–1943).* (New York: Doubleday & Company, 1948). [Translated by Louis Lochner].

Golovin, Nicholas, 'The Russian War Plan of 1914', *The Slavonic and East European Review,* Vol. 14 (42), 1936, pp. 564-584

Gorin, Nazim, 'Soviet Economic Integration or Industrial Colonialism?' *Heinrich-Böll-Siftung-Ukraine* (1st September, 2022); https://ua-boell.org/en/2022/09/01/Soviet-economic-integration-or-industrial-colonisation

Guardian Staff, 'UN nuclear inspectors shut down Russian 'dirty bomb' claim against Ukraine' *The Guardian* (4 November 2022); https://www.theguardian.com/world/22/nov/04/un-nuclear-inspectors-shut-down-russian-dirty-bomb-claim-against-ukraine

Guest, Frederick E., 'GENERAL DENIKIN (AIR SERVICE)', House of Commons: Written Answers to Questions, *Hansard,* Vol. 122 (2 March 1921), cc.56-57w

Hale, Henry E., 'Putin's Policy Positions' *Strengthening Democratic Institutions Project, Russian Election Watch* (Cambridge, Massachusetts: John F. Kennedy School of Government, Harvard University, 2000)

Hanousek, Jan and Matěj Bělín, 'Making Sanctions Bite: The EU-Russian Sanctions of 2014.' *CEPRA/VoxEU* (29 April 2019); https://cerpr.org/voxeu/columns/making-sanctions-bite-eu-russian-sanctions-2014

Harmsworth, Cecil, 'UKRAINE', House of Commons Debate (HC Deb), *Hansard,* (5 March 1919), Vol. 113, c.382

Hart, Peter, *The Great War 1914-1918* (London: Profile Books Ltd., 2014), ISBN 9-781-846-682-476

Hastings, Max, *Catastrophe: Europe Goes to War 1914* (London: William Collins, 2014), ISBN: 9-780-007-519-743

Hastings, Max, *Chastise: The Dambusters Story 1943* (London: William Collins, 2019), ISBN: 9-780-008-280-529

Hastings, Max, *Abyss: The Cuban Missile Crisis 1962* (London: William Collins, 2022), ISBN 9-780-008-364-991

Havlat, Denis, 'Western Aid for the Soviet Union During World War II: Part 1', *The Journal of Slavic Military Studies,* Vol. 30 (2), 2017, pp.290-320

Helm, Toby, 'Labour left breaks with Jeremy Corbyn over sending weapons to Ukraine.' *The Guardian* (26 February 2023); https://www.theguardian.com/politics/2023/feb/26/labour-left-breaks-with-jeremy-corbyn-over-sending-weapons-to-ukraine

Herman, Steve, 'Is Putin the New Hitler?' *Voice of America* (8 March 2022); https: //www.voanews.com/a/is-putin-the-new-hitler/6476408.html

Higham, Aliss, 'Has Putin gone mad? The "Putin Paradox" that will lead to his downfall.' *Express* (UK – 1 March 2022); https://www.express.co.uk/news/world/1572033/Vladimir-putin-mad-downfall-ukraine-invasion.

Hill, Alexander, 'Deep-rooted Russian fear of the West has fuelled Putin's invasion of Ukraine.' *The Conversation* (3 March 2022); https://theconversation.com/deep-rooted-russina-fear-of-the-west-has-fuelled-putins-invasion-of-ukraine -178351

Hitler, Adolf, *Closing speech at the NSDAP Conference in Nuremburg,* (12 September 1938); https:// der-fuehrer.org/reden/English/38-09-12.htm

Holzworth, Larry, 'This Spy Ring Betrayed the US and British to the Soviet Intelligence.' *History Collection: Cold War* (15 April 2021); https://historycollection.com/this-spy-ring-betrayed-the-us-and-british-to-soviet-intelligence/4/

Hopmans, Rob, 'Russian Brutality: Massacres by Russian Soldiers During WW2.' *WW2Gravestone* (30 April 2018); https://www.ww2gravestone.com/russian-brutality-massacres-russian-soldiers-ww2

HRW, 'Russia: Three Months of War in Chechnya.' *Human Rights Watch* (1 February 1995); https://hrw.org/news/1995/02/01/three-months-war-chechnya

HRW, 'Russia: with War, Censorship Reaches New Heights.' *Human Rights Watch* (28 February 2022); https://www.hrw.org/news/2022/02/28/russia-war-censorship-reaches-new-heights

HRW, 'Ukraine: Executions, Torture During Russian Occupation.' *Human Rights Watch* (18 May 2022); https://www.hrw.org/news/2022/05/18/ukraine-executions-torture-during-russian-occupation

Hunnicutt, Trevor and David Brunnstrom, 'Trump: If NATO members don't pay, US won't defend them.' *Reuters* (7 March 2025); https://www.reuters.com/world/trump-if-nato-members-dont-pay-us-we-wont-defend-them

ICRC, 'Additional Protocol 1 Relating to the Protection of Victims of International Armed Conflicts,' *Additional Protocols to the Geneva Conventions of 1949*. (Geneva: International Committee of the Red Cross, 1977)

IEOBM (International Election Observation Mission) (Russian Federation Presidential Election, 14 March 2004); https://www.osce.org/files/f/documents/5/b/25533.pdf (p.5)

Inozemstev, Vladislav, 'A Subtle Similarity Between Hitler and Putin.' *The Moscow Times* (16 April 2014); https://www.themoscowtimes.com/2014/04/16/a-subtle-similarity-between-hitler-and-putin-a34076

Johnson, Paul, 'Is Vladimir Putin Another Adolf Hitler?' *Forbes* (16 April 2014); https://www.forbes.com/sites/currentevents/2014/04/16/Is-vladimir-putin-another-adolf-hitler

Jones, Timothy, 'Berlin Marks East German Uprising of 1953." *Deutsche Welle* (17 June 2017); https://www.dw.com/en/berlin-commemorates-2953-uprising-in-east-germany

Jukes, Geoffrey, *Carpathian Disaster: Death of an Army*. (London: Pan/Ballantine, 1973), ISBN 13-978-034-509-800- 9

Keegan, John, *Barbarossa: Invasion of Russia 1941*. (London: Macdonald & Co., Ltd, 1971). ISBN-10: 0-356-037-479

Kelly, Lidia, 'Evidence suggests Russia blew Kakhovka dam in Ukraine: NYT.' *Reuters* (18 June 2023); https://www.reuters.com/world/europe/evidence-suggests-russia-blew-kakhovka -dam-ukraine-new-york-times-2023-06-18/

Kenez, Peter, *Red Advance, White Defeat: Civil War in South Russia 1919-1920*. (Washington, DC: New Academia Publishing, 2004), pp. 20–23. ISBN 9-780-974-493-459

Kennedy, Paul, *The Rise and Fall of The Great Powers: Economic Change and Military Conflict from 1500 to 2000*. (London: Fontana Paperbacks, 1990)

Khan, Mariam, 'Trump administration's 28-point Ukraine-Russia peace plan presented to Zelenskyy' *Abc News* (21 November 2025); https://abcnews.go.com/international/trump-administration-28-point-peace-plan-presented-to-zelenskyy

Khrushchev, Nikita S., *Khrushchev Remembers (Vol 1)*, (Harmondsworth: Penguin Books Ltd., 1971). [Translated and edited by Strobe Talbott, with Introduction, Commentary, and Notes by Edward Crankshaw].

Khvostov, Mikhail, *The Russian Civil War (1): The Red Army* (Oxford: Osprey Publishing Ltd., 1996) ISBN: 9-781- 855-326-088

Khvostov, Mikhail, *The Russian Civil War (2): White Armies* (Oxford: Osprey Publishing Ltd., 1997). ISBN: 9-781- 855-326-569

Kinetz, Erika, ' "Kill everyone!" Russian violence in Ukraine was strategic.' *Associated Press* (27 October 2022); https://apnews.com/article/russia-ukraine-kyiv-europe

King, Joseph, 'BRITISH AMBASSADOR (PETROGRAD)'. House of Commons Debate (HC Deb), *Hansard*, (12 November 1917), vol.99 c. 99

Kirby, Paul, 'Giorgia Meloni: Italy's far-right wins election and vows to govern for all' *BBC News* (26 September 2022); https://www.bbc.co.uk/news/world-europe-63029909

Klavana, Tomas, 'The Real Reason Putin Feels Threatened by NATO', *The Bulwark* (25 February 2022); https://www.thebulwark.com/p/the-real-reason-putin-feels-threatened-by-nato.

Knighton, Andrew, 'The Great Retreat: Germany Captured 1 million Russians in 1915.' *War History Online* (30 May 2018); https://www.warhistoryonline.com/world-war-i/the-great-retreat-germanys-gorlice-tarnow.html

Komorowski, Eugenjusz A., *Night Never Ending* (Washington D.C.: H. Regnery Publishing, 1974). ISBN-13-9-780-809-290-84

Kramer, John M., "Political Corruption in the USSR (Union of Soviet Socialist Republics)" *Western Political Quarterly,* Vol. 30 (2), June 1977, pp.213-224

Kristensen, Hans M., Matt Korda, and Eliana Johns, 'Nuclear Notebook: Russian nuclear weapons, 2023' *Bulletin of the Atomic Scientists* (9 May 2023); https://thebulletin.org/premium/20205/nuclear-notebook-russian-nuclear-weapons-2023

Kuromiya, Hiroaki, 'Ukraine and Russia in the 1930s', *Harvard Ukrainian Studies,* Vol. 18 (3/4), pp.327-341

Laker, Jeri and Barnett Rubin, '"Tears, Blood and Cries" Human Rights in Afghanistan Since the Invasion, 1979-1984.' *A Helsinki Watch Report* (New York and Washington: Helsinki Watch Committee, December 1984)

Latham, Pauline, 'UKRAINIAN HOLODOMOR' . House of Commons Debate (HC Deb), *Hansard,* (7 November 2017), Vol. 630, cc.544-560

Latsis, Martin, *Red Terror* [Krasnyi Terror] 1918 no 1 (Prague: Kazan, 1 November 1918), p.2

Lavrov, Sergey, 'West was covering up crimes of Kiev regime that led to Ukraine's tragedy, Lavrov says' *Military Operation in Ukraine,* TASS, (25 February 2022); https://tass.com.politics/1411067

Leggett George, *The Cheka: Lenin's Political Police. The All–Russian Extraordinary Commission for Combating Counter–Revolution and Sabotage, December 1917 to February 1922.* (Oxford: Clarendon Press, 1981), ISBN 0-198-225-520.

Li, Haishi, Yulin Wang, Zhi Li, and Jing Wu, 'To Comply or Not to Comply: Understanding Neutral Country Supply Chain Responses to Russian Sanctions,' *CESifo* Working Paper no. 11110 (5 May 2024); https://papers.ssrn.com./sol3/papers.cfm

Lieven, Dominic, *Nicholas II: Emperor of All The Russias* (London: BCA, 1994), ISBN 0-195-449-949

Lipman, Maria, (13 March 2015) 'How Russia has come to loathe the West.' *European Council on Foreign Relations (ecfr.eu)*; https://www.ecf.eu/article/commentary-how-russia-has-come-to-loathe-the-west311346

Llewellyn, Jennifer, Michael McConnell, and Steve Thompson, 'The Red Terror' *Alpha History* (5 March 2022); https://alphahistory.com/russianrevolution/red-terror

Lloyd George, David, 'PROVISIONAL GOVERNMENT'. House of Commons Debate (HC Deb), *Hansard,* (19 March 1917), Vol. 91, c. 1536

Lloyd George, David, *War Memoirs of David Lloyd George, Volume 1.* (London: Odhams Press, 1938)

Lowen, Mark, 'Georgia Meloni: Far-right leader poised to run Italy" *BBC News* (26 September 2022); https://www.bbc.co.uk/news/world/europe

Lucas, S. James, *War on the Eastern Front 1941–1945: The German Soldier in Russia* (London: BCA, 1979)

Luxmoore, Matthew, 'The Putin Constitution: How Will It Change Russia?' *Radio Free Europe/Radio Liberty,* (1 July 2021); https://www.rferl.org/a/the-putin-constitution-how-will-it-change-russia/30699899.html

Macdonald, Lyn, *1915 The Death of Innocence* (London: Headline Book Publishing, 1993) ISBN 0-747-204-322

Macmillan, Harold, *The Macmillan Diaries (Vol II- Prime Minister and After 1957-1966)* (ed. Peter Catterall) (London: Pam Macmillan, 2011), ISBN 9-780-330-433-099

Maeger, Herbert, *Lost Honour, Betrayed Loyalty: The Memoir of a Waffen-SS Soldier on the Eastern Front.* (London: Frontline Books, 2019). ISBN-13: 9-781-526-769-858

Malig, Kaela, 'How Russia's Press Freedom has Deteriorated Over the Decades Since Putin came to Power.' *Frontline* (26 September 2023); https://www.pbs.org/wgbh/frontline/article/russia-putin-press-freedom-independent-news

Malone, Cecil, 'UKRAINE', *Hansard,* House of Commons Debate (HC Deb), Vol. 113 (5 March 1919), c.382

Manning, Clarence D., *Ukrainian Resistance* (Bayonne, New Jersey: Jersey Printing Co., 1949)

Manoukian, Marina, 'The Truth About Vladimir Putin's KGB career' *Grunge,* 20 May 2022); https://www.grunge.com/441914/the-truth-about-vladimir-putins-kgb-career

Manvell, Roger and Heinrich Fraenkel, *Hitler: The Man and The Myth.* (London: Granada Publishing Ltd., 1978), ISBN 0-586-045-678.

Marcuse, Harold, 'Historical Dollars to German Marks Currency Converter.' Https://marcuse.faculty.history.Uscb.edu/projects/currency.htm

Marxsen, Christian, 'The Crimea Crisis: An International Law Perspective.' *Heidelberg Journal of International Law,* Vol. 7 (2), 2014, pp.367-391

Matthews, Owen, 'Vladimir Putin's new plan for world domination." *The Spectator* (22 February 2014); https://www.spectator.co.uk/article/Vladimir-putin-s-new-plan-for-world-domination

Mayhew, Freddy, 'Journalist John Pilger says ex-Russian spy poisoning case is a "carefully constructed drama in which the media plays a role"' . *Press Gazette* (20 March 2018); https: pressgazette.co.uk/publishers/nationals/journalist-john-pilger-say-ex—russian-spy poisoning-case-is-a-carefully-constructed-drama-in -the-media-plays-a-role/

McCormack, David, *The Galician Division 1943-45: Ukrainian Volunteers and Conscripts in the Waffen SS.* (Stroud: Fonthill Media, 2022) ISBN-13: 9-781-558-720

McKevitt, George, '"He is an Introvert – A Man of Deeds not Words": How Vladimir Putin Rose to Power in Russia.' *BBC* (30 December 2024); https://www.bbc.com/culture/article/20241220-how-vladimir-putin-rose-to-power-in-russia

McMeekin, Sean, *Stalin's War* (London & New York: Penguin Random House, 2021). ISBN 9-780-141-989-297

McNulty, Tim, 'Russian conscripts boarding buses to Ukraine drunk as soldiers "know they're cannon fodder"' *Express* (3 November 2022); https://www.express.co.uk/news/world/1691527/Russia-conscripts-drunk-video-ukraine-war-latest-Russian-soldiers-news-vn

Medvedev, Zhores A., 'Two Decades of Dissidence', *The New Scientist,* Vol. 72 (1025), (2 November 1976), pp.264–267

Mehrara, Maya, 'Russia's Staggering Losses in Three Years of Ukraine War', *Newsweek* (24 February 2025); https://www.newsweek.com/russias-staggering-losses-three-years-ukraine-war

Millard, Frank, Jonathan Swift, and Niall McCrae, 'Why the UAE is Becoming a Liability: The Case of Russian Sanctions Evasion.' *The Bruges Group and Tactics Institute* (London: The Bruges Group and Tactics Institute, 2024). ISBN 9-781-739-092-047

Melgunov, Sergey P., *'Red Terror' in Russia* (London and Toronto: J.M. Dent & Sons, 1925)

Moffat, Ian C.D., 'Forgotten Battlefields – Canadians in Siberia 1918–1919.' *Canadian Military Journal*; https://www.journal.forces.gc.ca/vo8/no3/moffat-eng.asp

Montaner, Carlos Alberto, '¿Está loco Vladimir Putin?" *El Independiente* (Colombia – 3 March 2022); https://www.elindependiente.com/opinion/2022/04/03/esta-loco-vladimir-putin.

Moore, Charles, 'What Putin has in Common with Hitler' *The Spectator* (26 February 2022); https://www.spectator.co.uk/what-putin-has-in-common-with-hitler

Nafziger, George F., *The German Order of Battle: Waffen SS and Other Units in World War II.* (Conshohocken, Pennsylvania: Combined Publishing, 2001), ISBN 1-590-970-583

NATO, 'Collective defence and Article 5' (https://www.nato.int/en/what-we-do/introduction-to-nato/collective-defence-and-article-5)

NATO, 'What counts as an 'armed conflict' under Article 5' (https://www.nato.int/en/what-we-do/introduction-to-nato/collective-defence-and-article-5)

Newman, Jack, 'Vladimir Putin "DOES have Parkinson's and pancreatic cancer", leaked Kremlin spy documents claim.' *Mailonline* (2 November 2022); https://www.dailymail.co.uk/news/article-11377825/Vladimir-Putin-DOES-have-parkinsons-pancreatic-cancer-leaked-kremlin-spy-documents-claim

Ng, Kelly, 'What we know about North Korean troops fighting Russia's war.' *BBC News* (24 December 2024); https://www.bbc.co.uk/news/articles/cm2796pdm1lo

Nohlen, Dieter, and Philip Stöver, *Elections in Europe: A Data Handbook*, (Oxford: OUP, 2010), ISBN 9-783-832-956-097

Nolan, Emma 'Which Companies are still trading with Russia?' *Naritatrading.com* (17 September 2022); https://naritatrading.com/which-companies-are-still-trading-with-russia?

Nollendorfs, Valters and Uldis Neiburgs, 'Soviet Mass Deportations from Latvia", *The Gulag Expedition* (2006); https://gulexp.weebly.com/latvian-citizens-in-the-gulag.html

Norris, Robert S., 'The Soviet Nuclear Archipelago', *Arms Control Today*, January/February 1992; https://nuke.fas.org/norris/nuc_01019201a_016.pdf

Novaia Zhizn, 'Executions Continue' *Novaia zhizn*, No. 71 (19 April 1918). Taken from the translation into English and published in James Bunyan and Harold H. Fisher (eds.), *Bolshevik Revolution, 1917-1918; Documents and Materials* (Stanford: Stanford University Press)

Ochab, Ewelina U., (2022) 'New Mass Graves Found in Ukraine as Putin's Atrocities Continue.' *Forbes* (22 September 2022); https://www.forbes.com/sites/ewelinaochab/2022/09/22/new-mass-graves-found-in-ukraine-as-putins-atrocities-continue

Ong, Danielle, 'Russian Soldiers Have To Buy Their Own Equipment For Ukraine War: Report' *International Business Times* (22 May 2022); https://www.ibtimes.com/russian-soldiers-have-to-buy-their-own-equipment-ukraine-war-report-3516842

Outhwaite, Robert, 'KERENSKY GOVERNMENT'. House of Commons Debate (HC Deb), *Hansard*, (12 November 1917), Vol. 99, cc 9-11

Paddock, Richard C., 'Lebed Says Russia Has Lost Track of 100 nuclear bombs" *Los Angeles Times* (9 September 1997); http://www.latimes.com/archives/la-xpm-1997-sep-09-mn-30448-story.html

Pásara, Luis, 'El Guano y la Penetración Inglesa', in Jorge Basadre (ed.) *Reflexiones en Torno a la Guerra de 1879* (Lima: Francisco Campodónico /Centro de Investigación y Capacitación, 1979), pp.15-42 *[Original Spanish: "Un país no gana una guerra solo cuando está major armado: primero es indispensable que sea un país."]*

Pashin, Nikolay, 'Did Allied assistance make a difference for Russia in World War I?' *Russia Beyond* (10 November 2018); htpps://www.rbth.com/history/329471-did-allied-assistance-make -difference

Paxton, Lcia, 'Ukrainian soldiers boast of high morale as troops cheered onto frontline in Kherson' *Express* (7 September 2022); https://www.express.co.uk/nes/world/1665938/Ukraine-soldiers-morale-Russian-invasion-Kherson-war-military-strategy

Pedler, Tayrn, "Secret declassified document reveals list of Vladimir Putin's assassination targets for the first time as memo accuses the Russian president of 'authorising killings abroad.'" *Mail Online* (24th November, 2024); https://www.dailymail.co.uk/news/article-14119891-vladimir-putin-assassination-targets-list-declassified. html

Peters, Cameron, 'Russian businessmen keep dying. No one knows why.' *Vox* (14 October 2022); https://www.vox.com/world/2022/10/14/russian-businessmen-oligarchs-putin-mysterious -deaths-windows

Philpott, William, *Bloody Victory: The Sacrifice of the Somme.* (London: Abacus, 2009), ISBN: 9-780-349-120-041

Pilger, John, *Hidden Agendas* (Vintage/Random House: London, 1999), ISBN 0-099-741-512

Pilger, John (2014) 'In Ukraine, the US is dragging us towards war with Russia.' *The Guardian* (13 May); https://www.theguardian.com/commentisfree/2014/may/13/ukraine-us-war-russi-john-pilger

Pipes, Richard (ed.), *The Unknown Lenin: From the Secret Archives* (New Haven: Yale University Press, 1996)

Pirie, Madsen, 'When Hungary Began Dismantling the Iron Curtain' *Adam Smith Institute* (2 May, 2019); https://adamsmith.org/blog/when-hungary-began-dismantling-the-iron-curtain

Plokhy, Serhi, *Forgotten Bastards of the Eastern Front.* (London: Penguin Random House UK, 2020), ISBN-13 – 9-780-141-991-100

Porutio, Theodor, 'Censorship in Russia: How to get around online Restrictions.' *Vpn Overview* (8 November 2022); https:vpnoverview.com/unblocking/censorship/internet-censorship-russia/

Power, Declan, 'State of Ukraine will "collapse within a fortnight" – security expert.' *Raidió Teilifís Éireann*, (3 March 2022); https://www.rte.ie/news/world/22/0303/1284234-ukraine-security

Powers, Thomas, *The Man Who Kept the Secrets: Richard Helms and the CIA.* (New York: Alfred A. Knopf, 1981). ISBN-13: 9-780-671-836-542

Putin, Vladimir, 'Russia at the Turn of the Millennium', *Signs of the Times* (31 December 1999); https://sott.net/article/310072-Vladimir-Putins-first-paper-as-president-Russia-at-the-Turn-of-the-Millennium-A-Strategy-for-Russias-revival

Putin, Vladimir, Interview with Editor of *Il Corriere della Sera* (7 June 2015)

Putin, Vladimir, 'On the Historical Unity of Russians and Ukrainians' (12 July 2021); en.Kremlin.ru/events/president/news/66181

Radchenko, Sergey, 'Why Were the Russians in Vietnam?' *New York Times* (27 March 2018)

Ratner, Paul, '39 Years Ago, a KGB Defector Chillingly Predicted Modern America', *The International Chronicles* (24 April 2024); https://www.theinternationalchronicles.com/2024/04/39-years-ago-a-kgb-defector-chillingly-predicted-modern-america

Reagan, Ronald, 'Address to the UK Parliament' (8 June 1982); https://millercenter.org/the-presidency-presidential-speech/June-8-1982-address-british- parliament

Reagan, Ronald, 'Address to the National Association of Evangelicals', Orlando, Florida, (8 March 1983); https://nationalcenter.org/ncppr/2001/11/04/ronald-reagan-eveil-empire-speech-to-the-national-association-of-evangelicals-1983

Reed, John, *Ten Days that Shook the World* (London: Penguin Classics, 2007), ISBN -13-9-780-144-421-29

Reid, Anna, *A Nasty Little War: The West's Fight to Reverse the Russian Revolution.* (London: John Murray Press, 2023), ISBN 9-781-529-326-789

Reitlinger, Gerald, *The SS: Alibi of a Nation* 1922-1945 (New York: The Viking Press Inc., 1957)

Reynolds, Maura, 'Russia Election Chief Rejects Fraud Claims in Presidential Vote' *Los Angeles Times* (13 September 2000); https://www.latimes.com/archives/la-xpm-2000-sep-13-mn-2017-story

Reuters, 'Kremlin says NATO expansion in Ukraine is a "red line" for Putin', *Reuters* (27 September 2021); https://www.reuters.com/world/kremlin-says-nato-expansion-ukraine-crosses-red-line-putin-2021-09-27

Reuters, 'Russia's oil and gas revenue windfall' *Reuters* (21 January 2022); https://www.reuters.com/markets/europe/russia-oil-gas-revenue-windfall-2022-01-21

Reuters, 'Conscripts sent to fight by pro-Russia Donbas, get little training, old rifles, poor supplies." *Reuters* (4 April 2022); https://www.reuters.com/world/conscripts-sent-fight-by-pro-russia-donbas-get little-training-old-rifles-poor-22-04-04

Reuters, 'Will Russia use nuclear weapons? Putin's warnings explained' *Reuters* (4 October 2022); http://www.reuters.com/world/Europe/qa-will-russia-use-nuclear-weapons-putins-warning-explained-2022-10-04/

Reuters, 'What we know about North Korean troops joining Russia's war in Ukraine.' *Reuters* 18 February 2025); https://www.reuters.com/world/Europe/what-we-know-about-north-korean-troops-joining-russias-war-ukraine-2025-02-18

Ring, Suzi, 'Over 100 British companies admit breaching sanctions on Russia', *Financial Times* (5 November 2023); https://www.ft.com/content/233891c0-2c8c-484a-88d3-866a-252d52d5b31

Ritgen, Helmut, *The* 6th *Panzer Division 1937-45.* (London: Osprey Publishing Ltd., 1982). ISBN 0-850-454-530

Roberts, Dan, Ian Traynor, and Alec Luhn, 'Obama extends sanctions against Russia to include wealthy Putin allies.' *The Guardian* (21 March 2014); https://www.theguardian.com/world/2014/mar/20/Obama-extends-sanctions-against-russia-ukraine

Rodriguez, Fátima, 'Russia: Importance of Diamond Industry', *Lupicino,* (19 December 2023); https://lupicino.com/en/russia-importance-of-diamond-industry.

Rosenberg, Steve, 'Strongman Putin stokes patriotism in small-town Russia', BBC News (15 January 2020); htpps://www.bbc.co.uk/news/world-europe-51103689

Roth, Andrew, 'It's not rational: Putin's bizarre speech wrecks his once pragmatic image' *The Guardian* (25 February 2022); https://www.theguardian.com/world/2022/feb/25/its-not-rational-putins-bizarre-speech-wrecks-his-once-pragmatic-image

Rudnytsky, Ivan L., 'The Soviet Ukraine in Historical Perspective' *Canadian Slavonic Papers/Revue Canadienne des Slavists,* Vol. 14 (2), 1972, pp. 235-250

Rummel, Rudolph J., *Lethal Politics: Soviet Genocide and Mass Murder Since 1917.* (Piscataway, NJ: Transaction Publishers, 1990), ISBN: 9-781-565-000-887-3.

Rutland, Peter and Neil Shimmield, 'Putin's dangerous campaign to rehabilitate Stalin.' *The Washington Post* (13 June 2009); https://www.washingtonpost.com/outlook/2009/06/13/putins-dangerous-campaign-rehabilitate-stalin

Salvoni, Elena, 'Why is Putin massing troops on the border of Finland? Military build-up similar to the prelude to Ukraine war sparks alarm in NATO.' *Mailonline* (12 May 2025); https://www.dailymail.co.uk/news/article-14703272/Satellite-images-reveal-Putin-gathering-forces-border-Finland-chilling-echo-Ukraine-war-launched-amid-fears-preparing-WW3.html

Samuel, Marcus, 'RUSSIA (BROADCASTS)'. House of Commons Debate (HC Deb), *Hansard,* vol 321 cc. 3-5 (1 March 1937) col. 4.

Sanders, Katie, 'Did Vladimir Putin call the breakup of the USSR "the greatest geopolitical tragedy of the 20th century"'? *Politifact* (6 March 2014); https://www.politifact.com/factchecks/2014/mar/06/john-bolton/did-vladimir-putin-call-breakup-ussr-greatest-geop/

Sandford, Daniel, 'Ukraine Crisis: what we know about the Kiev snipers.' *BBC News* (3 April 2014); https://www.bbc.co.uk/news/world-europe-26866069

Sandford, George, *Katyn and the Soviet Massacre of 1940: Truth, Justice And Memory* (London and New York: Routledge, 2005). ISBN 9-780-415-338-738.

Santayana, Jorge, *The Life of Reason: Reason in Common Sense* (New York: C. Scribner's & Sons, 1905)

Saradzhyan, Simon, 'When Does Vladimir Putin's Russia Send in Troops?' *Russia Matters* (7 August 2018); https://www.russiamatters.org/analysis/when-does-vladimir-putins-russia-send-troops

Saviano, Roberto, 'Georgia Meloni is a danger to Italy and the rest of Europe.' *The Guardian* (24 September 2022); https://www.theguardian.com/world/commentisfree/22/sep/24.giorgia-meloni-is-a-danger-to-italy-and-the-rest-of-europe

SBS News, 'Putin Announces "Special Military Operation" in Ukraine' *Special Broadcasting Service* (24 February 2022): https://www.bing.com

Sebestyen, Victor, *Lenin the Dictator: An Intimate Portrait.* (London: Weidenfeld & Nicholson, 2017), ISBN 9-781-474-600-446

Seidel, Jamie, 'Russia-Ukraine war: Vladimir Putin's bizarre claim Russia "saving" Ukraine from West's Nazi dictatorship.' *New Zealand Herald* (10 April 2022); https://www.nzherald.co.nz/world/russia-Ukraine-war-vladimir-putins-bizarre-claim-russia-saving-ukraine-from-wests-nazi-dictatorship

Service, Robert, *Stalin: A Biography* (London: Macmillan Publishers Ltd., 2004), ISBN: 9-781-447-201-830

Service, Robert, *Lenin: A Biography* (London: Pan Books Ltd., 2010), ISBN: 9-7-0-330-51838-3

Service, Robert, *Blood on the Snow: The Russian Revolution 1914-1924* (Picador: London, 2023), ISBN 978-1-529-065-855

Shapoval, Yuri and Marta D. Olynyk, 'The Holodomor: A prologue to Repressions and Terror in Soviet Ukraine.' *Harvard Ukrainian Studies,* Vol. 30 (1), pp. 99-121, 2008

Shepherd, Ben and Juliette Pattinson (Eds.), *War in a Twilight World: Partisan and Anti-Partisan Warfare in Eastern Europe, 1939-45.* (Basingstoke: Palgrave Macmillan, 2010). ISBN 978-0-230-57569-1

Sherbakova, Irina, 'Vladimir Putin's Russia is rehabilitating Stalin. We must not let it happen.' *The Guardian* (10 July 2019); https://www.theguardian.com/comment-is-free/2019/jul/10/vladimir-putin-russia-is-rehabilitating-stalin-soviet-past

Shevchenko, Vitaliy, 'Russia not on Trump's tariff list.' *BBC* (3 April 2025); https://www.bbc.com/news/articles/

Shoaib, Ali, 'Blinken issues warning to Kazakhstan. "Once Russians are in your house, it's sometimes very difficult to get them to leave."' *Business Insider* (8 January 2022); https://www.businessinsider.com/blinken-warns-kazakhstan-over-letting-russian-troops-in-your-house-2022.

Simha, Rakesh Krishna, 'Vietnam War: The critical role of Russian weapons" *Russia Beyond (Rossiyskaya Gazeta)* (30 April 2015); https://www.rbth.com/blogs/2015/04/30/vietnam-war-the-critical-role-of-russian-weapons-42917 [now deleted from website: it can be found at https://johndenugent.com/how-soviet-russia-beat-america-in-the-vietnam-war-by-massive-high-tech-help-to-the-north]

Sinclair, Archibold, 'ANGLO-RUSSIAN RELATIONS'. House of Commons Debate (HC Deb), *Hansard,* (3 March 1927), Vol. 203, cc599-675

Slisco, Aisla, '"Putin's Military Suffers Over 700 Deaths in One Day of War: Ukraine' *Newsweek* (11 September 2022); https://www.newsweek.com/vladimir-putin-russian-military-suffers-700-deaths-one-day-Ukraine-says-1758082

Smith, Joseph E., *Small Arms of the World (10th edition)* Revised. (Harrisburg, Pennsylvania: A& W Visual Library, 1973)

Snyder, Tim, 'Russia's Genocide Handbook: The Evidence of Atrocity and Intent Mounts', (translated from Russian propaganda article: 'What Should Russia Do With Ukraine?'), *Mgrublian Centre for Human Rights* (Claremont McKenna College), (14 April 2022); https://human-rights.cmc.edu/2022/04/14/russias-genocide-handbook.

Soldatov, Andrei, "The True Role of the FSB in the Ukraine Crisis." *The Moscow Times* (15 April 2014)

Srulevitch, Andrew, 'Why is Putin Calling the Ukrainian Government a Bunch of Nazis?" *Anti-Defamation League* (4 March 2022); https://www.adl.org/blog/why-is-putin-calling-the-ukrainian-government-a bunch-of-nazis

Staff Reporter, 'Stern words, economic sanctions and a diplomatic boycott: The action Obama took to deter Putin from invading Crimea' *MailOnline* (7 December 2021); https://www.dailymail.co.uk/news/fb-10285787/The-action-Obama-took-to-deter-Putin-invading-Crimea -in-2014

Staff Reporter, 'Indian police investigate Russian politician's hotel death' *The Guardian* (27 December 2022); https://www.theguardian.com/world/2022/dec/27/indian-police-investigate-russian-politicians-hotel-death

Staff Reporter, 'Russian journalist who attacked Putin's war live on TV may have been poisoned' *The Telegraph* (13 October 2023); https://www.telegraph.co.uk/world-news/2023/10/13/russian-journalist-poison-protest-putin-war-live-on- tv

Stalin, Josef I., 'On the Death of Lenin' (30 January 1924). Speech delivered at Second All-Union Congress of Soviets, Moscow (26 January to 2 February 1924). Printed in Pravda 30 January 1924

Stalin, Joseph I., 'Speech at Celebration Meeting of the Moscow Soviet of Working People's Deputies and Moscow Party and Public Organisation.' (Twenty-Fifth Anniversary of the October Revolution: 6 November 1942); https://www.marxists.org/reference/archive/stalin/works/1942/11/06.htm

Steinbuch, Yaron, 'Captive Russian troops claim commanders kill their own wounded soldiers' *New York Post* (16 May 2022); https://nypost.com/2022/05/16/russian-commanders-allegedly-kill-their-own-wounded-soldiers.

Stokols, Eli, 'Trump wants one thing from the NATO summit. Europe is going to give it to him. *Politico* (21 June 2025); https://www.politico.com/news/2025/06/21/trump-nato-defence-spending

Stone, Norman, *The Eastern Front 1914-1917* (Penguin Books: London,1975), ISBN 3579-10-864

Strachan, Hew, *The First World War* (London: Simon & Schuster UK Ltd., 2003), ISBN 0-743-239-598

Strauss, Barry, 'Pre-emptive Strikes and Preventive Wars: A Historian's Perspective." *Strategika*, Hoover Institution, Stanford University (29 August 2017); htpps://www.hoover.org/research/preemptive-strikes-and-preventive-wars-historians-perspective.

Strauss, Leo, *Natural Right and History*, Chicago: University of Chicago Press, 1953).

Strelinkov, Alexey and Alex Izmaylov, 'Trump's tariffs: why are Russia and Belarus not targeted?' *Deutsche Welle* (4 May 2025); https://www.dw.com/en/donald-trump-tariffs-russia-belarus-sanctions-imports-trade-goods

Soufan, Ali and Nathan A. Sales, 'One of the Worst Ways Putin is gaslighting the world on Ukraine' *Think: Opinion, Analysis, Essays* (5 April 2022); http://www.nbcnews.com/think/opinion/putin-nazi-pretext-russia-war-ukraine-belied- white- supremacy-ties-rcna23043

Suvorov, Victor, *The Chief Culprit: Stalin's Grand Design to Start World War II* (Annapolis, Maryland: Naval Institute Press, 2013), ISBN: 9-781-591-148-067

Tahir, Tariq, 'Putin thought he could take Ukraine in three days, leaked emails reveal', *The Sun* (23 February 2023); https://www.news.com.au/world/europe/putin-thought-he-could-take-ukraine-in-three-days-leaked-emails-reveal/news-story/bf4de32af600b8b653069cdc34c174c8

Taylor, Frederick, *The Berlin Wall: 13 August 1961 – 9 November 1989*. (London: Bloomsbury Publishing, Plc, 2007), ISBN: 9-780-745-785-541

Terraine, John, *Mons: The Retreat to Victory* (London: B.T. Batsford, 1960)

Thomas, Nigel, *Hitler's Russian & Cossack Allies 1941-45* (Oxford: Osprey Publishing Ltd., 2015) IBSN: 0-297-772-381

Thomas, Nigel, *Hitler's Eastern Legions 1942-45*. (Oxford: Osprey Publishing Ltd., 2020). IBSN: 9-781-472-839-541

Thomas, Ryan, 'Is Putin Comparable to Hitler? Who's the Closest Historical Match for Vladimir Putin?' *Hubpages* (12 March 2022); https://discover.hubpages.com/politics/Is-Putin-Comparable-to-Hitler-Whos-the-closest-historical-match-for-Vladimir-Putin

Timenote, 'Katyn Massacre: Russian Communists Authorize Order No. 394/5 Allowing NKVD to kill 22,000 Polish Army Officers.' *Timenote* (17' October 2022); http://timenote.info/en/events/Katyn-massacre

Tolstoy, Nikolai, *Victims of Yalta* (London: Corgi Books, 1979)

Toussaint, Eric, 'Russia: Origin and Consequences of the debt repudiation of February 10, 1918', *Committee for the Abolition of Illegitimate Deby (CADTM)*, (8 February 2024); https://www.cadtm.org/Russia-Origin-and-consequences-of-the-repudiation-of-February-10-1918

TNA, 'Deaths in the First and Second World Wars' *The National Archives* (2023)
https://www.nationalarchives.gov.uk/help-with-your-research/research-guides/deaths-first-and-second-world-wars

Treisman, Daniel, *The Return: Russia's Journey from Gorbachev to Medvedev* (New York: The Free Press, 2011) ISBN: 1-416-560-726

Tsvetkova, Maria, 'Some wounded Russian soldiers find compensation elusive, despite Putin's pledge' *Reuters* (29 July 2022); https://www.reuters.com/world/europe/some-wounded-russian-soldiers-find-compensation-elusive-despite-putins-pledge-2022-07-29

Tuchman, Barbara W., *The Guns of August* (New York: Bantam Books., Inc, 1976). ISBN-1-397-805-530-226-696

UKinform; https://www.net/rubric-ato/4056510-russian-army-losses-1190-soldiers-and-helicopters-in-war-against-ukraine

US Embassy, 'World War II Allies: US Lend-Lease to the Soviet Union, 1941-1945' *US Embassy & Consulates in Russia;* https://ru-usembassy.gov/world-war-ii-allies-u-s-enlease-to-the-soviet-union-1941-1945

Yevtushenko, Yevgeny, 'Foreword' in Brian Moynahan, *The Russian Century: A History of the last Hundred Years* (London: Pimlico, 1994), ISBN 0-712-673-091

Van Brugen, Isabel, 'Putin's Mobilization Backfires as 370,000 flee Russia in two weeks." *Newsweek*, (4 October 2022); https://www.newsweek.com/putin-mobilization-backfires-russians-flee-kazakhstan-georgia-eu-1748771

Van Brugen, Isabel, 'Russian Army Threatening to Shoot Deserters amid Low Morale: UK' *Newsweek* (4 November 2022); https://www.newsweek.com/Russian-army-threatening-shoot-deserters-low-morale-uk-1756880

Vaz, Keith, 'CHECHNYA" *House of Commons Debates*, (HcDeb) *Hansard*, vol. 340, (6th December, 1999), cc 400-401

Veidlinger, Jeffrey, 'The Killing Fields of Ukraine.' *Tablet* (23 February 2022); https://www.tabletmag.com/sections/history/articles/killing-fields-ukraine.

Velez-Green, Alexander, 'Russian Strategists Debate Pre-emption as Defense Against NATO Surprise Attack.' *Russia Matters*, (Cambridge, Massachusetts: Harvard Kennedy School, Belfer Center for Science and International Affairs (14 March 2018); https://www.russiamatters.org/analysis/

Vincent, Charles P., *The Politics of Hunger: the Allied Blockade of Germany, 1915–1919.* (Athens, Ohio: Ohio University Press, 1986), ISBN 1-008-214-083-13

Vogel, Steve, *Betrayal in Berlin: George Blake, the Berlin Tunnel, and the Greatest Conspiracy of the Cold War.* (London: John Murray, 2019), ISBN 9-781-473-647-510

Walker, Shaun and Andrew Roth, '"They took our clothes": Ukrainians returning to looted homes' *The Guardian* (11 April 2022); https//www.theguardian.com/world/2022/apr/11/Ukrainian-homes-looted-by-russian-soldiers

Wamsley, Laura, 'Rape has reportedly become a weapon in Ukraine. Finding justice may be difficult.' *NPR* (National Public Radio), Washington (30 April 2022); https://npr.org./2022/04/30/1093339262/ukraine-russia-rape-war

Watson, Katy, 'Brazil election: a moment in history as Lula returns" *BBC News* (31 October 2022); https://www.bbc.co.uk/news/world-latin-america-63452008

Way, Lucan A., 'Russian Foreign Election Interventions Since 1991', *PONARS Eurasia Policy Memo No. 520* (Washington D.C.). Institute for European, Russian and Eurasian Studies, Elliott School of International Affairs, George Washington University (March, 2018); https/www.ponarseurasia.org/Russian-foreign-election-interventions-since-1991

Werth, Nicholas, 'Dekulakisation as Mass Violence", *Mass Violence and Resistance* (23 September 2011); htpps://www.sciencepo.fr/mass-violence-war-massacre-resistance/en/document/dekaluisation-mass-violence-html

Weydemeyer, Joseph A., 'The Dictatorship of the Proletariat' *Turn-Zeitung*, New York (1 January 1852)

Wilson, Andrew, *Ukrainian Nationalism in the 1990s: A Minority Faith.* (Cambridge: CUP, 1996). ISBN: 0-521-574-570-9

Windrow, Michael, *Waffen SS* (London: Osprey Publishing Ltd., 1980). ISBN-10: 0-850-450-586

Wołek, Karol, 'A post-war War. The Years of 1944-1963 in Poland.' *The Warsaw Institute* (1 October 2018); https://warsawinstitute.org/post-war-war-years-1944-1963-poland

Workman, Daniel, 'Ukraine's Top Ten Exports.' *World's Top Exports* (2023); https://www.worldstopexports.com/ukraines-top-10-exports

Wright, Damien, *Churchill's Secret War with Lenin: British and Commonwealth Military Intervention in the Russian Civil War, 1918-1920.* (Warwick: Helion & Company, 2017). ISBN: 1-019-115-1210-2

Zaloga, Steven J., *The Polish Army, 1939-1945* (London: Osprey Publishing Ltd., 1982), ISBN 0-850-454-174

Zemaitis, Augustinas, (2024) 'The Occupation of Latvia (1940-1990)' *World War 2 And Later in Latvia*; https://www.onlatvia.com/the-occupation-of-Latvia-1940-1990-78

Ziemele, Inate, *State Continuity and Nationality: The Baltic States and Russia: Past, Present and Future as Defined by International Law.* (Leiden: Martinus Nijhoff Publishers, 2005). ISBN 9-004-142-959

Zukowski, Jerzy and Hubert Zawadzki, *A Concise History of Poland* (Cambridge: CUP, 2001). ISBN 1- 521-559-170

Index